Credit Scores
&
Credit Reports

How The System Really Works
What You Can Do

Evan Hendricks

Library of Congress Cataloging-in-Publication Data

Hendricks, Evan.
    Credit scores & credit reports: how the system really
    works, what you can do/ Evan Hendricks – 3rd ed.
    p. cm.
    ISBN 0- 96454864-X
    1. Consumer credit – Law and legislation – United States
    – Popular Works. 2. Finance, Personal – United States –
    Popular Works.

Third Edition, 2007 (First Printing)
Privacy Times, Inc.
P.O. Box 302
Cabin John, MD 20818
www.PrivacyTimes.com
www.CreditScoresandCreditReports.com

Editor-in-Chief: Pamela Stewart
Book Cover By Carlos Arrien

Acknowledgements

Many people assisted me in writing this book, and it is not possible to thank all of them. Certainly, all individuals and organizations that are mentioned in the book deserve thanks, either because I was in direct contact with them, or their Web sites made useful information available. Special thanks go to Joanne Faulkner and Richard Rubin, attorneys and founding members of the Natl. Association of Consumer Advocates; Chris Jay Hoofnagle, the Electronic Privacy Information Center; Craig Watts and Karlene Bowen, Fair Isaac Corp.; Ruth Koontz and Paul Wohkittel, of Lenders' Credit Services; CreditXpert, Inc.'s amazing trio – David Chung, Thierry Marbach and Peter Fitton; Ed Mierzwinski, U.S. Public Interest Research Group; Travis Plunkett, Consumer Federation of America; the staff of Consumers Union; Steve Baker and other staffers at the Federal Trade Commission; Stephen Gardner, Center for Science in the Public Interest; F. Paul Bland, Jr., Trial Lawyers for Public Justice, Bruce Daniel-son, First Stone Credit Counseling; and Terry Clemans, National Credit Reporting Association. Thanks to Pamela Stewart, Houston Law Office, Mark Durham, Joanne Faulkner, and Godhammer, for editing assistance. Thanks to ING Direct, Veracity Credit, I.D. Watchdog and the Natl. Association of Mortgage Brokers for their support in spreading the word.

Thanks also go to the many consumer attorneys who are doing pioneering work on credit reporting issues, including (but not limited to) Michael and Justin Baxter and Robert Sola, A. Hugo Blankingship III and Tom Christiano, Ian Lyngklip, Leonard Bennett, James Francis and John Soumalis, Sylvia Antalis Goldsmith, David Szwak, James Fishman, Terry Smiljanich, Chris Kittell, Christa Collins, Robert Stempler, Thomas Lyons (Sr. & Jr.), James Pietz, Penny Hays, Tom Stubbs, Robert Weed, Earl Underwood, and Michael Caddell. Finally, thanks to all the Hendricks help: Daniel, Steve, Rosario, Miles, Holly, Edward, Ardis and Heather.

Contents

To Mom & Dad
Gracias Por La Vida

To Rosario, Daniel & Diego-Miles
Razon de Vivir

Introduction:

Peering Into The 'Black Box'

Sunshine is the best disinfectant.

– Justice Louis Brandeis
Other People's Money & How the
Bankers Use It (1914)

A rather simple rule has emerged to dominate the American consumer economy: the worse your credit score, the more you pay for mortgages, loans, credit cards, and insurance. Conversely, the better your credit score, the more favorable terms you will get on interest rates and premiums.

For the first half of this decade, the "Credit Score Rule" was only of mild interest to many. The combination of easy credit and rising real estate prices meant that most Americans could get approved for home loans requiring little or no cash out of pocket. Those with lower credit scores simply paid more.

It was part of the new reality, known as "risk-based" pricing. In the old days, creditors would either approve you or disapprove you for credit—thumbs up or thumbs down. But with risk-based pricing in the easy-credit era, there was no need to reject you. Instead, they granted you credit or insurance at the rate that compensated for the "risk" reflected in your credit history. Your credit report, and the credit score derived from it, made this all possible.

The "Credit Score Rule" remains very much alive. But in the wake of the sub-prime lending crisis, tightening credit standards, and flat or falling real estate prices, the "Rule's" impact is all the more profound.

Since the late 1990s, a 620 FICO score was the sub-prime demarcation line, and anyone above could get a better quality loan.

In 2007, however, some lenders bumped up minimum scores for fully documented loans to 640, while others, like Webster Bank, a wholesale lender based in Connecticut, announced an increase of its minimum credit score to 680, and that was with full documentation of applicants' income and assets. Still other lenders said only those with a top-of-the-line 720 FICO score would be eligible for the faster and more convenient "low documentation" mortgages.

As a new era of more rigorous mortgage lending standards dawned, maintaining a positive FICO score became even more important. For many lenders, a bad FICO score meant consumers couldn't qualify for a loan they could afford. Would-be homebuyers were out of luck. Worse, homeowners struggling to pay high-interest adjustable mortgages couldn't refinance. That meant they had to hastily sell their homes, or face foreclosure. By 2007, foreclosure rates had risen dramatically.

FICO scores can directly impact credit card rates, sometimes when you least expect it. Take the case of Alan Cowan. Although never late paying his credit card bills, he found an "important notice" tucked into his monthly First USA bill advising him in small print that his 9.99% interest rate was going up to 19.49%. No reason was given for the increase, but when Cowan called for an explanation he was told that in spite of his spotless record at First USA,[1] he was many creditors, First USA routinely conducted monthly "account reviews" of customers' credit reports to spot any

---

[1] First USA was acquired by Bank One, which subsequently was acquired by Chase.

new problems that could portend greater risk.[2]

They can get you at the "front end" too. Kevin Washington (not his real name) He responded to a Capital One pre-approved offer for an introductory, zero-interest credit card. When he received the card, he noticed in the fine print that he would be charged a 12.99 interest rate for using the card. He discovered that in the initial offer's fine print, Capital One reserved the right to counter-offer with a less attractive card if it found something in his credit report that it didn't like. But Capital One never informed Washington that it pulled a bait-and-switch based upon his credit history.

Then there's insurance. Margaret Jones, a retired Floridian on a fixed income with a stellar driving record, was surprised to learn in April 2000 that Progressive had raised her auto insurance rate 20 percent. This didn't make sense to Jones, as she had not had an accident or moving violation since she first took out the policy. When she called to inquire, a Progressive operator "rudely" told her that it was all part of a general rate increase. Persistent digging by Jones revealed that Progressive had begun pulling customer credit reports to re-set premiums.[3]

In January 2003, Tony and Alethea Preston were preparing to buy a home in Clermont, Florida. They were advised they needed mortgage insurance, a common requirement for many people who prefer to pay less than a 20% down payment on their home purchase. Initially, the mortgage broker estimated the monthly premium would run between $100-$200. However, at the settlement table, they were shocked to learn that the monthly premium for mortgage insurance was $762.29. Neither the mortgage broker nor the settlement attorney could explain the whop-

---

[2] Caroline Mayer, "Read 'em and Weep; Cardholders See Rates Rise Based on Other Debts," *Washington Post*, December 20, 2001, pg. E1
[3] Cathryn Smith, et al. v Progressive Corporation: U.S. Dist. Ct. – Northern Dist. Of Florida (Gainesville) – Case No.: 1:00-CV-210-MMP; Plaintiffs lead attorney was Terry Smiljanich, of James, Hoyer, Newcomer and Smiljanich, of Tampa, Florida. Author was their expert.

ping discrepancy between the rather low estimate and the exorbitant premium. No notice or reason was provided by the insurer, Mortgage Guaranty Insurance Corporation (MGIC) of Milwaukee. Of course, MGIC jacked the rate after it pulled the Prestons' credit reports.[4]

One Last Check

If the volume is high enough, major creditors can check an applicant's credit reports and scores for a few dollars. It should not be surprising then that their use has spread.

In December 2004, the *Miami Herald* was the first to report that three major banks in Florida – Bank of America, SunTrust and Wachovia – were declining to open checking accounts for applicants with rock-bottom credit scores.[5]

Jean Ann Fox, of the Consumer Federation of America warned of a "Catch 22."

"Banks turn away checking account customers because they don't have a good credit score. But then you can't build up a financial identity, because you can't get a bank account, because you don't have one.''

Employers

Brenda Matthews learned the hard way that it was legal for employers to check credit reports before hiring job applicants. After Johnson & Johnson offered her a job in the patent office of its New Jersey headquarters, she gave her old

---

[4] Tony Preston and Alethea Preston, et al. v. Mortgage Guaranty Insurance Corp. of Milwaukee, et al.: U.S. Dist. Ct. – Middle Dist. Of Florida (Orlando) – Case No.: 5:03-CV-111-OC-10GJR; Plaintiffs represented by Smiljanich, op. cit. Like many of the FCRA cases cited in the book, the author was their expert.

[5] Harriet Johnson Brackey, "Banks Check Potential Customers' Credit," *Miami Herald*, December 5, 2004

employer notice. But two weeks later, Johnson & Johnson rescinded the offer because of her credit history.

Matthews, an African-American, filed a discrimination complaint with the Equal Employment Opportunity Commission. Her attorneys charged that the company's use of credit reports had a disparate impact on minorities. "It compounds an already unfair situation. African-Americans have been subject to historic discrimination in the credit market. For that to be compounded in the job market is a real inequity," said Rachel Geman, her attorney.

Johnson & Johnson told *CBS Market Watch* in a statement it couldn't comment on the EEOC filing, but said that Matthews applied for the position of tax specialist in the company's global patent office, a job "involving the timely payment of fees."[6]

Federal law requires employers to secure job applicants' permission before accessing credit files. But many job applicants are not in a strong position to say "no" when prospective employers "ask" to see their credit reports. Moreover, the Fair Credit Reporting Act does not require that credit reports only be used if they are relevant to the job in question.

CBS Market Watch reported that 35 percent of employers used credit checks in pre-employment screening, up from 19 percent in 1996, according to a survey of 208 companies by the Society for Human Resource Management.

Meanwhile, about 41 percent of retailers said they used credit checks in pre-employment screening, according to the 2003 National Retail Security Survey, conducted by the University of Florida. The study found about 10 percent of retailers said they planned to increase their use of credit checks in the coming year, putting it among the top five screening methods that retailers intend to ramp up.

---

[6] Andrea Coombes, "Are credit checks of job applicants discriminatory?" *CBS Market Watch,* November 17, 2004

The industries most interested in credit checks are defense, chemical, pharmaceutical and financial services, said Donald Girard, a spokesman with Experian, one of three credit-reporting agencies that sells reports to employers. Experian creates specific employment reports that don't include credit scores, birth dates or data on spouses.

Utilities

TXU Energy, the largest Texas utility company, in September 2004 proposed basing electric rates for its least profitable customers on credit scores. But TXU put the plan on hold after it sparked a storm of protest from consumer groups and a complaint by the Texas Public Utility Counsel.

"Electricity is not like any other commodity," the group's complaint stated. "It cannot be stored when prices are favorable, it has no substitutable product and it is a necessity and an essential service. The use of credit scores as a proxy for income levels, race, national origin, marital status, or other prohibited factors places the most vulnerable population groups at risk for electricity service."

Winning Scores, Losing Scores

These are just a few of the many little known ways in which credit scores and credit reports can determine how much you pay for a variety of necessities, or whether or not you get a job.

More and more Americans are waking to the fact that credit scores can have a dramatic and immediate impact. Although unusual, it is possible that one delinquent account could lower a credit score from 70 to 120 points, according to the Fair Isaac Corporation, the leading developer of credit scoring models.[7]

---

[7] Fair Isaac & Co. via *The Hartford Courant*,
http://banking.senate.gov/03_07hrg/071003/chart01.pdf

Typically, the impact is more incremental – a sliding scale. But the difference between the top and bottom of the scale can be huge.

Fair Isaac's Web site showed, for example, that on a $300,000 30-year, fixed-rate mortgage, a consumer with a 760 score would have a 6.072% interest rate and a monthly payment of $906, while a consumer with a 659 FICO score would get a 7.388% rate, and pay $1,051 monthly. Someone with a 619 score would get a 9.419% rate, paying $1,252 monthly. Bottom line: The difference between "top-of-the-line" and "sub-prime" is $346 per month, or $4,152 per year.[8] That's enough to cover a car payment.

A consumer with excellent credit (credit score of 740-850) would pay an 8.62% interest rate for a home equity loan, while a consumer with fair credit (640-659) would pay 10.2%, and one with poor credit (620-639) would pay a 12.95% rate.[9] The rate swings for a new car loan are even greater, with good credit risks paying a 7.148% rate, fair risks paying a 10.9% rate, and poor risks paying 14.2%.

Credit, Insurance & Employment

In general, one would expect credit scores and credit reports to play a key role in evaluating a consumer's credit worthiness. In fact, the federal law known as the Fair Credit Reporting Act (FCRA) specifies that credit reports can be used for "credit, insurance, and employment purposes."

The first problem, however, is that too many Americans do not understand how the credit reporting system works, how their credit scores are calculated, the important ways in which credit reports and scores can effect their financial well-being, or what they can do about it.

A second problem is the potential for inaccuracy in the credit report data that are used to calculate credit scores. Since the early 1990s, abundant evidence has emerged to

---

[8] www.myfico.com, visited September 10, 2007
[9] *The Hartford Courant*, see Footnote 6; (2003 data)

indicate that inaccuracy has been and continues to be a significant problem for the nation's credit reporting system. As we will see, damages to consumers stemming from credit report inaccuracy can range from the economic to the emotional.

A third problem is that identity theft, considered the nation's fastest-growing crime, poses a direct threat to the accuracy and integrity of data in the credit reporting system. Identity thieves typically steal an individual's identifiers, such as Social Security number, name, address, date-of-birth, and/or mother's maiden name, and then use them to obtain credit in that individual's name. When debts created by the identity thief go unpaid, creditors report the negative payment history to the credit report of the innocent victim. Consequently, the innocent victim's credit report is polluted by highly negative information that is inaccurate because it does not reflect that victim's activities. Multiply this dynamic by the million or so cases of identity theft each year and you will see why identity theft raises serious concerns about ensuring accuracy in credit report data.

Like your own credit score, the credit scoring and credit reporting system is a "work in progress." It would be inaccurate to characterize the system as totally or always unfair. But it clearly cannot be depicted as totally or always fair either. And, as we will see, when the system breaks down, the impact on individuals can range from inconvenient annoyance to life-altering devastation.

Spreading Awareness

This book is written to address these and a host of other issues concerning credit reporting in America. The book is designed to help readers gain a greater understanding of the credit reporting and scoring system, and how it impacts them.

It would seem that greater awareness is needed. According to a July 2003 survey by the Consumer Federation of America, "Only 25 percent of Americans—and less than 20 percent of those with incomes below $35,000—said they knew what their credit score was. But only three percent of Americans could, unprompted, name the three main credit bureaus—Experian, Equifax, and Trans Union—that provide both lenders and consumers with information from credit reports. Forty-three percent of Americans—only 35 percent of those with incomes below $35,000—said they had obtained a copy of their credit report from the three credit bureaus in the past two years."[10]

A March 2005 Government Accountability Office (GAO) report concluded that although the public's understanding of credit reports and credit scores was improving, it was far from universal, and a federal education campaign was still needed. It found that 60 percent of respondents had seen their credit reports, most often because they were making a large purchase or refinancing a loan. Most of these consumers said that they understood their reports, but about half (53 percent) were not aware that negative data could stay on their report for 7 or 10 years.

The GAO found that one-third of respondents had obtained their credit scores. While 70 percent correctly identified the definition of a credit score, only 28 percent could provide a number within a range of possible credit scores. Apart from late payments, about half did not know what factors determined a credit score.[11]

As the disclaimer states, this book does not give legal advice. Legal advice can only be given case-by-case by a lawyer, which this author is not.

---

[10] CFA Opinion Survey, July 2003, conducted by Opinion Research Corp.; www.consumerfed.org/072803creditscores.html
[11] Government Accountability Office, "Credit Reporting Literacy: Consumers Understood the Basics but Could Benefit from Targeted Educational Efforts" (GAO-05-223).
www.gao.gov/new.items/d05223.pdf

This also is not a "credit repair" book. This author repeats the advice of consumer protection officials: be very, very leery of outfits that call themselves "credit repair" clinics. Contrary to its literal meaning, the common use of "credit repair" connotes improving one's credit score through the removal of negative-but-*accurate* data. There is no guaranteed method for removing accurate information from a credit report, whether it is positive or negative. However, promising that you can do so and charging money in advance is a violation of federal law, according to the FTC. If you are contemplating using one of the many credit repair clinics, start by asking any of them whether they will provide you with copies of all letters they send to credit bureaus on your behalf. Odds are, they won't even answer.

This Book Covers...

The book is divided into chapters that cover the "basics" of credit scores and credit reports, and ones that cover "advanced" aspects of the systems, which create them.

Chapter 1 explains the basics of credit scores—beginning with Fair Isaac's explanation as to how they are calculated. Chapter 2 is more advanced, delving into little known—and sometimes surprising—details about credit scoring that should further increase your understanding. Chapter 3 goes even further by exploring the world of "resellers" and "re-scoring," a little known but valuable service for improving the credit scores of mortgage applicants, but which appears threatened by hostile economic forces.

We return to "basics" in Chapter 4, describing how you can obtain your credit reports for free under the 2004 Amendments to the FCRA, known as the Fair and Accurate Credit Transactions Act (FACTA). In addition, many other factors, like state laws, credit denials or identity theft, entitle you to free reports. You are also entitled to obtain one free report per year from a variety of "specialty" consumer reporting agencies, including employment and tenant screen-services like ChoicePoint, and check-approval services like TeleCheck and Certegy.

Similarly, Chapter 5 explains the basics of reading and understanding your credit report, and Chapter 6 describes the fundamentals of disputing inaccuracy. Chapter 7 offers a basic overview of identity theft, often described as America's fastest growing crime, and its impact on credit report accuracy. These "how-to" sections serve as a starting point for those who are ready to oversee their own credit histories.

Beyond 'How-To'

To fully appreciate the basics, one needs to understand the larger system. To that end, Chapters 8 and 9 examine how the three major credit reporting agencies (CRAs) compile credit data on 220 million Americans, and how they and credit grantors conduct, or sometimes don't conduct, reinvestigations upon receiving consumer disputes.

To help explain why credit reporting continually draws the attention of Congress, state legislators and enforcement officials, Chapter 10 traces the evolution of the industry, as well as the "mixed files" problem and other inaccuracy issues, and identity theft.

Chapters 11 and 12 address the controversial subjects of credit repair and debt collection. Chapters 13-15 explore the use of credit reports and scores by automobile, homeowners and mortgage insurers.

Chapter 16 focuses on the heated debate over whether credit scoring is tied to racial discrimination. Chapter 17 looks at some of the special challenges faced by certain groups, including Hispanics, students and the divorced.

One activity that affects most adult Americans, but is little understood, is the marketing of pre-approved credit card offers—the topic of Chapter 18. Chapter 19 covers the thorny issue of unauthorized access to credit reports, a problem that can arise in a number of settings, including car dealerships, for a number of reasons, including identity theft.

Chapter 20 explores the kinds of damages typically suffered by victims of inaccurate credit reports or identity theft, and provides a preliminary methodology for identifying and measuring those damages.

Chapter 21 recounts the exciting legislative debate of 2003, which resulted in major amendments to increase the FCRA's consumer protections. Despite the improvements, no one in Congress or elsewhere felt that the problems of credit report inaccuracy or identity theft would go away anytime soon. And they haven't.

Chapter 22 explores controversial policies of credit card companies that fail to report their card holders' credit limits to credit bureaus, a practice that can lower credit scores. It also examines credit card companies that practice "universal default," meaning they will raise card holders' interest rates if their credit scores drop too much – even if they've never had a late payment with that particular company.

Privacy

Credit scoring and credit reporting are inextricably linked to the fundamental privacy rights of consumers. As the U.S. Supreme Court has recognized, "To begin with, both the common law and the literal understandings of privacy encompass the individual's control of information concerning his or her person."[12]

In the "Information Age," privacy is defined by, and measured according to, the principles of "Fair Information

---

[12] U.S. Dept. Of Justice v. Reporters Committee, 489 U.S. 749 (1989)

Practices" (FIPs). As we will see in Chapter 10, these principles are at the core of information privacy laws, both in the United States and abroad, including the FCRA. They seek to ensure that individuals maintain a reasonable level of control over their personal information by ensuring accuracy, fairness, collection and use limitation, purpose specification, security, and enforcement. These principles form the basis for an international consensus[13] as to how personal data should be protected by law and by organizational practice. Enacted in 1970, the FCRA was the United States' first information privacy statute.

The credit reporting system contains detailed and sensitive financial information concerning an estimated 220 million consumers in the United States. The system is designed to facilitate the free flow of information for the purposes of credit, employment, and insurance. It enables thousands upon thousands of organizations, large and small, to make important judgments about consumers based upon their personal information. There are many benefits for consumers and for the economy.

All too often, however, this takes place without the knowledge or consent of consumers. Problems arise for individuals' privacy, and for our economy and society, when judgments are made based upon inaccurate, incomplete, or irrelevant information. Privacy is damaged when personal information is used or disclosed for impermissible purposes. Moreover, privacy suffers when others gain unauthorized access to our credit reports.

The purpose of this book is to increase consumers' understanding of the system, and thereby increase their ability to exercise control over their personal information.

The more the system is subjected to public scrutiny, and the more consumers gain control over their data, the better the system works. The goal is privacy, which is some-

---

[13] "Principles of Fair Information Practices, Organization of Economic Cooperation and Development (OECD), 1980

times explained as "informational self-determination."[14] The goal is more readily reached by adhering to Brandeis' instruction that, "Sunshine is the best disinfectant."

This book answers many questions. But it will raise many more. Here are a few to keep in mind as you continue reading:

- Should our society and our system of law continue to treat our personal data like a commodity?
- Should we have a "property interest" in our data?
- In the current "information age," is our personal information better viewed as a "resource," both public and private?

These questions ultimately go to the fundamental importance of credit reports and personal information in 21st Century America.

But first things first. Let's start with the basics.

---

[14] As noted by Dr. Spiros Simitis, Professor of Law, Johann Wolfgang Goethe-Universitat, Frankfurt, Germany, this right is recognized by the German Constitution and was affirmed by the German Supreme Court in a national case involving the Census. Also see the writings of Law Professors Paul M. Schwartz and Joel R. Reidenberg, including Data Privacy Law (Michie, 1996)

Chapter 1

Basics of The Credit Score

If winning isn't everything, why do they keep score?

– Vince Lombardi

All right, everyone, line up alphabetically, according to your height.

– Casey Stengel

A Brief History

The Fair Isaac Corporation first developed models for calculating credit scores in the late 1950s. Credit scores started gaining widespread use in the late 1980s and came to consumers' attention in the late 1990s when mortgage lenders began considering credit scores in their loan underwriting. They helped usher in today's era of "automated underwriting" and "credit decisioning," in which large organizations can decide, via computer, whether or not to grant you credit or insurance—no human involvement necessary.

Despite their importance and growing popularity among businesses, to consumers, credit scores were shrouded in mystery. It was not clear how they were calculated or who was using them. In fact, the Federal Trade Commission (FTC) put out an opinion stating that federal law did not require the credit bureaus to reveal credit scores to consumers who requested their credit reports. This was in part, because the 1996 revisions to the Fair Credit Reporting Act (FCRA) specified disclosure was not required of "any information concerning credit scores or any other risk scores or predictors relating to the consumer."[15]

Public criticism of this policy mounted as the vital role of credit scores in credit and insurance decision-making became evident. The changing environment was best illustrated by a situation that arose in February 2000 at E-Loan, an Internet lender that could quickly approve mortgage and auto loans, in part because credit scores facilitated automated decision-making. To better advise consumers where they stood, E-Loan decided to tell prospective loan applicants their FICO scores—a radical move at the time. Within a month, thousands of people took advantage of the service.[16]

But the move sparked an uproar in the credit industry, as two of the three national credit reporting agencies (CRAs) moved to cut off E-Loan's use of credit scores. E-Loan ultimately prevailed when California passed a state law, sponsored by State Senator Liz Figueroa, requiring lenders to provide California mortgage and home equity applicants with the score used in their loan decision. The law also required Equifax, Experian and Trans Union to disclose credit scores to consumers who requested them.

"The passage of this law is a giant step forward for California consumers, but there's still more that needs to be done," said Chris Larsen, E-Loan's Chairman and CEO. "This is information that should be readily and freely available to consumers nationwide. There should be very little difference between getting information about a stock or mutual fund and finding out your credit score. Just like consumers can research an investment before they commit their money to it, consumers should have free access to information about their credit score *before* they apply for a loan."[17]

---

[15] 15 U.S.C. Sect. 1681g(a)(1)

[16] E-Loan Opens Over 10,000 Personalized Loan Management Accounts In First Month," E-Loan Press Release, March 23, 2000

[17] E-LOAN, Inc., A Full Credit Score Disclosure Pioneer, Calls For National Legislation," E-Loan Press Release, June 27, 2001

Larsen's plea was fulfilled—well, almost. Although scores won't exactly be "freely available," federal law now requires credit bureaus, for a "fair and reasonable" fee, to disclose to consumers their credit scores and how those scores are determined. The FTC was supposed to set rules instructing the credit bureaus how to do this. The federal law also requires mortgage lenders to disclose scores. However, the new law appears not to require CRAs to provide consumers with the scores that lenders *actually use*. Instead, they can disclose "educational scores," meaning FICO "knock-offs" that approximate scores used by lenders, but which can differ significantly. (More on this later.)

Critics said even the California law fell short of its goals, as CRAs initially did not publicize its requirements, made it difficult for consumers to learn about their scores, and charged rather high fees.

What Is A Credit Score?

A credit score is a number that reflects your credit worthiness *at a given point in time*. For most models, the higher the score, the better the risk.[18] People with higher scores often can obtain mortgages, credit cards, loans, and insurance at more favorable rates. Conversely, the lower the score, the less favorable the terms will be in any offer that is made. The credit score is based entirely on data in your credit report, which is why the bulk of this book is devoted to credit reports, and the system that creates them.

Each Bureau Has Its Own

Although similar in many aspects, each of the three major credit bureaus has a different name for their FICO credit score. There's Equifax's "Beacon," Trans Union's "FICO Classic," and the "Experian/FICO Risk Model."[19]

---

[18] The bankruptcy score runs from 0-1000 with higher being worse.
[19] Up until 2004, the TU FICO score was called "Empirica"

The general scoring range is 300-850. Fair Isaac divides the scoring range into five risk categories:

- 780-850 – Low Risk
- 740–780 – Medium-Low Risk
- 690–740 – Medium Risk
- 620–690 – Medium High Risk
- 620 and Below – High Risk or "sub-prime."

All of these generalities come with a note of caution. First, a credit score can change quickly for several reasons, including late payments or significant increases in credit balances. Second, each credit bureau might not have identical data about you, in large part because many creditors only report to one or two bureaus rather than all three, resulting in different credit scores among the three. Third, some creditors and insurers use their own formulas, or "templates," to calculate credit scores, either in conjunction with a general-purpose model like FICO, or by themselves. For example, a mortgage lender will want the formula to zero in on one set of a consumer's payment characteristics, while an insurer or sub-prime credit card issuer will emphasize a different set. Fourth, the credit score itself might play a different role in different contexts. For some types of credit, the score could be the predominant factor in setting interest rates and credit limits. But in the insurance context, the "credit-based insurance score," typically is one of many factors determining whether a policy is underwritten or at what premium. Some lenders and insurers, along with using a score, also scan the credit report for major "derogatory" terms like bankruptcy, judgment, foreclosure, or collection.

How Is the Credit Score Calculated?

Like the Coca-Cola formula, the precise formulas that are used for calculating various kinds of credit scores are well-guarded trade secrets. Nonetheless, Fair Isaac has released enough information to give a very general idea of how scores are calculated.

Remember, the score is calculated by analyzing the "whole" of *credit information* in the report and the various factors that make up that whole. No singular piece of information or factor by itself determines your credit score.

Factor 1: Payment History (35%)

Your payment history is the first and most important factor because, obviously, "The first thing any lender would want to know is whether you have paid past credit accounts on time." On the other hand, Fair Isaac says that this usually only amounts for 35% of the score on average. Late payments are not an automatic "score-killer," as an overall good credit picture can outweigh one or two late credit card payments. At the same time, having no late payments in your credit report does not mean you will get a "perfect score." Some 60%–65% of credit reports show no late payments at all, the company says.

The factors that are considered in calculating your payment history include:

- **Track record with various lenders.** Do you pay all your credit obligations on time, including mortgages, credit cards, store charge cards, home equity loans, auto loans, finance companies, and personal loans? The greater the number of accounts without late payments, the better the score.
- **Length Of Positive Credit History.** The longer the better.
- **Length of Time that has Passed Since the Most Recent Negative Item.** It is vital to realize that the more recent a public record or delinquency, the more that delinquency will lower your credit score.

- **Severe Unpaid Debts – Public Records.** The most negative credit failures are reflected in public records, as the account(s) at issue resulted in court action. Bankruptcy, foreclosure, court judgments, wage attachments, tax liens, and collection lawsuits, particularly if recent, can cause a credit score to plummet.
- **Severity & Quantity of Delinquencies.** While one 30-day late payment from four years ago would have a minimal impact on an otherwise positive credit history, the presence of three separate 90-day lates in the past year would have a major detrimental effect. Also severe are unpaid accounts that are sent to collection agencies or are "charged off."

Factor 2: Amount Owed—Extent of Indebtedness (30%)

How much debt is too much? How "maxed out" are you on your credit cards? The FICO system wants you to have debts, but not too many. It gauges whether you *manage your debt responsibly.* As Fair Isaac puts it: "Owing a great deal of money on many accounts can indicate that a person is overextended, and is more likely to make some payments late or not at all. Part of the science of scoring is determining how much is *too* much for a given credit profile."

- **Quantity of Credit Accounts.** Too many credit cards can lower a score because FICO sees it as increasing risk. On the other hand, if you have no credit accounts, you will not be able to build a credit history. Fair Isaac warns against thinking there are an "optimal number" of credit cards.
- **Ratio of Credit Balance To Credit Limit.** Are you using a fraction of the credit that is available to you, or are you "maxed out" on your credit cards every month? The ratio of your credit bal-

ance to your credit limit is a key factor in scoring your indebtedness. Some experts say that using only one-third of your available credit is optimal.

- **The amount owed on all accounts.** How much are you dipping into debt? Remember, even if you pay off your credit cards in full every month, your credit report may show a balance on those cards. The total balance on your account at the time the credit card company reported it to the bureau often is the amount that will show in your credit report.

- **How Much Is Owed On Each Type of Account?** In addition, for the overall debt total, FICO scores the amount you owe on specific types of accounts, such as credit cards and installment loans. Fair Isaac says: "In some cases, having a very small balance without missing a payment shows that you have managed credit responsibly, and may be slightly better than carrying no balance at all. On the other hand, closing unused credit accounts that show zero balances and that are in good standing will not raise your score."

- **How Much of Mortgage or Other Installment Loans Are Paid Off?** How much was the original loan amount, and how much have you paid off so far? Fair Isaac says: "Paying down installment loans is a good sign that you are able and willing to manage debt responsibly."

Factor 3: Length of Credit History—The Longer, The Better (15%)

Fair Isaac breaks this category down accordingly:

- **Overall Length of Credit History (In General).** How many accounts, how long?

- How long have specific credit accounts been established?
- How long has it been since you used certain accounts?

Factor 4: How Much New Credit? (10%)

This category basically is to flag people who suddenly are seeking new lines of credit, possibly indicating they are about to overextend themselves, or possibly already are getting in over their heads. As Fair Isaac says: "Research shows that opening several credit accounts in a short period of time does represent greater risk—especially for people who do not have a long established credit history."

- **How many new accounts, particularly credit card accounts?**
- **How long has it been since you opened a new account?**
- **How many recent requests for credit have you made, as indicated by inquiries to the credit bureaus?** Inquiries remain on your credit report for two years, although FICO scores only consider inquiries from the last 12 months. Fair Isaac emphasizes it only considers inquiries for which you were applying for different kinds of credit, as opposed to the multiple inquiries that might result if you were shopping for the best mortgage rate or car loans.
- **Length of time since credit report inquiries were made by lenders.**
- **Whether you have a good recent credit history, following past payment problems.** This is a biggie for people hoping to re-establish their credit by making payments on time after a period of late payment behavior to help raise a score over time.

Factor 5: Type Of Credit (10%)

Fair Isaac refers to this as measuring whether you have a "healthy mix" of installment (mortgages and loans) and revolving credit (credit cards). It's not entirely clear what's "healthy" and what isn't. Loans from banks are considered positive, while finance company loans are not.

Inquiries—Fair Isaac's Clarification

At one point in the 1990s, many people believed that inquiries to their credit report caused their credit scores to drop. Some felt they were being "responsible consumers" by shopping for the best mortgage rate. But the multiple applications prompted a flurry of inquiries, making it appear that the consumer was trying to buy the whole neighborhood, not just one house.

Some consumers who saw their credit reports worried that inquiries resulting from pre-approved offers were lowering their scores. In fact, these inquiries only appear on the report disclosed to the consumer, and are not printed on the report seen by creditors. They are not used in scoring.

Accordingly, Fair Isaac emphasizes that it only counts inquiries that are caused by consumers applying for credit. Here's what else Fair Isaac says:

- **Inquiries don't affect scores that much.** For most people, one additional credit inquiry will take less than five points off their FICO score. However, inquiries can have a greater impact if you have few accounts or a short credit history. (In other words, the system is designed to flag inexperienced people who could be in danger of overdosing on the joys of credit.) Large numbers of inquiries also mean greater risk. People with six inquiries or more on their credit reports are eight times more likely to declare bankruptcy than people with no inquiries on their reports, Fair Isaac said.

- **Many kinds of inquiries aren't counted at all.** The score does not count it when you order your own credit report or score. Also, it does not count inquiries related to "pre-approved" credit offers, or routine account reviews by your current creditors. Employment-related inquiries are not counted either.

- **The score doesn't penalize "rate shopping."** Looking for a mortgage or an auto loan may cause multiple lenders to request your credit report, even though you're only looking for one loan. To compensate for this, the score counts multiple auto or mortgage inquiries in any 45-day period as just one inquiry.[20] In addition, the score ignores all inquiries made in the 30 days prior to scoring. If you find a loan within 30 days, the inquiries won't affect your score while you're rate shopping.

What Fair Isaac Says It Doesn't Consider

Fair Isaac says its scoring model complies with the Equal Credit Opportunity Act prohibition against using racial or ethnic data in credit decisioning. It also claims: "Independent research has shown that credit scoring is not unfair to minorities or people with little credit history. Scoring has proven to be an accurate and consistent measure of repayment for all people who have some credit history. In other words, at a given score, non-minority and minority applicants are equally likely to pay as agreed."

---

[20] This protection can break down if auto or mortgage inquiries are not properly coded, recorded or communicated by credit grantors or CRAs.

In a broader context, however, credit scoring can disadvantage *disadvantaged* people who are not familiar with the system. For instance, poor and low-income people are usually not mobile and tend to utilize stores and credit grantors within their communities. As these tend to be small, privately owned stores that do not report to credit bureaus or finance companies rather than large banks, these consumers have credit files that suffer from the limited menu of credit options available to them. Many poor and low-income communities have higher concentrations of minorities.

Specifically, Fair Isaac said it does not consider:

- **Race, color, religion, national origin, sex, or marital status.** Receipt of public assistance, exercise of any consumer right under the Consumer Credit Protection Act.
- **Age.** (Clearly, underwriting scoring models used by insurers consider age, but these are not Fair Isaac models.)
- **Salary, occupation, title, employer, date employed, or employment history.** Lenders may consider this information, however.
- **Place of residence**
- **Any interest rate being charged on a credit card or other account**
- **Any items reported as child/family support obligations or rental agreements**
- **Certain types of inquiries (i.e., certain requests for your credit report or score)**
- **Any information not found in your credit report**
- **Any information that is not *proven* to be predictive of future credit performance**

Chapter 2

Credit Scoring – Advanced

> *You can observe a lot by watching.*
> – Yogi Berra

Fair Isaac Corporation's explanation is a good starting point, and for some, it will suffice. But of course, there's more to the system – much more. This chapter, as well as Chapters 3 and 4, will provide more detail.

Fair Isaac actually has several scoring systems or models. The most widely used is the **"classic risk model."** Equifax's version of classic is called "Beacon." Formerly called "Empirica," Trans Union's version in 2004 was renamed "TU FICO Classic." Experian's version is known as the "Experian/Fair Isaac Risk Model."

Classic is used by the majority of mortgage lenders. It is also the version you buy when you go to www.myfico.com. More than 70% of the 100 largest financial institutions use FICO scores to make billions of credit decisions each year, including more than 75 percent of mortgage loan originations, according to Fair Isaac.

In addition, there are variations of the model that are tailored to different kinds of credit: auto, bank card, personal finance and installment loans. Some mortgage lenders and credit card issuers have developed their own credit scoring models, which they use alongside of the FICO model when evaluating an application.

Classic was first developed in 1989, but its use increased sharply in 1995 when the two major mortgage underwriters, Fannie Mae and Freddie Mac, endorsed them for use by mortgage lenders. In 2001, Fair Isaac introduced its more advanced "Next Generation," or "NextGen," scoring model. NextGen is supposed to be more precise and more reliable, but it has not yet been widely adopted, in part because Fannie Mae and Freddie Mac have not endorsed it.[21]

How It Works: 'Variables' and 'Score Cards'

In creating its Classic model, Fair Isaac identified about three hundred possible characteristics on consumer credit reports that might be predictive of future credit risk, according to Craig Watts, Fair Isaac's Consumer Affairs Manager.[22] These included combinations of data types, such as Factor A divided by Factor B. Fair Isaac score developers then winnowed that list down to a couple dozen of the most predictive characteristics, which were then incorporated into the Classic FICO scoring model. These two-dozen or so characteristics are listed in Chapter 1 and can be found at the MyFico Web site.[23]

Fair Isaac's Classic uses 10 "Scorecards" to calculate the credit score. The scorecards find key attributes in the consumer's credit report and then groups the consumer with other consumers who have the same key attributes. Watts said the scorecard approach greatly improves the predict-ability of the scores.

---

[21] Equifax's trademarked version of "NextGen" is called "Pinnacle;" Trans Union's is "Precision" and Experian's is the "Experian/Fair Isaac Advanced Risk Score."

[22] Craig Watts and Karlene Bowen consistently and helpfully responded to a series of questions from the author.

[23] http://www.myfico.com/myfico/CreditCentral/ScoreConsiders.asp

"For one thing, consumers are compared with like-consumers so the model can be sensitive to subtler distinctions between them. Here's how it works. The FICO formula first checks to see which of the 10 consumer groups your credit report best matches. Let's say you have a serious delinquency on your report. You will be put into a group with other consumers who also have at least one serious delinquency on their reports, and your FICO score will be calculated using a scorecard customized to the credit risk features found in that group," he said.

Fair Isaac said the NextGen model is more precise because it breaks the consumer population into 18 groups or scorecards. As with classic FICO scores, the groups are based only on the credit history data from their credit reports.

Impact On Mortgage, Refinance Rates

Although actual use varies greatly among lenders, for some mortgages and refinancing, the cut-off line for your interest rate can come at 20-point intervals. Again, depending on the lenders or refinanciers, the FICO Classic score qualifying you for the best rate can range from 680-760. Remember our first "general rule," the lower the score, the more you pay. Anything below a 620 is considered "sub-prime," which means the borrower is considered "very high risk" and must pay much, much higher interest rates.

Fair Isaac has its roots in risk assessment. The first purpose of the FICO score is to show how likely you are to become at least 90 days late in making payments in the next 24 months based upon patterns in your credit history, compared with patterns of millions of past consumers.

The Importance Of Being Recent

Fair Isaac scoring models place a great deal of weight on *how recently* you had a credit problem. As the following chart illustrates, in a proportional sense, a major delinquency in the past year has a 93% negative impact, while a major delinquency between 1-2 years-old has about a 60% negative impact; a major delinquency between 2-3 years-old has a 44% negative impact; a 3-4 year old delinquency has a 33% impact; any delinquency older than 4 years has only a 22% negative impact. (See Fair Isaac slide.)

Previous credit performance

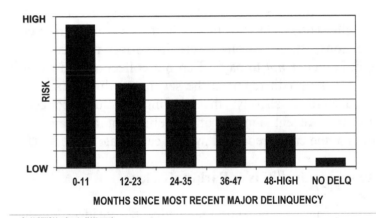

MONTHS SINCE MOST RECENT MAJOR DELINQUENCY

In fact, under the FICO scoring system, sometimes how recently the event occurred is more important than the event itself. This is true for all derogatory items, from a 30-day late payment to a collection or judgment. A 30-day late payment from last month is going to reduce your score significantly while a judgment from 6 years ago, while still reducing the score somewhat, is insignificant. The *amount of money* involved in the event is *not* always significant. While the amounts of delinquent balances are important to a score, the "recency" of the event can be more important. So even if it is only for $25, if you have a collection or public record in the past few months, it does serious damage to your credit score. In other words, a $40 balance on an account that is currently 60 days late, in some cases can do more damage to your credit then a $3,000 collection account that appeared on your credit report four years ago. Delinquencies are also scored according to "severity." Is the delinquency a "first-ever" event or the latest in a series? Is it 30-days or 90-days?

Another little known fact is that if you pay off an old collection account, it can "update" to your credit report and once again becomes a "recent" event that is highly damaging to your credit score. That is, a collection from the year 2003 that is paid off in February 2007 might very well be re-scored in March 2007 by FICO as a very recent, highly damaging entry. Thus, while it's best to pay off very recent collections, strictly from a credit-scoring perspective, it might be better *not* to pay off an old collection and to let it drop off the credit report at the seven-year limit. Fair Isaac has disagreed sharply that paying an old collection constitutes recent activity on a delinquent account,[24] but quirks in the credit reporting system can create that effect.

Unpaid Medical Bills & Parking Tickets

This is why some knowledgeable insiders feel that minor medical collections can unfairly drag down credit scores and undeservedly make people look like greater credit risks than they really are. Moreover, it's not uncommon for medical bills to go unpaid and be sent to collection agencies because of mistakes on the part of health insurers or HMOs. As a consumer, it is important to understand that a minor medical collection, or any collection or default judgment, can seriously damage a credit score. This is significant because researchers are learning that medical bills may account for more than 50 percent of collections.

---

[24] There appears to be disagreement between Fair Isaac and some credit bureaus on this issue.

Whether it is a service bill or mail order product, it is not uncommon for consumers who feel they did not receive the service or product that they ordered, or who feel they simply are not responsible for a debt, to refuse on principle to pay the debt. Some people who think they were wrongly given a $20 parking ticket, refuse to pay, and move out of the jurisdiction where they were ticketed. They might think that one minor item will not damage their credit that much.

But many collectors and creditors already know that it is damaging, and will use the threat of reporting to the credit bureaus as a means of pressuring consumers into paying debts. For many major forms of credit, like a mortgage, a consumer must resolve all outstanding collections and negative public records before a loan will be approved. Accordingly, creditors view credit reporting as an arm of debt collection – a sort of last resort that will catch up with non-paying consumers sooner or later. This practice "crosses the line" when creditors and collectors threaten to report debts – or actually report debts – that they know or should know are not the responsibility of the consumer.

Heavy Credit Card Use

Another common misconception about credit scoring is that paying off your credit card balances in full every month guarantees a top-notch credit score. If fact, if the balance is high on the day of the month that your credit card company reports to the credit bureaus, that will be the amount reported. The fact that the balance is paid off with each month's billing statement and returned to "zero" might not be reflected on your credit report. Many self-employed or small business people, or those who make many business- or profession-related purchases on their credit cards and then pay off the balances each month, fit this profile.

Say for instance, that by the end of the month, you make $7,000 worth of purchases using a credit card with a credit limit of $8,000. In the middle of the month, at the time of the due date, you pay off the entire balance that appeared on your last statement.

But from a credit reporting perspective, you *aren't* paying off the entire balance: by the time your payment arrives at the credit card company, your true balance has changed due to incoming charges. While you may pay the full amount shown on your statement, the account never reaches a true zero balance, unless you cease charging for a month. Since the credit card companies choose a particular day of each month to report to the bureaus, whatever the *balance on that day* is the one that goes on your credit report. Your credit score may remain unchanged if your purchases are consistent month to month, or the score may drop if the balance is higher, or rise if that balance is lower.

So, *if you know* the date that your credit card company reports to the bureaus, and you want to raise your credit score at least temporarily, then paying off your balance a few days before that date could achieve that goal.

The Fair Isaac slide below charts the impact on credit scores of the balance-to-credit limit ratio:

Current level of indebtedness

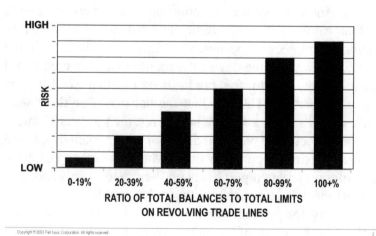

This is but one example of how someone who in reality handles their credit very responsibly is in fact penalized by the credit scoring system, in part because of the timing or reporting cycles and the current inability of the system to accommodate people who regularly pay off high balances, or at least dramatically reduce them. This also why Fair Isaac advises consumers to keep their card balances low.

This comes under "Factor 2: Amount Owed – Extent of Indebtedness" that we discussed in Chapter 1. The categories within Factor 2 are: "Ratio of credit balance to credit limit," "the amount owed on all accounts," and "the amount owed on each type of account." In other words, you might think of yourself as a responsible user of credit, but your credit score is taking a hit in all three of these categories.

Store Cards & Instant Discounts

Credit scores can also drop when a consumer accepts or signs up for a department store charge card and then uses the card to take advantage of an instant discount. Such charge cards usually start with very low credit limits, so any purchases likely will result in a high ratio of "credit balance to credit limit." Next, your score drops because you have opened up a new line of credit and then because of the department store's inquiry to your credit report. Also, the credit scoring system looks less favorably on store charge cards, which give you limited buying potential, than it does on credit cards from major banks, which give you much broader buying potential. Again, your score can take a hit from three different directions.

The department store scenario can have an unforeseen impact when the consumer receives preliminary approval for a mortgage application and then to celebrate, goes shopping. The subsequent drop in credit score forces the mortgage lender to withdraw its approval or make another offer at a less favorable rate.

But, Don't 'Close' Your Unused Credit Cards

In addition to the balance-to-credit limit calculation made on each individual account, the scoring module also makes a separate calculation using all of your revolving accounts. This means closing unused or little-used credit cards can cause your score to drop because it raises, unfavorably, that overall ratio between the balances on all your revolving accounts against the limits on all of your open revolving accounts. It can also have a negative impact because it can shorten the length of time you have credit. Also, the FICO model looks more favorably on major credit cards, like a Visa or MasterCard from a major issuer, or an American Express or Discover Card. So if you feel compelled to close some accounts, close the department store or specialty cards, and the cards with the lowest credit limits.[25]   Certainly one of the ironies is that the FICO model penalizes you for not having credit cards, but also penalizes you if you use them too much, or in the "wrong" way – as the scoring model defines it.

Inquiries

The impact of inquiries on credit scores has evolved over time, as FICO has made important adjustments (this was mentioned in the previous chapter). In the early days, shopping for a mortgage or auto loan meant that many lenders would pull the applicant's credit report, thereby creating a slew of inquiries that promptly lowered the applicant's score. This left a lasting impression, as to this day too many people mistakenly assume that inquiries are the main cause of a falling credit score. But Fair Isaac agreed with critics that it wasn't fair to penalize people who shopped for better rates. Initially it changed FICO classic so that all mortgage-related and auto-related inquiries within

---

[25] Singletary, Michelle, "Play Defense In the Credit Game," *Washington Post*, Jan. 25, 2004; pg. F1

any 14-day period that occurred more than 30 days prior or
less than one year prior would only count as one inquiry.
Now, both Classic and the NextGen model allow for all
inquiries within a 45-day period to count as just one inquiry,
giving consumers more time to rate-shop without being
penalized.

'Classic' vs. 'NextGen'

A more general and ongoing problem relates to the
fact that although Fair Isaac over the years has regularly
updated its credit scoring models, many lenders continue to
use the older versions. In fact, the latest model, dubbed
"Next Generation," was rolled out in 2001. But as Kenneth
Harney of the *Washington Post* reported, it has not been
adopted by most lenders and investors.[26] Fair Isaac
recognized the problem but said it could not require any
creditor to use a specific version of its software. There were
substantial computer system costs to integrating new FICO
models into lenders' underwriting programs, "and we are
very sensitive to that," said Fair Isaac's Craig Watts.

Variations between the older and newer FICO models
can lead to significant differences in credit scores. In 2002,
the National Association of Mortgage Brokers issued a
warning to its 13,000 members. Ginny Ferguson, chair of the
group's credit-scoring committee, told the *Washington Post*
that "when lenders use [outdated FICO models] for pricing
of loans, we can run into major problems."

It's not just Classic vs. Next Gen – there can be
significant differences within Classic itself. For example,
instead of incorporating changes made to Classic by FICO
into one version, Equifax released the changes as a newer
version. At one point you could sign up for the original
"Beacon," or its successor, "Beacon Enhanced," or the third

---

[26] Kenneth Harney, "Outdated Credit-Scoring System Can Penalize
Potential Borrowers," Feb. 23, 2002, pg H01,
www.washingtonpost.com/wp-dyn/articles/A53198-2002Feb22.html

generation "Beacon 96." Currently, Beacon 5.0 is the most commonly used, as Beacon 6.0 has not yet caught on.

The FICO models have evolved regularly for various reasons. In the mid-1990s, the FICO model would penalize applicants for having "finance company" loans on their credit histories, or for multiple "inquiries" resulting from a consumer shopping for the best mortgage or auto loan rate. The most recent NextGen model ignores any collections or public record for an amount under $100In some cases, the older the version, the lower the credit score. However, the majority of lenders don't use the most recent NextGen model.

A potential conflict arises when a lower credit score results in a higher mortgage rate, which in turn generates higher fees for loan officers, and higher rates for the lender when it sells the loan on the secondary market.

Richard Le Febvre, who for years ran AAA American Credit Bureau Inc. in Flagstaff, Ariz., said he often saw mortgage applicants get hurt by older FICO scoring.

A mortgage broker would order a score on an applicant through a small credit bureau like Le Febvre's, which used an updated FICO model. But then the lender to whom the broker intended to sell the loan ran the same applicant through an old model, and the score came out lower. The lender's lower score dictated what the borrower paid, Le Febvre said.

Sometimes it works the other way. An online lender had received more applicants than it could handle. So the online lender sold the names of those consumers with qualifying FICO scores to a second mortgage lender. However, the online lender used a FICO version that produced higher scores than the FICO version used by the second mortgage lender. Thus, most of the leads turned out to be worthless because they failed to qualify under the second lender's version of FICO. Neither the online lender nor the second lender was aware that there could be such significant discrepancies.

TrueCredit Is Not Truly A FICO Score

Further complicating matters is the fact that consumers can buy credit scores from companies other than FICO. At times, these "knock-off" scores can mislead consumers because 1) consumers think that they are actually FICO scores, and 2) they are higher than the FICO score. Accordingly, the consumer thinks he has a high score, but is only offered a mediocre rate when he applies for credit. This is because the real FICO score used by the lender was much lower than the imitation score obtained by the consumer.

If you find this a bit confusing, well, you're not alone. For instance, at Experian's Web site the credit score available for purchase is your "PLUS Score," a proprietary model developed by Experian and introduced in early 2004. TransUnion sells the "TrueScore" through it affiliate, www.TrueCredit.com. Neither the Experian nor TransUnion Web sites clearly explain, in an easy-to-find place, that the credit score that you buy from them could differ significantly from the FICO score that your lender is likely to use. They also don't explain that lenders do not use TrueCredit or PLUS scores when making credit decisions.

Equifax's Web site sells the FICO score, but the problem is that there are five industry-specific versions of Classic FICO. The bottom line is that a borrower cannot rely on the score bought at a Web site, even if it is a true FICO, to match the industry-specific score that will be provided to a mortgage company or auto dealer.

Mortgage industry sources say consumers regularly complain that the FICO score actually used by their lender was lower than the scores they bought at any of the Web sites, including the true FICO score available at Equifax.

At www.myFico.com, you can buy your FICO score for each of the three bureaus. If you are just trying to get a general idea of where you stand, the Experian and Trans Union knock-offs are probably good enough. But if you are applying for a mortgage, or an auto loan, or to refinance, a few points can make a big difference. Thus, the prudent thing to do is to make sure you get your actual FICO score, keeping in mind that even that might not be identical to the one that determines your interest rate.

VantageScore: Contender or Pretender?

To confuse matters more, in March 2006, Equifax, Experian and TransUnion jointly unveiled their new "VantageScore," which they touted as a new and improved scoring model. Because it was developed cooperatively by the Big Three CRAs, they claimed it would eliminate inconsistencies caused by differences in existing scoring models. They said lenders would prefer it because it would be more predictive. While there were similarities to the factors making up the FICO model (listed in Chapter 1), there were differences in the VantageScore model:

- Payment History (32%)
- Utilization (23%)
- Balances (15%)
- Depth of Credit (13%)
- Recent Credit (10%)
- Available Credit (7%)

VantageScore used a different scoring range, 500–900, which the Big Three said would be easier to understand for lenders and consumers because each 100-point segment corresponded to a "letter grade":

901 - 990: **"A"**
801 - 900: **"B"**
701 - 800: **"C"**
601 - 700: **"D"**
501 - 600: **"F"**

Fair Isaac responded by filing an anti-trust lawsuit against Equifax, Experian and TransUnion. Fair Isaac licenses it scoring model to each CRA, which then uses the model to score the raw data it keeps in a consumer's file. The CRA then sells the FICO score to the lender. Each of the three bureaus has contracts in place that prevent Fair Isaac from selling scores directly to lenders. Instead, Fair Isaac collects royalties from the bureaus when they price and market the scoring products to lenders.

Fair Isaac CEO Tom Grudnowski said in a press release that the credit agencies were "using their position to drive adoption of their own score to the detriment of our competing FICO score product," and were "in conflict with their obligations to distribute our product."[27]

The unanswered question was whether lenders would migrate to VantageScore. There were some signs of interest. In July 2007, Experian announced that 1,500 companies had bought VantageScore, up from 800 in January. Equifax said that 60 major financial firms were in various stages of evaluation, while four institutions had already implemented it.

There were still reasons to be skeptical that changes would come anytime soon. After all, it was not a trivial matter for lenders to change scoring models, given that their systems were designed around the model. As noted earlier, Fair Isaac rolled out a new-and-improved "NextGen" model, but lenders were slow to adopt it. Moreover, VantageScore had not been approved by Fannie Mae or Freddie Mac, the two government-sponsored mortgage underwriters that endorsed FICO and expedited its use by lenders.

On its Web site, Lending Tree.com said financial institutions were not obliged to purchase the new model. "Since lenders have long relied on FICO scores to approve borrowers and set interest rates, they may find it too disruptive or too expensive to adopt a new system," it said.

---

[27] The suit was pending in September 2007. The CRAs and the joint venture, VantageScore Solutions, LLC, vowed to vigorously defend their rights to sell an alternative score.

VantageScore's least credible claim was that it would bring consistency to credit scoring. As discussed below, the primary cause of score discrepancies were the differences in data that each CRA maintained on any given consumer.

Independent Research: The CFA-NCRA Study

Perhaps the most comprehensive research on credit scores and credit reports to date, found significant differences in credit scores for the same consumer among the Big Three CRAs. The research was published jointly in December 2002 by the Consumer Federation of America (CFA) and the National Credit Reporting Association (NCRA), which represents the smaller, independent credit bureaus and resellers.

In one phase, the groups set out to learn if there were significant differences between Equifax, Experian and Trans Union. To do this, they compared the credit reports and credit scores from each of the three major bureaus pertaining to 1,500 individuals. The study focused on a 620 score, as that was the line below which consumers paid dramatically higher-priced "sub-prime" loans. Researchers felt that wide disparities between credit scores reflected major differences in the underlying data of Equifax, Experian and Trans Union.[28]

Specifically, "Phase 1" of the study found that among the three credit reports actually pulled for 1,500 consumers:

- 29% of the credit reports had a range of 50 points or more between the highest and lowest scores.
- 11% had a middle score between 575 and 630 and had a range of 30 points or more between the highest and lowest scores. This meant that one CRA would have a consumer pegged below "sub-

---

[28] Consumer Federation of America and National Credit Reporting Association, *Credit Score Accuracy and Implications for Consumers*, December 2002

prime" while another would have him above "sub-prime."

- 16% had high scores above 620 and low scores below 620.

Overall, the NCRA-CFA study found that

- 21%, or one in five files, could be considered "extremely consistent," with a range of fewer than 20 points between the highest and lowest scores.
- 31%, or one in three files, had a range of 50 points or greater between scores.
- 5%, or one in 20 files, had a range of 100 points or greater between scores.

In Phase 2, researchers did not pull full credit reports. Instead, they did an automated comparison of the credit scores among all three bureaus for 502,623 individuals. The resulting differences were remarkably similar to Phase 1.

- 24%, (compared to 21% in Phase One) could be considered extremely consistent, with a range of 20 points or fewer between the highest and lowest scores.
- 43% had a 21-49 point difference.
- 29%, (compared to 31% in Phase One) had a range of 50 points or greater between scores.
- 4%, (compared to 5% in Phase One) had a range of 100 points or greater between scores.

Considering that mortgage rates can change at 20-point, credit-score intervals, the NCRA-CFA study revealed the importance of knowing your credit score before you apply for credit. The study also tested differences between Equifax's and Trans Union's older and newer FICO scoring models, and found the differences to be negligible.

The Phase I comparison discovered another unexplained occurrence: in 10% of the cases, instead of there being three credit reports for each individual (one each for Equifax, Experian and Trans Union), a fourth, or fifth, or even sixth credit report would be returned, most of which had credit scores.

These reports were not duplicates. In some cases, the "extra" credit reports clearly were reporting the credit activity of an entirely separate person, as none of the accounts matched with those on the three primary reports. But it was very common for the additional report to contain a mixture of credit data, some of which belonged to the applicant and some of which clearly did not. In still other cases, applicants had split files that appeared to be the result of applying for credit under variations of their name. It was unclear to researchers exactly how various lenders and their systems would interpret these additional credit reports and scores.

Credit Scores Rule

What is clear is that credit scores are a key factor in credit granting, be it automated or manual decision-making, especially in the all-important home mortgage loan business. To understand why, it is necessary to understand how the mortgage market works. Once a mortgage is approved, mortgage brokers and other "originators" of home loans generally look to sell them on the "secondary market." To do so most profitably, they want to sell these mortgages quickly, and that requires the financial guarantees of Freddie Mac's and Fannie Mae's automated underwriting process (AU).[29]

As the CFA study put it, "In this market, where record volumes of loans are being originated, there is a tremendous incentive to deal only with the loans that will be approved the fastest – the loans that pass the credit score/ automated underwriting test."

---

[29] The FICO score is one of 15 factors set by Fannie's and Freddie's automated underwriting systems.

It Was Different Before

Of course, it did not start out this way. Freddie Mac, in a 1995 letter to mortgage lenders, described FICO scores as only "one of the selection factors in our quality control sampling procedures." This, of course, was before Automated Underwriting took off.

"After reviewing a number of alternatives, we determined that, within the manual underwriting process, one of the easiest and most readily available tools to assist you in managing the challenging credit-risk environment is the use of either FICO bureau or MDS bankruptcy scores. Using these scores can help you better assess and manage the quality of your loan originations, reduce servicing costs and sustain profitability," Freddie Mac continued.

The 1995 Freddie Mac letter virtually closed out what now seems like a quaint era in which human judgment was required, and numbers weren't everything. The letter continued:

> We want to emphasize that there is no single FICO bureau or MDS bankruptcy score that means an individual borrower will default. However, these scores can help you identify loans that may require a closer look by your underwriter. If your underwriter is able to establish the borrower's willingness to repay as agreed, then we encourage you to consider this is in your investment-quality decision, regardless of what the credit score alone might suggest. Remember that you are still responsible for underwriting the credit reputation, as well as the file as a whole, to make your investment-quality decision.

In the years following this letter, advances in information technology, coupled with Freddie Mac's and Fannie Mae's satisfaction with FICO scores, allowed automated underwriting to take off. This coincided with falling interest rates and resulted in tremendous growth in both home sales and mortgage refinancing, benefiting millions of consumers and the economy as a whole.

In the meantime, the FICO score had emerged as the most important, and at times, the only determinant in the credit granting process.

'Reason' Codes

The FICO models most commonly in use offer several dozen "Reason Codes" as to why your FICO score is less than perfect. (See listing on pages 43-44.)

As you look over these codes, keep in mind that some of these codes should not be acted upon, as they do not represent "stand-alone" categories, but are scored against the broader credit history. In fact, under the newer scoring models, there is one code for "too few bank revolving accounts" and another code for "too many bank or national revolving accounts."

Also, under the new models, the number of scoring factors or reason codes has expanded.

In addition, the three major credit bureaus' scoring models generally can produce special messages after a credit report is analyzed. Below are some examples of so-called "Scoreability criteria" from TU's old Empirica model:

- **Not Scored** -- Insufficient credit; when a credit file does not contain a tradeline opened for at least six months and a tradeline updated within the last six months;
- **Not Scored** – Deceased; when the subject's Social Security number matches the Social Security Administration's deceased SSN file.
- **Alert** – When a credit file contains one or more of the following: previous bankruptcy, derogatory public record, collection activity, or a status of 150-days late or worse.

Reason Statement	All Bureaus Unless other	Equifax (BEACON^{sm})	TransUnion (EMPIRICA^{sm})	Experian (Alpha/Num) (FICOII^{sm})
Amount owed on accounts is too high	01	•	•	A/•
Level of Delinquency on accounts	02	•	•	B/•
Too few bank revolving accounts	03			C/•
Proportion of loan balances to loan amounts is too high	03	33	•	I/33
Too many bank or national revolving accounts	04	•		D/•
Lack of recent installment loan information	04	32	•	Y/32
Too many accounts with balances	05	•	•	E/•
Too many consumer finance company accounts	06	•	•	F/•
Account payment history is too new to rate	07	•	•	G/•
Too many inquires last 12 months	08	•	•	H/•
Too many accounts recently opened	09	•	•	J/•
Proportion of balance to credit limits is too high on bank revolving and other revolving accounts	10	•	•	K/•
Amount owed on revolving accounts is too high	11	•	•	L/•
Length of time revolving accts. have been established	12	•	•	M/•
Time since delinquency too recent or unknown	13	•	•	N/•
Length of time accts. have been established	14	•	•	O/•

Lack of recent bank
revolving information ....15 .... • .... • .... P/•

Lack of recent revolving
account information ....16 .... • .... • Q/1

No recent non-mortgage
balance information ....17 .... • .... • .... R/•

Number of accounts
with delinquency ....18 .... • .... • .... S/•

Too few accounts
currently paid as agreed .....19 .... • .... 27 .... T •

Date of last
inquiry too recent ....19 .... • ....

Time since derogatory
public record or collection
too short ....…................20 .... • .... • .... V/•

Amount past
due on accounts ....21 .... • .... • W/1

Serious delinquency,
derogatory public
record or collection ......…......22 .... * .... * .... X/*

Number of bank or national
revolving accts. with balances .23 .... • .... /•

No recent revolving balances ..24 .... • .... • U/1

Length of time installment
loans have been established ....25 .... I/O .... I/O

Number of revolving accounts.26 .... I/O .... I/O

Number of bank or other
revolving accounts ....26 .... I/O .... I/O

Secret Data?

Important aspects of the system remain a secret.
Sources have told this author there are raw data in credit
reports – regularly scored by FICO scoring models – that are
never seen by consumers because these data do not appear
on their credit reports. These raw data show up on "machine
readable" credit reports used by lenders and their scoring
models, but not on the more familiar reports disclosed to
consumers.

For example, one major credit bureau has one code to denote the most recent negative item; a second code marking the previous most recent negative item, and a third code denoting the most recent, worst negative that is more than 24 months old. If consumers are to become more educated about their credit reports and credit scores, shouldn't this kind of information be disclosed as well?

Generation Gap

In late 2001, Fair Isaac announced the rollout of its "Next Generation" scoring models with some fanfare. Fair Isaac's Karlene Bowen predicted before the National Credit Reporting Association that the new "NextGen" model would bring more precision and would rapidly be adopted by banks and mortgage lenders in 2002.[30]

Bowen said the key to the "Next Generation" score was that it used complex statistical models to "see through" credit file data to better identify loan applicants who represented the highest risks of delinquency or foreclosure. Based on new analyses of tens of millions of consumer credit files, the Next Generation scores "reward" some people -- moving them into the heretofore rarefied "800" and higher score category. But it also pushed other people below the "600" level that often triggers higher interest rates and fees.[31] The ranges changed as well. While "800" might be rare under FICO classic because the top score was "850," under NextGen, the top score is now "950" – and the default rate classes are probably adjusted as well. Fair Isaac's Craig Watts indicated for many consumers, the change would not be that great. "NextGen scores correlate to classic FICO scores, so a score of 620 from either model indicates the same likelihood the consumer will become seriously delinquent within 24 months," he said.

---

[30] Kenneth Harney, "Higher Credit Scores On the Horizon," *Realty Times*, November 12, 2001
[31] *Id.*

But lenders for the most part have not adopted Next Generation. Fair Isaac attributed their reticence to the cost of integrating new software. But another important factor is that Fannie and Freddie have not endorsed it. Until they do, don't expect many others to. It took six years for Fannie and Freddie to endorse FICO classic after its unveiling in 1989. There's no telling if and when the two influential mortgage organizations will recognize "NextGen" in the same way.

This means that there will continue to be a pronounced lack of uniformity in the market, which, at a minimum, will generate confusion for consumers trying to understand their actual status in the credit-scoring hierarchy.

Where Do We Stand?

There appears to be a discrepancy in how Fair Isaac and Experian rate the creditworthiness of the U.S. population. Fair Isaac said as of early 2004, this was how U.S. consumers' FICO scores were distributed nationally:

- 800 or higher – 11 percent
- 750-799 – 28 percent
- 700-749 – 19 percent
- 650-699 – 16 percent
- 600-649 – 12 percent
- 550-599 – 8 percent
- 500-549 – 5 percent
- 499 and under – 1 percent[32]

If Fair Isaac's estimates are accurate, then nearly 60 percent of U.S. consumers are qualifying for top-notch credit, with credit scores of 700 or above.

However, in March 2004, Experian rated the nation according to its PLUS score, which uses a range similar to the FICO model. However, the PLUS score was not used by

---

[32] Fair Isaac Corp., "National Distribution of FICO Scores;" (Slide)

lenders, sources said. Still, Experian claimed its survey used the most up-to-date information, and found that the average PLUS credit score was 678. Moreover, it gave the following regional breakdown:

- New England – 699
- West North Central – 695
- Mid-Atlantic – 690
- East North Central – 684
- East South Central – 677
- South Atlantic – 675
- Pacific – 674
- Mountain – 670
- West South Central – 656[33]

It was worth noting that New Englanders had the most credit card and installment debt (per capita, $13,566), had the most credit cards, had the highest minimum monthly payments ($575), and the most credit usage, according to Experian. But they had the fewest late payments. [34]

The "West South Central," on the other hand, had the lowest per capita debt ($9,297), but the most late payments.

Who Knows?

One key question is whether the credit-scoring system so lacks in transparency, fairness or reliability that a stronger public policy is needed to protect consumers.

Because Congress dedicated much of 2003 to a major updating of the Fair Credit Reporting Act, and because the FTC and federal banking agencies continued working to establish new enforcement rules and guidance, it was not seen as likely that Congress would move to further regulate credit-scoring before the end of the decade.

---

[33] www.nationalscore.com/USScore.aspx, click on "View All Graphs."
[34] Excluding real estate/mortgage loans

Thus, despite any problems with the current credit-scoring and credit-reporting systems, it appears that they are here to stay. Many of the changes passed by Congress, coupled with the financial industry's response to them, should help make the system more transparent and fair to consumers. But as much of this book should make clear, there's a long way to go. A primary goal of this book is to narrow the "knowledge gap" so consumers can gain an in-depth understanding of how these all-important systems work and what consumers can do to improve their lot.

Does Credit Scoring Really Work?

In the 2002 NCRA-CFA study, which was one of few known independent research efforts on credit scoring validity, the authors noted the lack of non-industry assessment of credit-scoring methods.

> Despite the gatekeeper role that these scoring systems play regarding access to credit, housing, insurance, utilities, and employment, as well as pricing for those essentials, exactly how the formulas perform the transformation from credit report to credit score is a closely guarded secret. For consumers, regulators, and even industry participants who rely on the computations in their decision-making, the scoring models largely remain a "black box." No scholarly reviews of this extremely powerful market force have been permitted, and apart from reviews by federal banking regulators to protect against discrimination, no government regulator has insisted that they be examined to ensure that they are adequate and fair.

Stephen L. Ross and John Yinger, both professors of economics at University of Connecticut and Syracuse University, respectively, made a similar observation in their

2002 book, <u>The Color of Credit</u>:

> No existing credit-scoring scheme, let alone a fully automated underwriting system, has been subjected to the scrutiny of disinterested scholars. There is significant literature (reviewed in Thomas, 2000) on the technical dimensions of credit scoring, that is, on the best method for devising a credit score. As Thomas points out, however, "comparisons [across methods] by academics are often limited as some of the most significant data like the credit bureau reports are too sensitive or too expensive to be passed to them by users." As a result, the accuracy of credit-scoring schemes remains an open question.[35]

Fair Isaac said it's never really been a factory for "white papers," a reference to the lengthy, seldom read

How do we know it works?

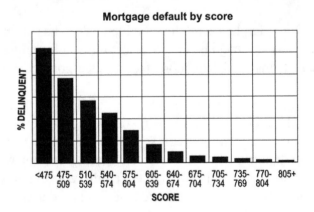

Mortgage default by score

---

[35] Stephen L. Ross & John Yinger, <u>The Color Of Credit</u> (MIT 2003); the passage refers to Lyn C. Thomas, "A Survey of Credit and Behavioral Scoring: Forecasting Financial Risk of Lending to Consumers," *International Journal of Forecasting*, 16(2) (April-June): 149-172.

research papers that some technology companies are known to churn out. But Fair Isaac is confident that its system helps lenders improve their decision-making, and that it's an overall plus for consumers and for the economy.

Most important, Fair Isaac said that its scoring model has been tested over and over in the market by nearly every creditor in the country, and has passed with flying colors, as demonstrated by the company's chart on page 51.

One dissenting voice was Golden West Financial's Herb Sandler, who with his wife, ran one of the most profitable mortgage lenders in America. Sandler told *Forbes Magazine* that Golden West, based in Oakland, California, doesn't use or trust FICO scores. He said the models were too dependent on borrowing histories accumulated during a relatively benign economy with strong housing prices. Golden West's bad loan rate was just 0.5% of assets compared with 0.7% for the thrift industry, *Forbes* reported March 1, 2004.

"Obviously we're doing something right," Sandler said.

Other lenders said that Golden West has a special situation, as it specialized in short-term adjustable rate mortgage loans, and had more face-to-face contact with its clientele.

One thing that Fair Isaac is crystal clear on: All of its models rely exclusively on information in consumers' credit reports when calculating credit scores. That is why to gain a full understanding of how the credit scoring system works, one needs to examine the source: the credit reporting system. While next two chapters provide additional details about credit scoring, the balance of this book is devoted to an examination of the credit reporting system and how credit reports are used, and at times, misused.

Chapter 3

Re-Scoring

"If at first you don't succeed . . ."

– Old Saying

When it comes to new mortgages or refinancing, there is a cost-effective, professional service available to improve your credit score in a way that could very well save you thousands of dollars by getting you a better interest rate.

It's called "Re-Scoring," but hardly anybody knows about it.[36] How could that be?

Re-scoring is offered by the smaller, independent credit bureaus, sometimes referred to as "resellers." But the contracts these resellers have with Equifax, Experian, and Trans Union prohibit them from offering their services directly to consumers. In other words, if you call a reseller, they can't help you—no matter how much you'd be willing to pay them. If that seems like a restraint on trade, don't get your hopes up just yet. An anti-trust lawsuit was not well received by a federal court.

Meanwhile, to use a reseller, you have to abide by a kind of "food chain," meeting the following three conditions set by the contracts issued by the Big Three CRAs:

---

[36] See two articles by Kenneth Harney of the *Washington Post*, "Bad FICO Mark? Re-score Your Credit." *Washington Post*, July 14, 2001, pg. H1; and "Credit Re-scoring: How To Know If It's For You," July 21, 2001; pg. H1.

(1) You have to be a prospective customer of a lender or mortgage broker;

(2) That lender or broker must be a customer of the reseller; and

(3) The mortgage broker must request the reseller's help on your behalf.

Take Time Out

The lender or mortgage broker is under no obligation to tell you that it uses a reseller that could improve your score. If the lender or broker is most concerned with speedy approval, and feels that using a reseller would slow down the mortgage-granting process, then they are not likely to tell you about re-scoring. For some lenders and brokers, the worse the credit score, the higher the interest rate, the larger the loan, the bigger the commission. If you, the customer, are in a hurry and don't know about re-scoring, what you don't know could cost you, and your "haste makes waste." By the way, only a fraction of lenders or brokers use resellers.

The re-scoring system was created because of pressure on the Big Three CRAs from the mortgage granting industry. This happened for two basic reasons. First, the mortgage industry saw that credit report errors were hampering mortgage granting, sometimes causing unjust rejection of applicants. Often, delays were caused and expenditure of extra time and effort was necessary to correct mistakes so a loan could be approved. Second, as the industry moved towards automated underwriting, and loan approval was reduced from months to days—sometimes to hours or minutes—virtually nobody was willing to wait the 30 to 45 days it took to correct credit report errors.

The re-scoring contracts give re-sellers special privileges that allow them to review credit reports and, within a day or so, submit corrections or other changes to a "dedicated" desk at the CRA. Because the changes are made directly to the Big Three CRAs, the consumer's amended credit report can be pulled and verified by Fannie Mae, Freddie Mac or other loan guarantors.

In general, the process is rather simple.

(1) The lender or broker forwards the file of a potential re-scoring candidate to the reseller. The reseller reviews that candidate's credit report and advises the lender/broker whether re-scoring will result in enough improvement to make it worth it. Unless the credit report is a overrun by derogatories, it's usually worth it, as sometimes just improving a few points will qualify the borrower for a better rate.

(2) The reseller identifies a strategy for changing or correcting the report so the score will be improved.

(3) Because the strategy involves actions that the borrower must take, like paying down debt or obtaining documentation from creditors, the reseller prepares a set of recommendations based on the contents of the credit file, the goal score, and the borrower's situation, and sends instructions to the borrower, through the loan officer.

(4) The borrower follows the recommendations, obtains proof of the changes from their creditors (including collection agencies or courts if applicable), and supplies the documentation proving the changes to their loan officer.

(5) The loan officer forwards the documentation to the reseller, who then verifies the documentation is legitimate and forwards the documentation to the re-score desk at the CRA(s) selected by the reseller or determined by the loan program.

(6) The reseller confirms that the changes have been made at the CRAs and that the credit-report

containing the amended data is now available to the lender and loan guarantors like Freddie and Fannie. In most cases, the new score will be improved by the amended data. It is important to remember that during the re-score process, other creditors may issue reports to the bureaus changing the data in trades other than the trades selected for re-score. If the change is negative it could possibly cancel out or event reduce any increase the file may have gained from the changes put through by re-scoring work. In a few cases, it may cause a reduction greater than the increase, resulting in a drop in the score. Because of this, and the "black box" of secret algorithms and calculations, there can never be a "guaranteed" increase.

Depending on how much work needs to be done on the credit report, the cost of this process usually ranges from $150-$300, but can run over $1,000 in dramatic cases. Under Equifax's contract, resellers are not allowed to pass through costs to the borrower. This means that the mortgage broker or lender has to eat the costs. Clearly this might dissuade the broker or lender from making it known to their applicant that the service is available, even if their borrowers are perfect candidates for the process, and despite the fact that any borrowers could benefit greatly from reduction in their interest rate.

A reputable reseller, like Lenders' Credit Services, Inc.(LCSI), in Baltimore, Maryland, will carefully screen a borrower's history and only attempt to re-score those for whom success is likely.

But the results can be impressive. LCSI re-scores the credit reports of an average of 25 borrowers per week. The company estimates the results as follows:

- On average, the score improves 30 points. This is significant because the mortgage rates generally improve at 20-point FICO intervals.
- About 1-2 cases a week improve 50 points.
- About 1-2 cases a week improve 70 points.
- About 3 cases a month improve 100 points.
- About 2 cases a week cannot be improved.

The extent of the savings can depend on your starting FICO score, but they can add up quickly. According to Fair Isaac, for a $300,000 30-year, fixed-rate mortgage, a consumer with a 760 score would have a 6.072% interest rate and a monthly payment of $906, while a consumer with a 619 score would get a 9.419% rate, paying $1,252 monthly. The difference between "top-of-the-line" and "sub-prime" is $346 per month, or $4,152 per year.[37]

The two most common ways of improving a score are by (a) correcting mistakes, like late payments or outdated balances that make the borrower appear more in debt than he really is, and (b) by "manipulating" debt, either by paying down the amount owed on credit cards (revolving debt), or redistributing debt so it's at least below 50% of the credit limit on each revolving account and as a total of all accounts.

Here are the seven most common reasons to re-score a credit file, and some of the actions the reseller, working with the borrower, must take for each item.[38] Clearly the following is useful for anyone who doesn't have access to a reseller and wants to do it on his own. But here's something you'll want to remember: <u>resellers cannot affect changes to accounts the consumer has recently put "in dispute" with the CRA</u>. The CRAs also won't allow a reseller to effect changes due to a "mixed file," that is when a file appears to

---

[37] www.myfico.com, visited September 10, 2007
[38] The seven points were provided by Ruth Koontz and Paul Wohkittel of Lenders Credit Services Inc. (LCSI). This author signed an agreement with LCSI confirming that I was not shown, and did not see, any confidential consumer data.

include identification data on more than one consumer.[39] (Resellers are permitted to change a balance or remove a late date that is incorrect, not a trade that "doesn't belong" to the consumer, if the evidence is present that the file is "mixed.")

1. **Payment history is incorrect.** Letter from creditor, on creditor's letterhead, stating what the correct history should be, or a "Universal Data Correction" (UDC) form (a standard form used by most creditors reporting information to the CRAs) completed and signed by the creditor.

2. **Account reports a delinquency that has been brought current or can be brought current.** Letter from creditor (all such letters should be on letterhead) stating that the account is now current, and/or with a correct lesser balance, or a UDC form completed and signed by the creditor.

3. **Account reports a balance that in fact has already been paid in full.** Letter from creditor or UDC form. However, caution is needed in regard to collections and "charge-offs." The older an item, the less effect it has on scoring. Paying off, and/or marking a five-year-old collection or charge-off as "paid-in-full' could cause the score to drop instead of rise. This is because the change makes the "date of last activity" become "recent," instead of "five-years-old." In such cases, it's better to let "sleeping dogs" lie and let them quietly drop off the report at the seven-year mark. The exception to this is when the change is being made not to increase a score, but instead to change something that is interfering with an automated underwriting approval. Remember, Fannie Mae, Freddie Mac, and others automatically scan credit reports for

---

[39] See Chapters 8 and 10 for more information on "Mixed Files"

major derogatories, like bankruptcy, foreclosure, and tax liens.

4. **Credit report includes an account that does not belong to the borrower.** This is a challenge, given the CRAs' refusal to let resellers change mixed files. Still, resellers can re-score when another the problem account was created by another's fraud. A letter from the creditor or UDC form is needed. For judgments, a copy of the judgment from the correct court showing the same case number and defendant, is required.

5. **Includes an account that belongs to the consumer, but should not show up on the credit report.** This includes accounts that are too old to report as defined by the FCRA's seven-year limit. Another example would be a collection that was paid prior to being placed with the collection agency issuing the report, either to another agency or to the original creditor. Some medical collections resulting from insurance disputes can be deleted if the original service provider instructs the collection agency to close the collection file. This usually requires that the debt be paid, and the insurance dispute be documented. Multiple references to the same account can cause problems, especially if there are negative remarks associated with the account. Even good accounts that are duplicated can cause problems. For example, a lost or stolen credit card can result in the old account, complete with its balance and credit limit, continuing to be included (but not updated by the creditor) on the file, along with the replacement account.

6. **Includes an account on which the borrower is only an "authorized user."** "Co-signers" and "joint users" of credit card accounts are legally obligated for their payment. "Authorized users,"

on the other hand, are not. Yet the FICO model traditionally has scored authorized user accounts as if they were joint users. Fair Isaac announced in 2007 its new model would stop scoring unauthorized users, but it was unclear how quickly the change would be implemented in the market.

7. **Revolving accounts (credit cards) that are "maxed out" or close to it, but which can be paid down or paid off.** There are two calculations made on revolving debt involving credit limit vs. balance. First, each account's balance-to-limit ratio is analyzed individually. Second, the average balance-to-limit ratio is calculated by dividing the sum of balances of most open and closed accounts by the sum of credit limits for the same accounts. Avoiding a high balance-to-limit ratio in both of these categories is crucial. While there is no "magic" number, Lenders' Credit Services said it achieved the best results when the balance was brought to less than 50%of the credit limit. Other re-scorers said that three credit cards, with balances at 1/3rd or below credit limits, was a good target.

"Perfection" in credit scoring is nearly impossible. One re-scorer had three platinum cards with limits of $20,000. Two cards had zero balances, and the third never had a balance over $3,000. Still, this professional's FICO score was slightly over 750—top notch, but far from a "perfect 850." Two of the "Reason Codes" given were "relationship of balance-to-credit limit on revolving accounts" (despite having a very low balance), and "too many open revolving charge cards" (despite only having three underused platinum cards).

"I guess the ideal consumer for FICO is one card with a zero balance," she said. "But who can live like that?"

Payoffs, Big & Bigger

Lenders Credit Services, Inc. (LCSI) said on average it improves credit scores about 30 points, or two levels (1/8 percentage point per level) in the lenders' index, for an average improvement of 1/4 percentage point.

Even a change of two or three FICO points can translate into savings, particularly for the larger mortgages. This is because the mortgage rates can change at 20-point intervals. For example, your original score was 698, which translated into a good interest rate, but not the best available. Because the cut-off used by the lender for the next best rate was 700,[40] the re-scorer only needed to improve your score two points to get you a better deal. But if the re-scorer could boost your score 22 points to 720, you would jump two levels. If all the negative drag on your credit score was based on inaccuracies that could be corrected, or revolving debt that could be paid off, you could probably jump 60-100 points and qualify for the best loan rate the lender had to offer.

At LCSI, Koontz tells of the single mother whose score was ambushed by a charged off auto loan. This was caused by the bank misapplying the final payment to someone else's account. The account was coded as a "charge off" about one month before she applied for a mortgage. The incident occurred without her knowledge because at the same time she made the final payment, she also moved. The bank reversed the payment from the incorrect account, applied it to the correct account, and adjusted all of the late fees and interest, along with the payment history on the account, which was returned to its pristine state. Once all the necessary documentation was gathered and submitted, the collection was deleted from the mother's report and her credit score improved by 100 points. Without the change, the borrower would not have qualified for the mortgage because

---

[40] The FICO cut-offs used by mortgage lenders vary greatly. Moreover, FICO is not the only factor.

the interest rate she would have been paying would have pushed her payments too high for her to qualify based on her income. After the change, she got the best rate available, saving her thousands of dollars.

Harney, of the *Washington Post*, reported the case of Alexandria C. Phillips, a Los Angeles area lawyer who sought to refinance her Newport Beach condo and purchase a new home in Laguna Beach. Phillips' broker said her FICO scores were: 597 (Experian), 569 (Trans Union) and 580 (Equifax). Considering that 620 and below was "sub-prime," Phillips' scores were horrible. Phillips' broker turned the case over to Richard Le Febvre, whose company, AAA American Credit Bureau in Flagstaff, Arizona, was still doing re-scoring at the time.

Working with Phillips, Le Febvre removed three inaccuracies that were dinging her credit: an erroneous delinquent credit card payment, a "repossessed" Mercedes that actually belonged to someone else, and an incorrectly listed collection action from 1995. Phillips also regularly purchased law office and other professional items with her credit card, thus driving the balance near the "maxed out" point at the time the credit card companies reported to the Big Three CRAs. In five days, Le Febvre had improved Phillips' FICO score from a 580 to a 780, making her eligible for the best loan available.[41]

Why Isn't Re-Scoring Available To Everyone?

Equifax, Experian, and Trans Union probably permitted re-scoring to come into existence because a portion of their subscriber base—mortgage lenders—demanded it. But as mentioned before, the Big Three contracts prohibit resellers from offering their services directly to consumers.

---

[41] Harney, July 14, 2001, op. cit.

Price Squeeze

Although they adamantly deny it, there was some evidence that the Big Three were trying to squeeze the resellers out of the re-scoring business. In the past three years, they had put a "price squeeze" on the resellers, steadily hiking the price they charge resellers for credit reports and for re-scoring. For example, Trans Union was charging a reseller in the Midwest $2.30 each credit report, or $4.60 for a married couple's report, plus 70 cents for a credit score, if he pulled fewer than 500 credit reports per month. But Trans Union offered a commercial bank, which happened to be a customer of the reseller, a rate of $1.60 per individual report, $3.20 for a husband-wife report and 40 cents for a credit score, if they pulled fewer than 1,500 reports per month. For anyone paying attention, this created the appearance that Trans Union was trying to squeeze the reseller out of the market and lure away one of its key customers.[42]

According to a September 2003 report by the American Antitrust Institute (AAI), Equifax also tried to put a price squeeze on resellers and then "poach" away their customers. A California reseller was approached by a home-equity lender about purchasing 10,000 single-bureau reports per month. The cost to the reseller was $1.75 for each report, plus 50 cents for the credit score, or $2.25. The reseller offered the reports to the home-equity lender at $2.50 apiece—a 25-cent markup. Equifax contacted the home-equity lender directly and offered to sell its reports for $1.90 a piece. Equifax, Experian and Trans Union know all of the resellers' customers and the volume because the FCRA requires resellers to identify end-users to the CRAs.[43]

---

[42] Jonathan L. Rubin and Albert A. Foer, "Competitive Conditions in the Mortgage Credit Reporting Industry: A Report By the American Antitrust Institute (AAI)., September 8, 2003
[43] *Id.*

A Massachusetts reseller who bought 3,000-4,000 Equifax reports per month paid $1.70 per report and 35 cents per credit score. Equifax offered to provide credit reports <u>and</u> credit scores to one of the reseller's bank customers for a combined price of $1.30—even though the bank's volume was only 100-300 reports per month.

A Florida reseller discovered that Experian's exclusive affiliate for the State of Florida, Credit Data Services, Inc., offered one of the reseller's customers a merged Equifax/Experian report for $1.50—less than half the reseller's wholesale cost for a two-bureau report.[44]

In 2001, Trans Union informed a reseller that it was raising his wholesale prices between 29 to 250%.[45]

Moreover, Equifax and Trans Union have "dramatically" jacked the prices they charge resellers for re-scoring. In 2000, the charge was $5.00-$7.00 per tradeline. In 2001, within 60 days of each other, they hiked the price to $15.00-$30.00 per trade line. Meanwhile, Trans Union and Equifax, through their mortgage reporting subsidiaries, continued offering lenders re-scoring services at $5.00-$7.00 per trade line.

'Baseless Policy'

Along with these price hikes, the three CRAs have specific clauses in their contracts with resellers prohibiting resellers from passing along to consumers any of the prices that the CRAs charge resellers. This means that the reseller must either absorb the cost, or be paid by the reseller's customer, the mortgage lender.

Naturally, this has created friction between resellers and their mortgage broker customers. In the March 2003 issue of the official publication of the National Association of Mortgage Brokers (NAMB), one official wrote:

---

[44] *Id.*
[45] *Id.*

"It seems to me that the fastest way to spoil this wonderful new service by making it look like credit repair would be for repositories to insist that credit resellers restrict mortgage brokers and lenders from charging a fee to the consumer for the upgraded credit report."

The NAMB official called this restriction a "baseless policy." The AAI concluded that resellers were caught between the proverbial "rock and a hard place."

"Resellers, faced with the prospect of audits and termination by the repositories, are understandably reluctant to deviate from the express terms of their contracts. But at the same time, they are loath to be perceived by their customers as 'holding the line on a baseless policy' which costs their customers money. The repositories have been asked to clarify the rules, but have so far refused to do so. Thus, while re-scoring is a permissible business for resellers, the repositories have made it difficult or impossible for resellers to profit from it without risking the alienation of its customers."

As mentioned, if indeed the Big Three are putting the squeeze on independent resellers, they might be doing so to take over that portion of the market. But the motivations could run deeper. The AAI report noted that major creditors, even though they often are the cause of inaccuracy, do not want to have to deal with resellers.

"At least one national credit card issuer flatly refuses to accept inquiries from smaller credit reporting agencies," AAI wrote. "The single largest concern of the repositories is to maintain the inflow of credit data, so it is to be expected that they would be protective of large credit furnishers. Thus, smaller resellers engaged in updating and correcting errors created by reporting creditors are often viewed as a liability by the repositories."

The AAI added: "Smaller resellers are also a liability to repositories in another sense. With their primary emphasis on customer service, smaller resellers often shed light on repository practices and the extent of their compliance with laws and regulations. They expose inaccuracies and errors in credit data and also educate the public about the industry and about the legal rights of consumers."

In March 2004, the National Credit Reporting Association and its members filed separate anti-trust lawsuits in federal court in California and California state court against Equifax, Experian, and Trans Union. Some of the suits were dismissed. After the lawsuits were filed, some re-sellers complained of retaliation, as at least one of the major CRAs suddenly exercised its right under their contracts to conduct audits.

Unless the lawsuit results in major changes – an unlikely prospect – consumers should not expect all mortgage brokers to inform them about re-scoring. Those mortgage bankers or brokers who make higher commissions on sub-prime borrowers actually have a disincentive, as re-scoring could cut into their incomes when the borrowers get better rates.

Moreover, because of all the price hikes, cost can be a major factor for brokers and mortgage companies that are expected to absorb the cost of re-scoring. In 2000, the average re-score, consisting of two tradelines corrected on reports issued by two of the three CRAs, would cost the re-seller $28.00 (using the high of 7.00 per trade), a figure that was palatable to most mortgage bankers/brokers. That same re-score would now cost the reseller approximately $120.

Chapter 4

Obtaining Your Credit Report

> *We'd like to know a little bit about you for our files,*
> *We'd like to help you learn about yourself...*

>   – Simon & Garfunkel
>   "Mrs. Robinson"

    In this chapter, we will explain how to order copies of your credit report[46] and credit scores from the newly created "Centralized Source," either by mail, by phone, or via the Internet. We will also explain how to order them directly from Equifax, Experian, Trans Union, and Fair Isaac. If you want contact information right away, go directly to page 75, and to page 85 for Fair Isaac.

    All Americans are entitled to obtain one free copy per year of their Equifax, Experian, and Trans Union credit reports from the "Centralized Source" (**credit scores are not included and always come with a price**). The free report and the Centralized Source were mandated by Congress when it passed the Fair and Accurate Credit Transactions Act of 2003 (FACT Act). The goal of the law is to improve credit report accuracy and fairness by encouraging Americans to review their credit reports.

---

[46] Technically, the CRAs define the report they give to you as a "consumer disclosure." The version that is given to their subscribers, the credit grantors, when you apply for credit, is defined as a "credit report." For simplicity and stylistic purposes, we will generally refer to "consumer disclosures" as "credit reports."

To further the goal of Americans reviewing their credit reports, Congress left in place all of the existing reasons that consumers were entitled to free reports (see pages 75-76).

The bottom line: If you know your rights, you can regularly check your credit report throughout the year at little or no cost. This is a significant advance, considering that Equifax, Experian, Trans Union and others each charge between $89-$119 annually for ongoing credit report monitoring services.

This chapter should help cost-conscious consumers figure out the most economical way to obtain their credit reports. For those whom "cost is not an issue," this chapter should help them decide the fastest way to get the most complete picture.

Also remember, Americans are entitled to one free credit report from "specialty" reporting agencies like ChoicePoint, LexisNexis' Accurint, the Medical Information Bureau, TeleCheck and other check verifying companies. But these must be requested directly from those companies and cannot be obtained through the Centralized Source.

The Centralized Source – Contact Information

Remember, you can order your free report from one, two or all three of the CRAs by mail, by phone or over the Internet. Here's the contact information.

Annual Credit Report Request Service
P.O. Box 105281
Atlanta, GA 30374-5281
1-877-322-8228
www.annualcreditreport.com

One At A Time, Or All Three At Once?

Once you are eligible, you can request your free report by mail, by phone or over the Internet. You can choose to order your Equifax, Experian and Trans Union reports all at once, or, you can order only one of three bureaus first, and then request a second one months later, and the third one after that. If you stagger your requests by four months, you effectively monitor your credit report three times per year. If you are not planning a major credit transaction like a mortgage, refinancing or auto purchase, then the staggered approach might be best, as it permits you to periodically monitor your credit report for signs of identity theft (see Chapter 7).

However, if you are planning a major credit purchase in the coming months, it's probably best to get all three at once. Remember, authoritative research by the Consumer Federation of America (CFA) and the National Credit Reporting Association (NCRA) showed there could be major discrepancies between the three bureau reports for any given consumer (see Chapters 2 & 10).

Consider Ordering Via Toll-Free Number

Since its inception in December 2004, many people have reported glitches that prevented them from getting all three of their free credit reports at the official Web site.

Accordingly, if you have lived at the same address for a while, it might be best to order via the toll-free number. That way, the paper version of your credit report is sent to your home address, and you avoid the glitches that have prevented some people from obtaining their reports online.

How To Order Through The Centralized Source

When you first go to www.annualcreditreport.com, you are asked to provide your identifying data: name, date-of-birth, Social Security number (SSN), address, city, and zip code. There is a box to click if you only want your report to list the last five digits of your SSN. If you have lived at your current residence fewer than two years, it asks for your previous address. For security purposes, a random, seven-digit number that is displayed must be read and typed into a box.

Then you go to the page where you choose which of three bureau reports you want to get first. The names of Experian, Equifax and Trans Union rotate so each takes its turn at the top of the list. After you finish ordering your report from the first bureau of choice, you can order a report from a second bureau by finding the link: "Return to AnnualCredit-Report.com."

Equifax – Online

Equifax's Web site first authenticates the identifying data you provided to the centralized source, and then proceeds to ask an additional question for authentication purposes, for example, the name of the company to which you pay your mortgage. Accordingly, *prior to using the centralized source, it is a good idea to review your financial accounts, including credit cards, mortgages and auto loans, so you can answer these types of authentication questions.*

When you pass the authentication test, Equifax then informs you that its site is the only one connected to the centralized source where you can buy your FICO score. It advises visitors as to why the FICO score is important.

The price: $6.95.

Next, you are asked if you would like to be able to view your credit report online free for 30 days. If you answer yes, you then must enter a user ID and password. Finally, you are offered free access to "Equifax Credit Rankings," which shows where your FICO score ranks (if you purchased it), or where your level of debt ranks (if you don't buy your FICO score).

Equifax also asks you if you want to receive offers and information. **If you don't want this, make sure you check the "opt out" box.**

The online credit report is divided into eight sections: (1) Personal (identifying) information; (2) Credit summary; (3) Account information; (4) Inquiries; (5) Collections; (6) Public Records; (7) Dispute File Information; and (8) Summary of FCRA Rights. You can click on any of these categories to view your data; toward the bottom, there's a button for printing out the entire report. (Next chapter, we'll discuss reading and understanding your report.)

Experian – Online

For authentication, Experian first asked for the last four digits of the SSN. Then it asked four multiple-choice questions:

(1) county of residence,

(2) street,

(3) company holding my auto loan and

(4) amount of monthly auto loan payment.

(Interestingly, the correct answer to the last three questions was "None of the above.")

The Experian report was divided into six categories: (1) Report Summary; (2) Potentially Negative Items; (3) Accounts in Good Standing; (4) Requests for Your Credit History; (5) Personal Information, and (6) Your Personal Statement.

The difference between Experian and the other two was that Experian did not try to start selling you additional products or services before you obtained your credit report. Instead, it promoted these items on the left and right sidebars of the front of your credit report. These services included your PLUS Credit Score for $5, and "Triple Alert," in which ConsumerInfo.com "watches over all 3 of your national credit files and scans for key changes." ($4.95 per month) At Triple Alert, you must opt out from receiving promotional offers.

On the right sidebar, "Credit Score Basics" takes you to an explanation of what's in a credit report and lets you view a sample report. It also introduces you to "Ask Max," a free, online column in which Maxine Sweet, Experian's vice president of public affairs, answers questions about credit scores and credit reports. Another sidebar has tips about disputing errors in your report online. (In Chapter 6, we discuss the advantages and disadvantages of disputing in writing, by phone or online.)

Experian's Credit Report Basics also promotes "Credit Manager," its online monitoring service that includes the Plus Score ($9.95 per month; $119.40 per year); as well as the Three-bureau report and Plus Score ($34.95). One offering you should not want is the Experian credit report and Plus score for $14.95. By coming through www.annualcreditreport.com you received your report for free, and could have purchased your Plus score for $5. And, if you sign up for the Credit Manager 30-day trial, you get the Plus score for free – provided you remember to cancel your subscription before the trial expires.

Trans Union – Online

One type of glitch that was known to frustrate many people happened to our tester on "Opening Day" (Dec. 1, 2004). We were part way through being authenticated at

TransUnion when the system froze and would not let us complete the order for a free credit report. When we returned a few days later, the TransUnion site kept asking for additional authentication information, including credit card account numbers. The problem was that even when the correct American Express account number was provided, TransUnion would still not authenticate our tester. We also saw that the tester's Experian report had an incorrect American Express account number. This showed how inaccuracies can prevent authentication, and thereby prevent consumers from gaining access to their reports. Eventually, we gave up on the Web site and ordered his report through the toll free number (see below).

The Trans Union Web site charges $5.95 for a TrueScore, but does not sell a FICO score.

In order to send you promos in the future, the site has a box checked next to the statement, "You will receive a free monthly newsletter loaded with important credit education as well as valuable product offers provided by our subsidiaries and partners."

If you don't want this, you must <u>uncheck</u> this box.

By Phone (1-877-322-8228)

When you call the toll-free number for ordering your report, the automated voice menu walks you through a series of steps to authenticate your identity. If you pass the authentication test, it will send the report or reports you ordered to your home address. After it confirms your home phone number, the automated voice advises that you can get your report instantly at www.annualcreditreport.com. Also, you can get instructions on how to order your reports in writing by pressing "1."

To continue, it asks you to press "1" if you are calling from your home phone. (When you call toll free numbers, a technology known as Automatic Number Identification (ANI) records the number you're calling from, much like Caller ID captures the caller's phone number). If you are not calling from home (press "2"), you can still go to the next step by entering your home phone.

Then, the automated voice says the address it has for you and asks if it is correct (Press "1"). It repeats this process for your last name and first name. Next, it asks if you have been at your current address for more than two years. If you press no, it asks for your previous address. Then, you must say or punch in your SSN. You can also tell them to only include the last four digits of your SSN on the credit report they send you.

Next, enter your date-of-birth. Provided that everything checks out, you then choose whether you want one, two, or all three of your credit reports mailed to you.

To order in writing, send a letter with your full name, including middle initial and generational suffix (i.e., Sr./Jr.), current address, SSN, and date-of-birth. You must specify which bureau report you want, or whether you want two or all three.

At the Web site, you can download a "Request Form" for requesting your report(s) in writing: www.annualcreditreport.com/cra/requestformfinal.pdf

How Did It Work?

Considering that on its first day the centralized source was receiving up to 500 requests per minute, it should be no surprise that it got off to a rocky start. None of the 10 people who contacted this author said they had a problem-free experience, as none were able to obtain all three credit reports online. Still, these people had the option of ordering them through the toll-free telephone number or by mail.

Consistent with our tester's experience, MSNBC reported that Equifax's system had performed the best. At Experian's site, it was common to get an error message: "No backend server available for connection: timed out after 10 seconds."

One major frustration raised by several MSNBC.com users: They got about halfway through the process of getting their Experian report, then were booted out of the system, and when they returned they were told they already had received their free report for the year. A message on the Web site then urged them to pay for a fresh copy.[47]

Another frustration was that the centralized source installed a security measure that blocked pro-consumer Web sites, including those of the Consumer Union, Privacy Rights Clearinghouse and the Electronic Privacy Information Center (EPIC), from linking to the centralized source. But within a few days, EPIC's Chris Jay Hoofnagle came up with a method to bypass the block so visitors to www.epic.org could link to the centralized source. The method was promptly adopted by www.ConsumersUnion.org and www.privacyrights.org.

Nonetheless, those groups and others sent a Dec. 7, 2004 letter to the FTC protesting the link-blocking as a violation of FACT Act because it undermined the Centralized Source's purpose of facilitating consumer access to their free credit reports.[48]

They scoffed at the security rationale, stating, "If there is a justification to block links to the free site, why are the credit reporting agencies not blocking links to their for-profit sites?"

The groups assailed the Centralized Source for using the term "free annual credit file disclosures," instead of "free credit report," because it reduced the likelihood of consumers finding the Web site through search engines. The Source also lacked "meta tags," the key words that enable Web surfers to find what they're looking for through search engines, the groups charged.

---

[47] Bob Sullivan, "Glitches Mar Launch of Free Credit Report Site," MSNBC.com, Dec. 2, 2004; www.msnbc.msn.com/id/6576905/
[48] Letter to Joel Winston, Assoc. Dir., FTC Financial Practices Div.; www.epic.org/privacy/fcra/freereportltr.html

"Indeed, a Google search for 'free credit report' leads to an array of free-to-pay conversion sites that advertise free credit reports, but really deliver expensive, unnecessary credit monitoring, such as Experian's Consumerinfo.com."

"Whether intentional or not, every subtle and not so subtle web design tactic has been employed to make www.annualcreditreport.com difficult to find and use. It appears this is unlikely to have occurred by accident, because many of the tactics represent bad web design, mistakes that only beginner HTML authors would make," the groups wrote.

The protest worked. By March 2005, after an inquiry by Rep. Barney Frank (D-MA) the three CRAs agreed to cure many of the problems.

Despite the glitches, by June 2007, 52 million credit reports had been disclosed through the Centralized Source, according to industry testimony. Interestingly, the CRAs said they had provided over 160 million total disclosures, indicating they had *sold* twice as many reports or monitoring service subscriptions. Thus, Congress's Free-Report requirement became a great marketing tool for the CRAs.

Obtaining Your Credit Report Directly From 'Big Three'

If you are not yet entitled to a free report from the centralized source, or if you've already used yours up, then you need to order reports directly from the Big Three CRAs. Make sure you review all of the reasons that you are entitled to free additional reports (they're listed after the contact information). For instance, if you live in one of seven states granting you a right to an annual free report from each CRA, then you can monitor your reports throughout the year without paying.

Here are the toll-free phone numbers,[49] mailing addresses and Web sites for ordering your report directly

---

[49] The CRAs have changed the toll-free number from time to time.

from the three "major repositories," and the separate numbers and addresses for reporting fraud:

Equifax - www.equifax.com
To order your report, call: 800-685-1111 or write:
P.O. Box 740241, Atlanta, GA 30374-0241
To report fraud, call: 800-525-6285 and write:
P.O. Box 740241, Atlanta, GA 30374-0241
Hearing Impaired: 1-800-255-0056, ask operator to call
1-800-685-1111 to request a copy of your report.

Experian - www.experian.com
To order your report, call: 888-EXPERIAN (397-3742) or write: P.O. Box 2002, Allen TX 75013
To report fraud, call: 888-EXPERIAN (397-3742) and write:
P.O. Box 9530, Allen TX 75013   TDD: 1-800-972-0322

Trans Union - www.transunion.com
To order your report, call: 800-888-4213 or write:
P.O. Box 1000, Chester, PA 19022
To report fraud, call: 800-680-7289 and write:
Fraud Victim Assistance Division, P.O. Box 6790,
Fullerton, CA 92634 TDD: 1-877-553-7803

Additional Rights To Free Reports

Here are the other reasons that consumers are entitled to free reports *in addition* to their annual free report under the FACT Act.

- You've been turned down for credit or insurance or otherwise experience an unfavorable change (known as an "adverse action") in the terms of your credit or insurance in the past 60 days.
- You are a victim of identity theft or have reason to believe that inaccurate data are in your credit report because of fraud.

- You are unemployed and intend to apply for employment in the next 60 days.
- If you are on public welfare assistance.
- If an adverse decision related to your employment has been made based in whole or in part on information contained in the report.
- If your report has been revised based upon an investigation you requested.
- You live in a state with a free credit report law: Colorado, Maine, Massachusetts, Maryland, New Jersey, or Vermont, and Georgia (Georgians are entitled to two free reports per year).

After Free Reports Used Up: $10

If you've already obtained all of the free reports to which you are entitled, then the federally-regulated price for buying an additional credit report is $10.[50]

Prior to the FACT Act, these states capped the prices accordingly: Minnesota ($3); Connecticut ($5); California, ($8), and Montana ($8.50).[51]

It's generally easy to order your credit report directly from the Big Three CRAs. If your address matches the one they have on file, you can order over their toll-free numbers by following the push-button prompts. Their Web sites ask you the same type of authentication questions as does www.annualcreditreport.com. If you order your report by mail, your request must include your name, address, SSN, and copies of a driver's license and current utility bill.

---

[50] The price is set by the statute, the FCRA, 15 U.S.C. Sect. 1681, and by FTC regulations.

[51] A complete listing of state prices can be found at http://annualcreditreport.transunion.com/pdf/DisclosureRequest.pdf

Extra! Extra! Credit Scores Not Included

As mentioned before, the FACT Act did not mandate free credit scores. It only required that CRAs charge a "fair and reasonable price" for them.[52] When the Centralized Source launched, Equifax charged $6.95 for a FICO score; Trans Union charged $4.95 for a True Credit score; Experian charged $5.

One of the only ways to get a free score was to sign up for a 30-day trial at Experian's Web site entitling you to a PLUS score. Remember, the PLUS score is not a FICO score, and could vary significantly. Even the FICO score you get from Equifax can differ from the score ultimately used by a lender to whom you have applied for credit. Moreover, if you don't cancel before the 30-day trial, Experian will charge your credit card for an annual subscription. If cost is your priority, then these subscription services are probably not the best deal.

Credit Monitoring and Other Web Site Services

It should be no surprise that the three major CRAs try to push the monitoring services. After all, they've discovered it's a great way to make money. This is a major shift, as the CRA traditionally looked at consumers as an added cost of doing business,[53] and only made money by selling credit reports and other data to businesses. Starting in 2001, all three CRAs said that the direct sale of credit reports and

---

[52] The FTC must determine what is "fair and reasonable," but had not done so by the time this book went to print. The FTC appeared to lean in favor of the $5-8 market price for credit scores, even though lenders often pay well under $1 for them.

[53] In one lawsuit, Equifax estimated it costs $7.50 to process a request and send a consumer his credit report. Clark, et al. v. Equifax, et al. (U.S. District Ct. For S. Carolina – No. 8:00-1217-22)

credit scores had "taken off nicely."[54] One analyst said CRA direct-to-consumer sales would reach roughly $600 million in 2002 and could easily reach $1 billion by 2005.   In September 2002 Experian's Consumer Direct websites had 9.79 million unique visitors, Equifax had 922,000 hits, Trans Union 523,000, and TrueCredit 239,000.[55]

Both Equifax and Experian offered 30-day free trials for their monitoring services, but only Experian included a PLUS credit score. This meant it was one of the few places you could obtain a credit scores for free – provided that you remembered to cancel your subscription before the 30-day trial period ended. PrivacyGuard offered a two-month trial for $1 that included ongoing access to all three reports, and FICO scores from all three CRAs. If you forgot to cancel, your credit card was billed $12.95 per month for a year.[56]

If you sign up for a monitoring service, and you don't want to receive spam or junk mail offers from these companies or their affiliates, you must remember to "opt out" from having your name sold or used for these purposes.[57] Other potential pitfalls to watch out for are "binding arbitration clauses," designed to block you from going to court if there is a dispute.

The Equifax Credit Watch Gold includes notification to either your e-mail, cell phone or other wireless device within 24 hours of changes in your credit report. The Equifax Web page also contains an archive of past newsletters that explain updates of products and services, as well as testi-monials from subscribers and other news.

---

[54] Elayne Robertson Demby, "Letting Consumers Know the Score - and More." Credit and Collections World (undated) http://www.creditcollectionsworld.com/cgi-bin/readstory2.pl?story=20030203CCRU943.xml.

[55] *Ibid*

[56] www.privacyguard.com is owned by Trilegiant Corp., (877) 202-8828

[57] At www.equifax.com, go to "Member Center;" at www.experian.com, go to "privacy" and then to "opting out;" www.transunion.com says that TU does not sell data to outside parties and is silent on sharing with affiliates.

Experian's 'Credit Manager'

The monthly price for Experian's Credit Manager is $9.95 (or $119.40 per year). It offers email notification when new data are added to your credit report, **ongoing access to your Experian credit report** and your PLUS **credit score**, along with a **score simulator**, **explanations** about your score, "**helpful tips**," other consumer education material, and an **online dispute process**. Another feature at the Experian Web site is "Ask Max," a biweekly column in which Maxine Sweet, Experian's Vice President of Public Affairs answers questions from consumers.[58]

A drawback of this service is that the PLUS Score is not the same – and can differ significantly – from the more widely used FICO score.

The online version has a completely different layout than your traditional paper credit report. In fact, if you've never seen your paper report, and your first access is to the online version, you might not know what to look for, or you might overlook important details.

High Risk vs. Low Risk

The Experian Credit Manager shows your PLUS Credit Score at the top right half of the computer screen, with an arrow indicating where you stand on a scale from a positive "low risk," to "medium-low risk," to "medium risk," to the more negative "medium-high risk," and the sub-prime "high risk." The Manager offers explanations as to how your credit score was calculated and what you can do to improve it. (More on this in a bit.)

At the top left, it lists your current debt:

- Revolving (credit cards and store cards)

---

[58] Maxine Sweet headed the Experian Consumer Advisory Council, on which this author had served as a member from 2002-2004.

- Installment (fixed payment loans, like personal or auto loans)
- Real Estate (mortgages)
- Total Debt

The next column is the Credit Monitor, which is supposed to notify you if there have been significant changes or new activity on your credit report.

The next column lists your credit information.

- Percentage of Credit Currently Available (total of credit limits on all of your accounts or "trade lines," subtracted by total credit used)
- Satisfactory accounts (paid on time)
- Delinquent/derogatory accounts (failed to pay on time)
- Amount still past due (still owed)
- Public records (usually very negative: bankruptcy, court judgments over collection accounts, etc.)
- No inquiries in past 6 months (if there were inquiries, they would relate to companies that pulled your credit report in order to evaluate you because you applied for credit with them)

Online Disputes

The Credit Manager permits you to dispute trade lines while you are online. To file a dispute, select an account or public record item and click the blue "Dispute this item" button next to the inaccurate account or public record. You can then choose one of Experian's ten dispute reasons (e.g., "Payment Never Late," "Belongs To Ex-Spouse," "Unauthorized signature") or provide a written explanation. The advantage is, it allows the information to be forwarded immediately to the creditor and can help your credit score improve at least temporarily. The disadvantage is that online, you are unable to provide supporting documentation, which may bolster your dispute and, theoretically, persuade Experian or the creditor to delete the disputed account.

You can click on each of these categories to check the accuracy of information. Clearly, you want to pay close attention to delinquent/derogatory trade lines, and to any public records data, which are usually negative. Also, check to see if all of your creditors are reporting your positive payment history, or if they are reporting it in the most positive way.

Capital One

For example, it was revealed in 2003 that Capital One, a leading credit card company, did not report credit limits to the CRAs, only the amount owed. If you owed $3,000 on your Capital One account, but had a credit limit of $6,000, by not reporting the credit limit, Capital One could make it appear that you had reached your limit and were "maxed out" at $3,000. Generally, the high balance is substituted for the missing credit limit. So, if in future months, you continued to run up your balances just short of $3,000, you would continue to appear to be "maxed out." (After years of criticism, Capital One announced in the summer of 2007 that it would change this practice. See Chapter 22 for details.)

'Credit Header' Data

It's also important to check your identifying information, known as "Above The Line," or "Credit Header" data because it's the first thing you see on a paper credit report.[59] Click on the "View My Credit Report" tab, and click on the link to "personal information." This is where you check the accuracy of your name, SSN, date-of-

---

[59] This is true for Equifax and Trans Union; Experian lists identifying data towards the end of its paper version.

birth, address, previous addresses, type of residence, employer, drivers' license number, and telephone number (it's not unusual for the credit report to include unlisted or unpublished numbers). Inaccurate identifying information has been known to cause the mis-merging of two separate credit histories. Even accurate identifying data can lead to mis-merging if there are enough similarities between you and another person. (More on this in Chapters 8 & 10).

Credit Score Simulator

The Credit Score Simulator is a useful tool for gaining an idea of how your credit would go up or down if you took certain actions. Caution! This is only a general education tool, as the simulator will not tell you precisely what your credit score is. Precision can be important for major credit moves, like mortgages, refinancing, and auto loans. The lack of precision is particularly evident when using non-FICO scores, like Experian's PLUS Score, or the TrueCredit Score available at Trans Union's Web site.

Still the Experian simulator will give you a general idea how much your credit score will rise if you reduce your credit card debt, delete a derogatory payment, or make any number of moves.

Scoring Factors

Also helpful are all the explanations of the factors that affect your score provided by Experian's credit manager. Web sites of Equifax, Trans Union, and Fair Isaac (myFico.com) provide similar services.

Here are some random examples of positive factors provided by Credit Manager.

- Having higher than average credit *limits* on your bank cards indicate that most lenders consider you a lower risk and are willing to trust you with more credit compared to others in your credit category. (*Credit utilization ratio*, pg. 20.)

- With three or more credit accounts on your report, you have established significant number of credit relationships—a fact that is favorably viewed by lenders.

- You do not have derogatory information, such as collection, charge-off, or bankruptcy reported on your credit report. Continue to pay all your bills on time, allowing you to maintain and improve your credit score. (*Payment history*, pg. 19.)

- On average, your accounts have been open more than five years. This positively affects your credit score. Having long-term credit accounts that you consistently pay on time is one important indicator of stability to lenders. (*Length*, pg. 21.)

- Having few, if any installment loans, reduces your number of fixed payments. This makes it easier for you to meet other debt obligations and positively influences your credit score. (*Amount owed*, pg. 20)

Here are some random examples of negative factors provided by Credit Manager.

- Outstanding credit balances on your revolving accounts are higher than the average consumer in your credit category. Most lenders view this negatively because it may show that you are taking on too much debt. By avoiding taking on too much debt and paying down your total debt as soon as you can, your credit score will usually improve. (*Credit utilization ratio*, pg. 20.)

- You are (or have been) late by 30 days or more in paying one or more of your credit accounts. Being late on any bill, for any length of time, is a possible indication of future non-payment and is almost always viewed negatively by lenders.

- Any late payments will remain on your credit report for up to seven years. Paying any overdue bills immediately and paying all future bills on time can help avoid further erosion to your credit score. (*Payment history*, pg. 19 .)

- Applying for credit in the last two years—even once—can negatively affect your credit score because it may indicate that you are taking on new debt. Therefore, it is best to apply for new credit only when it is truly needed. (*Inquiries.*)

In addition to the Credit Manager (30-day free trial, $89.95 per year thereafter), Experian at its Web site sells:
- $14.95 – Experian Credit Report and PLUS Score
- $34.95 – TU, Equifax, & Experian (3-in-1) Report and PLUS Score

Trans Union

- $14.95 – TU Credit Report, plus TrueCredit score, "personalized tips for improvement and custom analysis of your debt and income."
- $29.95 – TU, Equifax, & Experian (3-in-1) Tri-Merge Credit Reports, plus TrueCredit Score from TU Report.
- $39.90 – The above package, plus TrueCredit scores for all three bureaus.
- $10.95 – Three-month credit report-monitoring service, including "quarterly online access to your credit report with analytical tools, weekly fraud-watch emails, $25,000 in identity theft insurance, and toll-free **ID Theft Specialists** with fraud resolution service."

For a summary of all TU's offers, go to:
http://www.transunion.com/Personal/PersonalSolutions.jsp

Equifax

- $14.95 – 30-day online access to a snapshot of your credit report,[60] plus FICO score, explanation and tips.
- $29.95 – All Three Bureaus' (3-in-1) Report
- $39.95 – Equifax 3-in-1 with FICO Score. Includes simulator allowing you to see what your score would be if you paid off debt or took other actions, self-help tips, and toll-free access to "customer care."
- $99.95 (Annual) or $9.95 (Monthly) – Equifax Credit Watch Gold: Daily e-mail alerts of key changes in credit reports, $20,000 in identity theft insurance, access to live customer support and unlimited credit reports (30-day free trial available).
- $49.95 (Annual) or $4.95 (Monthly) – Credit Watch Silver: Weekly alerts of key file changes, $2,500 identity theft insurance (deductible applies), and one initial credit report.

Fair Isaac (www.myfico.com)

- $39.95 – All Three Bureaus' (3-in-1) Credit Report with FICO score (based on TU report), plus "dynamic score simulator," explanation of score, and helpful tips.
- $12.95 – Any one bureau report, plus FICO score, including online access to one "snapshot" of your credit report for 30 days.
- $38.95 – All Three Bureaus' (3-in-1) Credit Report with FICO score at each bureau, including online access to one "snapshot" of your credit.

---

[60] "Snapshot" means that for 30 days, you can keep accessing the credit report as it appeared the first day you accessed it.

report for 30 days—plus "dynamic score simulator," explanation of score, and helpful tips.

- $24.95 – FICO Savers For Homebuyers. Claims to give you "inside information that mortgage industry professionals use;" allows you to print a "financial certificate" to share with lenders and obtain a detailed property report for the home you're considering.

- $89.95 – ID Fraud Intercept. Provides e-mail alerts. Analyzes TU credit report, plus 400 different sources of public and commercial data, looking for (unauthorized) changes in your personal data. In addition to credit bureaus, the service searches "utilities, property deeds and assessment, bankruptcy filings, vehicle data, and other public sources."

The Sky's The Limit

This brief description illustrates that you have the option of spending a lot of money to monitor your credit information. As some have noted, the consumer reporting agencies are well-positioned, as they receive consumer data from creditors for free, and then make money selling the information back to both creditors and consumers. As the saying goes, that's good work if you can get it.

But as this chapter should also make clear, a well-informed consumer can at least occasionally check his or her credit report at minimal or no cost. For some consumers, obtaining their credit report is the easy part. The real challenge begins when they discover errors and try to get them fixed.

Chapter 5

Reading Your Credit Report

> *In a sense a person is defined by the checks he writes. By examining them the agents get to know his doctors, lawyers, creditors, political allies, social connections, religious affiliation, educational interests, the papers and magazines he reads and so on ad infinitum. These are all tied to one's Social Security number . . .*

> – Justice William O. Douglas (Dissenting)
> <u>California Bankers Assoc. v. Shultz</u>
> (416 U.S. 735, 1974.)

Years ago, a major complaint about credit reports was that they were hard to read and hard to understand. In recent years Equifax, Experian, and Trans Union, the Big Three consumer reporting agencies (CRAs), have changed the format of the reports to make them more readable and understandable. Still, significant numbers of consumers say they have trouble understanding all or part of their credit report. This brief chapter will go over the basics of what is in a credit report and what to look for. You will want to note that each of the CRA's reports include at the top a **"confirmation number,"** (Equifax), or **"report number"** (Experian) or **"File Number"** (Trans Union). If you find errors in your report and dispute them, you will want to refer to this number when communicating with each CRA.[61]

To complicate matters further, "credit report" is not the official term. Under the Fair Credit Reporting Act, it's called a *"consumer report."* The industry refers to the version they provide you as a *"consumer disclosure."* The industry refers to the report they sell to creditors as a *"credit*

---

[61] This number is not available on the reports pulled by merchants.

report" or *"subscriber version."* For purposes of readability and common understanding, we will continue to refer to it as a "credit report."

The Credit Report consists of three (or four) basic sections:

(1)   Your identifying information—name, address, Social Security number, date of birth, previous address, employer, and sometimes phone number. This is known as "Credit Header" data.

(2)   Your payment history, including mortgage, auto and installment loans, credit cards and department store cards and collections.

(3)   Public records, i.e., bankruptcies, tax and other liens, and court judgments (when applicable).

(4)   Inquiries, showing which companies accessed your report and for what purposes.

In addition, attached to the credit report is
(1) A form for disputing errors, and
(2) A statement of your rights under the FCRA.

Mostly Similar, Some Differences

Each of the Big Three CRAs uses a slightly different format. On the first page, Experian lists a helpful summary, of "potentially negative items," including "public records," "accounts with creditors and others," and the number of "accounts in good standing." Experian does not list identifying data until the final page, where it typically provides a list of the variations as to how your name is reported, i.e. with middle initial or without, or with a "Jr." designation. It also includes the spouse's name when it has one. Experian then leads with public records, collections, and accounts that are negative because of late payments.

By contrast, the Trans Union report lists the SSN, date of birth, and phone number in the upper right-hand corner, and also posts the "date since" that information about you has been in TU's files. On the upper left-hand side, it lists name, address, former addresses, employment information, and the date it was reported. Like Experian, the TU report opens with the most negative items, public records, followed by collections and accounts that are negative because of late payments.

In some ways the Equifax report is the hardest to read because of its "line-and-box" format for listing accounts. On the other hand, the Equifax report more fully explains the categories and other factors that determine your credit worthiness. More on this later.

What's In A Name? (The Credit Header)

It's important to make sure that your identifying information is accurate. The CRAs use identifying information to determine to which consumer's file credit accounts are routed. As we will see later, misapplication of identifying information can result in mixed files and other inaccuracies. This is particularly true of the SSN. If the SSN listed in the "credit header" of your credit report isn't yours, you will want to put this on the top of your dispute list and make a copy of your Social Security card so it can be attached.

If you're a "Sr." or a "Jr.," or you have a name very similar to a family member, particularly one who lives at the same address, you want to make sure that your relative's information is not being mixed on to your file.

Caution: if your report lists current or previous addresses that you've never heard of, that's another possible indicator that your file might be mixed with someone else's. The CRAs often refer to identifying information as "indicative data."

Your Credit History

Bankruptcies can remain on your report for 10 years; other negative data can remain for seven years. Unpaid tax liens can stay on forever; once paid, they must come off in seven years. The credit report typically lists the worst items first, more or less in this order:

- **Public records.** Bankruptcies, court and default judgments, liens, foreclosures
- **Collections.** Accounts that are so delinquent that they have been turned over to a collection agency or the collection arm of a major creditor
- **Charge-offs.** Accounts that are in default of the original terms of the contract. Some consumers mistakenly think they don't need to pay charge-off debts, but such accounts could be subject to further collection action. Technically, "charge-off" is a bookkeeping term used to indicate the date the creditor reports it as a loss on their business taxes; if it gets paid, it then gets reported as "recovery."
- **Late payments.** Usually falling into one of three categories, 90-days late, 60-days and 30 days.

Then, the report lists your accounts in good standing. Equifax reports it as "pays as agreed;" Experian and Trans Union report "never late." Clearly, you will want to check to ensure accuracy. As we saw in earlier chapters, recent public records can be extremely damaging to your credit score, as can recent collections, charge-offs, and major delinquencies.

After discussing inquiries, we will use the Equifax format to explain the credit history in more detail.

Inquiries

The "Inquiries" section shows which companies have accessed your report. Basically, there are two types of legitimate inquiries: "soft" and "hard."

"Soft" inquiries do not affect your credit score. These include promotions (PRM) by creditors that sent you a "pre-approved" credit card application or other credit offer. You can stop these offers by calling 1 888 OPTOUT (see Chapter 17 for more details).

They also include "account reviews" (AR) by creditors with whom you already have accounts. Creditors often conduct an automated scan of their customers' credit reports to see if there is any deterioration in payment performance. Some credit card issuers have been known to raise interest rates after account reviews showed a consumer's credit rating was falling, even though the consumer never had a late payment with that particular company. There have been instances when even though a consumer closes an account, the creditor continues to pull that consumer's report to do account reviews. One court has ruled that conducting account reviews on non-customers is a violation of the FCRA.

Account History Status Codes

The Equifax report lists the codes showing how consumers are classified when they don't pay their bills on time. Along with these numeric codes, a credit report can have a letter showing the type of credit, i.e., "R" for revolving (credit card) and "I" for installment (personal loan). The code for someone who always paid her credit card on time would be "R1." Here are the numeric codes.

- 2 : 30-59 Days Past Due
- 3 : 60-89 Days Past Due
- 4 : 90-119 Days Past Due
- 5 : Over 120 Days Past Due
- 7 : Included in Wage Earner Plan
- 8 : Repossession
- 9 : Charge Off
- Blank : No Data available for that month
- 0 : Too new to rate, or unrated
- 1 : On Time

Description of Accounts

The Equifax report, through its "Account Column Title Description," lists many of the categories of information considered by creditors and FICO when judging your credit worthiness. On a typical credit report, many of the "boxes" under these Account Columns will be blank because there was no "Balloon Payment Date" or a "Charged Off Amount." Remember, in addition to the negative data about late payments or non-payments, there are several key factors affecting your credit report. One such factor is the difference between the balance, which is the amount owed, and the credit limit. The closer you are to being "maxed out" on your credit card, the worse it is for your credit score. Moreover, some credit card companies report to the credit bureaus on the last day of the month. Thus, that's the balance owed that gets reported. That means that paying off credit card balances by the due date in the middle of the month does not improve your credit score as much as most people think. In fact, if the end-of-the-month balance is very high, this factor is likely to lower your credit score.

Here are the Account Column Title Descriptions As listed on the Equifax report:

- Company Name – The Creditor
- Account Number (Equifax and Experian don't include last four digits; Trans Union lists entire account number)
- Date Account Opened
- High Credit – The highest amount charged
- Credit Limit – The highest amount permitted
- Terms Duration – The number of installments or payments
- Number of Months Reviewed

- Date Reported – The month and year of last account update
- Balance – Total amount owed as of the date reported
- Past Due
- Date of Last Payment
- Actual Amount of Last Payment
- Scheduled Payment Amount – The requested amount of last payment
- Activity – The most recent account activity
- Date of Last (Account) Activity
- Date that first major delinquency was reported
- Charge off amount
- Deferred payment date – Date the next payment was moved to
- Balloon payment amount
- Balloon payment due date
- Creditor Classification
- Date Account Closed

Three other important factors are included on the Equifax report below the row of boxes describing the Accounts. The first is the **"Current Status."** If there are no late payments, it states "Pays As Agreed." If there are late payments, there is an additional row of boxes showing which months and year you were either 30- or 60-days late.

The second factor is the **"Type of Account,"** (i.e., "revolving" for credit card vs. "installment," for personal loans, vs. mortgages). Equifax seems to describe mortgage loans as "installments," and then in an "Additional Information" line, state "Real Estate Conventional Mortgage."

The third factor is **"Whose Account,"** which refers to the "ECOA code,"[62] meaning, are only you—the individual—responsible? Or is it a "joint account" with your spouse? Or is your spouse an "authorized user?" The "Authorized User" is sometimes problematic. When a spouse is an authorized user, he or she is authorized to use the card, but is not always responsible for paying. Nonetheless, FICO traditionally has scored authorized user accounts. This meant that if you were the authorized user on an account that was always paid on time, you benefited. If payments were regularly late, however, you were penalized for an account that you were not responsible for paying. It's worse when there is a divorce, and one spouse's score drops because he or she is still tagged as an authorized user on an ex-spouse's account that is unpaid and sent to collection. Creditors have been known to send debt collectors after the non-responsible authorized user, and to unfairly report the unpaid debt to the user's credit report as a means of pressuring that consumer into paying the ex-spouse's debt.

Several Internet-based businesses exploited this once little-known scoring anomaly by offering to help consumers improve their credit scores by making them authorized users on accounts of strangers with high credit scores. For hefty fees ranging from $350 to $1,000 dollars, these upstart businesses enabled struggling consumers to improve their lot by piggybacking on others credit histories.

In response, Fair Isaac announced in 2007 that it would cease scoring authorized users. However, since such scoring was embedded into so many existing models it was unclear what impact Fair Isaac's announced change would have.

---

[62] Equal Credit Opportunity Act code

Secret Data?

Of course, you can't read what you can't see. As noted in Chapter 2, Sources have told this author there is raw data in credit reports – regularly scored by FICO scoring models – that are never seen by consumers because these data do not appear on their credit reports. These raw data show up on "machine readable" credit reports used by lenders and their scoring models, but not on the more familiar reports disclosed to consumers.

For example, one major credit bureau has one code to denote the most recent negative item; a second code marking the previous most recent negative item, and a third code denoting the most recent, worst negative that is more than 24 months old. If consumers are to become more educated about their credit reports and credit scores, shouldn't this kind of information be disclosed as well?

Conclusion

Getting your credit report is fairly easy when the system works as it should. Reading your report is not too difficult if you know what to look for. Disputing errors and getting them corrected should not be that difficult, and sometimes it isn't.

Unfortunately, sometimes it is.

Chapter 6

Disputing Errors

> *As every man goes through life he fills in a number of forms for the record, each containing a number of questions. There are thus hundreds of little threads radiating from every man, millions of threads in all . . . Each man permanently aware of his own invisible threads, naturally develops a respect for the people who manipulate the threads.*
>
> – Alexander Solzhenitsyn, <u>Cancer Ward</u>

Disputing errors and otherwise improving both your credit score and credit report is an art and a science. It can also be a "crap shoot"—meaning, sometimes you cannot be sure what will happen.

There is no magic wand that can be waved. There usually is no "quick fix." There is no "one perfect way" to do it. To understand many of the reasons why this is true, you need to read the "advanced" chapters of this book covering the way that credit reports are assembled and the way the three major credit bureaus operate.

There is one potential shortcut: get your credit grantor to tell the credit bureaus that your dispute is valid and that the error should be removed immediately. While credit bureaus are often skeptical of consumer disputes, they almost always trust the word of creditors, their paying customers.[63]

---

[63] One company that has adopted the direct-dispute-to-creditor approach is Consumer Direct, <u>www.ConsumerDirect.com</u>.

You should be very cautious about using a "credit repair clinic." The Federal Trade Commission has charged some credit repair clinics with violations of the Credit Repair Organizations Act. On the other hand, thousands of consumers regularly pay credit repair clinics and do not complain about the service they get. (See Chapter 11 for more on credit repair, and on a few companies that say they ethically help consumers clean up their reports and handle their debts.)

In this "beginners" chapter, we will explore many of the straightforward ways that *you*, by yourself, can go about correcting errors or otherwise improving your credit score and credit report. This chapter will give you the basics of what you need to know and what you need to do to dispute errors and get them corrected. If the system works the way it is supposed to, this chapter may tell you everything you need to know. Sometimes the system actually works as it should—errors disappear within 30 days of a dispute, never to return. If you're lucky, it will work, as it should in your case too.

But proceed with caution and realistic expectations. The reason that credit report errors emerged as a political issue, and the reason Congress has twice amended the Fair Credit Reporting Act in the past seven years, is that the *system for correcting inaccuracies does not always work as it should.* A few of the well-known problems include:

- Credit bureaus refuse to delete disputed, inaccurate data because the credit grantor, through an automated system, "verified" it was "accurate."
- Disputed information actually was deleted, but later was reinserted because the credit grantor thoughtlessly re-reported it, and the credit bureaus' "screens" failed to catch it.

- The credit bureaus' algorithms cause them to wrongly mix into your credit report data about people with similar names or SSNs.

Another important consideration is the tremendous volume of disputes that the bureaus must handle and the challenges this presents. According to deposition testimony, approximately 350 credit bureaus employees must process between 7,000 and 10,000 consumer disputes per day. Because there is an average of three items disputed by each consumer, the credit bureau employees only have a few minutes for processing each disputed item.

To handle this volume, credit bureau employees must quickly enter a two-digit code describing the consumer's dispute, which is then sent via computer to the furnisher of the information. Most creditors, through a semi-automated system, merely check to see if the information disputed by the consumer is pretty much the same as that which currently resides in the creditors' files, and which previously was furnished to the credit bureau. If it is the same, the credit grantor "verifies" its "accuracy" and the credit bureau refuses to delete it. But if the furnisher's original information is inaccurate, this automated exchange between it and the credit bureau fails to uncover the inaccuracy.

The approaches recommended in this chapter are designed to maximize your chances for resolving disputes with the minimum amount of time and effort. However, if credit bureaus or credit grantors initially fail to correct inaccurate information, these approaches should enhance your ability to enforce your basic right to an accurate credit report.

With these caveats in mind, we can proceed to discuss the basics of the dispute and correction process.

First Steps—A System For Documenting Your Disputes

Whether you look at it as a "project" or "part-time job," it is wise to keep careful track of your dispute-related communications with the three major repositories. You should create a *folder* for each of the three credit bureaus in which you can store copies of letters and attachments. It also is wise to maintain a *log* that records the date and time of your communications. The log is particularly important if you choose to conduct your disputes mainly over the Internet or by phone.

The *fastest* way to dispute errors is online, through each CRA's Web site. The *second fastest* way to dispute is over the telephone. But unless you are forced by the circumstance of a pending mortgage application or other high-pressure deadline, it is generally *most prudent* to conduct all disputes in writing via First Class *certified mail*. It will cost you $2.65 for each certified letter (or $7.95 for three). With the number on the certified mail receipt, you can go to the U.S. Postal Service's web site (www.usps.com) and verify that each credit bureau received your dispute letter. Print out a copy and place it in your newly created folder. For an extra $2.15 per letter ($6.45 for three), you can go the extra step of a "return receipt requested," which you can include in the folder upon its return from the credit bureau. Remember, keep copies of all letters, receipts, and attachments in the folder corresponding to Equifax, Experian, or Trans Union. If credit grantors like Chase or MBNA are causing inaccuracies, you will want to create folders for them as well.

Some might find such recordkeeping chores to be a "pain in the neck," but it's a greater pain down the road to have to prove that you disputed something when you don't have the documentation. As we will see, the FCRA imposes *deadlines* on the credit bureaus and credit grantors, and these deadlines can work to your advantage. Your recordkeeping system can help show that you did what you were supposed to do, but that they did not meet the deadlines. Under the FCRA, if they don't meet the 30-day deadline for verifying disputed information, they are supposed to delete it and not reinsert it.

The Nature of Your Dispute

An important consideration in deciding how to proceed is the nature of the error or errors that you are planning to dispute. Again, if you are under a high-stakes deadline, where errors have lowered your credit score to the point that a mortgage will cost an extra several hundred dollars per month, you will probably want to dispute the errors online through the credit bureaus' Web sites. You may even want to involve an attorney. If you are applying for a mortgage or refinancing, ask your mortgage broker or lender to enlist the help of a reseller so you can benefit from "rapid re-scoring" of your credit report (see Chapter 3). If you are facing a mortgage or other deadline, say so in your dispute letter. The bureaus prioritize emergency disputes.

On the other hand, let's say you are not faced with a deadline and you have discovered Chase is reporting that last year, you were once 60-days late, and once 30-days late. To the best of your recollection, this was a result of a mistake by Chase, as it sent the bill to the wrong address. You found out about it because Chase called you at the correct phone number. You paid the bill right away. Chase admitted it was their mistake and apologized.

Because you finally obtained your credit report, you've discovered the mistake is showing up on two of your three credit reports. Because you used the online credit score simulator at the Fair Isaac or credit bureau Web site, you see that removing these derogatory tradelines will bump you up to a better risk category. In other words, it's worth getting it deleted because in a few months, you'll probably apply for some kind of credit or be up for an insurance renewal. In this case, it could be most effective to send a friendly, written dispute to the two credit bureaus, along with any supporting documentation, preferably a letter from Chase confirming your story. Again, it's even better if Chase directly notifies the credit bureau that the information should be deleted. In any event, if things work as they should, the information is deleted from your credit report and your credit score improves.

Three Avenues—Mail, Phone, or Online

All right. We have gotten most of the qualifiers out of the way. For the most part, it's best to do your disputes in writing. Here are the three avenues for disputing credit report errors, with a brief summary of their advantages and disadvantages:

- **Certified First Class Mail.** *Advantage*: Allows you to prove the credit bureau received your dispute. Allows you to attach supporting documentation. *Disadvantage*: Takes longer, usually requires more paper shuffling.
- **By Phone.** *Advantage*: Allows you to explain your case to a human being. Involves less paper shuffling. *Disadvantage*: Could make it more difficult to later prove you disputed errors. Requires that you take careful notes of your conversation. Does not allow you to provide supporting documentation unless you can provide it via fax machine. Also, it's possible, and some folks think likely, that CRAs record consumer dispute phone calls.
- **Online.** *Advantage*: Dispute is immediate, and is instantly forwarded to the credit grantor, triggering its investigation. *Disadvantage*: Could make it more difficult to later prove you disputed errors. Requires that you take careful notes, print out computer screens. Does not allow you to provide supporting documentation unless you can provide it via fax machine later.

Here are the addresses and phone numbers for disputes. Please note that the P.O. Box numbers and telephone numbers for disputes are different from the ones used for requesting a copy of your credit report.

Equifax
P.O. Box 740256
Atlanta, GA 30374
(800) 797-7033
[9am – 5:00pm In Your Time Zone]
www.equifax.com/online-credit-dispute/

Experian – Allen, TX 75013
(Will not publish mailing address "because the address changes." The dispute address can only be found on the credit report you obtain from Experian.)
(800) 583-4080 [9am – 5:00pm In Your Time Zone]
www.experian.com/disputes/index.html

Trans Union
P.O. Box 2000
Chester, PA 19022-2000
(800) 916 8800 [8:30am – 4:30pm Your Time Zone]
www.transunion.com/investigate

Disputing In Writing Via First Class Mail (Certified)

One advantage to getting the paper version of your credit report is that the last page is the bureau's form for disputing errors in your credit report. In general, the most effective manner for disputing errors is to:

- **Fill out the bureau's dispute form**, including the **confirmation number** from your credit report. Be as specific as possible about what information you want deleted or changed, and why. If you prefer not to use the dispute form, integrate all specifics into a concise dispute letter. Avoid poorly focused or rambling letters that don't quickly identify the specifics of your dispute. Limit your dispute to one page and rewrite it until it is that short.

- **Attach any supporting documentation**, like a copy of a cancelled check, showing that a trade line was paid on time or paid in full.

Attach your own version of "Dispute Sample Letter 1" (see Page xyz)

- **Send your dispute "package" Certified First Class Mail to <u>both the credit bureau and the credit grantor</u> (furnisher)**
- **Keep all copies and the mail receipt in a dedicated folder**
- **Note the Activity on your Log**
- **Mark on your calendar 35 days from when you send the letter to check for a response and to send a follow up letter** (if necessary)

    Fill Out The Dispute Form. One advantage of the dispute form attached to your credit report is that it has your identifying information pre-filled-in, thereby authenticating you. The form also makes it easy to fill in the company name and account number of the trade line you are disputing.

    It includes boxes you can check explaining the reason why the information is inaccurate, including **"Not My Account," "Paid In Full," "Payment Never Late,"** or **"Payment Status Incorrect," "Account Closed,"** and **"Account in Bankruptcy,"** or **"Paid Before Sent To Collection."** Importantly, these forms include the category **"Other,"** and space to explain in more detail.

    If there are details that support your dispute, concisely write them on the form. Also important, if there are <u>documents</u>, like cancelled checks, or user agreements that support your dispute, <u>attach copies</u> and make it part of the dispute package. The FCRA requires that the credit bureaus provide to the credit grantor (furnisher) *all relevant information* provided by the consumer so that the credit grantor can see that the dispute is supported.

Testimony before courts and Congress suggested that the credit bureaus were not always complying with this requirement. As noted before, the bureaus try to cope with the volume by describing the dispute with a two- or three-digit code that can be sent via computer to the furnisher.

This automated message exchange does not very well accommodate transmission of paper attachments provided by the consumer. But the FCRA mandates that the credit bureaus "provide" all of your relevant material to the credit grantor. Thus, there is a tension between customary industry practice and what seems to be an obvious legal requirement, which has not yet been resolved by the courts.

Another potential tension is the requirement that credit bureaus forward the consumer's dispute to the furnisher within five business days. Testimony before Congress raised questions as to the extent this was happening.

I mention this so you will know to fashion your dispute to fully take advantage of the rights afforded you by the FCRA. That brings us to the "Sample Dispute Letter."

Sample Dispute Letter

This letter serves two purposes. First, it puts the credit bureau and credit grantor on notice that you are serious about getting errors corrected and that you know your rights. Second, it provides an opportunity to provide any extra details or explanations that you were unable to fit on the dispute form. (If you do not use the dispute form, include the identifiers needed to authenticate you: Name, address, SSN, date of birth, previous addresses, and spouse's name.)

You will also notice that the sample letter takes on a respectful, non-threatening tone. Remember, a human employee, likely trying to handle huge volumes in a stressful environment, must process your dispute. Credit bureau officials state that a threatening or nasty tone does nothing to encourage their employees to effectuate your ultimate goal of correcting errors. They also say that it helps to get right to the point and not ramble. On balance, it is always better to treat other humans with respect, particularly when you want them to facilitate the correction of errors. (*See sample letter.*)

Sample Letter[64]

To: Equifax, Experian and/or Trans Union (Address)
Dear Credit Bureau:

I am writing to dispute the following inaccuracies in my credit report:

1) Chase Account No.: 123456789-01 –
   Dispute: Never late
   (Canceled check showing timely payment attached)
2) MBNA Account No. 987654321-03 –
   Dispute: Not Mine -- My ex-spouse's account
   (Statement of Divorce & Confirmation letter from ex-spouse attached)
3) Previous Address – Dispute: I never lived at
   444 Elm St (Utility bill with current address is attached. I've lived at this address for four years).

Please forward this letter and the enclosures to any of the creditors. If you do not send a copy of my letter and the enclosures to any of the creditors, I request that you promptly advise me so I can take additional steps to protect myself. Thanks for helping me in this very important matter.

Sincerely Yours,
The Concerned Consumer

---

[64] This letter was drafted with the help of James Fishman, an attorney and FCRA specialist in New York with Fishman and Neil, and by attorney Joanne Faulkner of New Haven, Connecticut.

Send To Both Credit Bureau & Credit Grantor

Even if you think your creditor is the main cause of the problem, you need to send the dispute to the credit bureau that is including the errors in your credit report. This is because the FCRA directs consumers to route their disputes through the credit bureaus. The credit bureau in turn is responsible for notifying the credit grantor of the dispute and for forwarding to the creditor all other relevant information. By sending the dispute to the credit bureau, the consumer increases the duty on the credit grantor to reinvestigate and increases its liability if it fails to do so.

In most cases, it's also a good idea to send the dispute data directly to the credit grantor. There have been cases in which the credit grantors have claimed they never received the credit bureau's notice of the consumer's dispute. Sending it directly to the credit grantor also puts it on notice that you are serious about getting the error corrected.

And don't forget the "shortcut" mentioned before. If you think your creditor will believe you and promptly instruct the credit bureau that the disputed data should be deleted or corrected, that could be the most efficient way to accomplish this goal. After all, *you* are the creditor's customer. Sometimes, that gives you leverage.

Send all letters Certified First Class Mail. In a few days, go to the U.S. Postal Service's Web site (www.usps.com) and using the number on your Certified Mail receipt, confirm receipt of your dispute. Note all the activity in your "Activity Log."

The FCRA requires the credit bureaus to complete their investigation in 30 days and send you the results of their investigation. Mark your calendar so you will know to send a follow up letter if they fail to meet that requirement. Generally, you want to avoid sending additional dispute letters within the 30-day period, as that grants the credit bureaus an extension. The credit bureaus must forward your dispute to the credit grantors within five business days.

Following Up

Within 30 days or so, you are supposed to receive at least a letter from each credit bureau advising you the results of the investigation. If your dispute is successful, the bureaus will respond by informing you that "trade lines" (information about accounts) will be deleted or otherwise corrected. If you don't receive a response by day 40 or so, then write a follow-up letter basically stating:

Dear Credit Bureau:

Since you did not advise me within 30 days about your investigation of my dispute, please confirm that you have deleted the disputed account (insert creditor name and account number). Please do this promptly and send me a corrected copy of my credit report. Also please ensure that this deleted trade line is not reinserted into my credit report at some future date. Thank you very much for your prompt assistance in this matter. I hope you have a great day.

> Sincerely Yours,
> Happy Consumer

If the credit grantor insisted that its original report about you was correct, the credit bureau will advise you that the disputed trade line was "verified as reported." If this is the case, and you are not willing to give up, it's time to escalate. Before we discuss the escalation process, let's say a few words about disputing by telephone and via the Internet.

Telephone

You can dispute errors over the phone by calling the toll-free numbers listed in this chapter. There might be certain errors that lend themselves to resolution by telephone. For example, if you are 22-years-old and your credit report shows you owe an unpaid, 7-year-old auto loan, you could probably convince a credit bureau operator that you are not responsible and that this is a mistake.

But if you are trying to resolve the kinds of disputes where your "word" is not sufficient then you need to prepare before you make the phone call.

First, you want to gather and have ready all documentation supporting your dispute. Second, you want to be ready to keep detailed notes of your conversation. Some state laws permit you to record phone conversations without first getting the other person's consent, but overall, it's usually better to obtain someone's consent before recording a phone conversation.

Finally, you should ask the credit bureau employee for a fax number so you can fax any supporting documentation. Keep a copy of the fax machine's "activity record" showing the time and date that you faxed the information to the bureau's fax number. Keep in mind, the CRAs outsource much of their dispute handling to low-wage countries like The Philippines, India, Jamaica and Costa Rica.

Place all records related to this communication in your dedicated folder.

Internet

After obtaining your credit report online at the credit bureau's Web site, you can click on specific derogatory trade lines, find the "dispute" button, and click on that to dispute it. When you do this, the credit bureau says it instantly forwards your dispute to the furnisher. This should speed the dispute resolution process, but there are no guarantees of that as of this writing. Print all relevant computer screens and save them in a dedicated folder.

Escalating After A Refusal To Correct

If, like many other consumers, you found that the system did not work the way it was supposed to, and that inaccurate information remains on your credit report, your situation is considerably more serious, and it's time to take it to the next level. If possible, it's best to get expert legal advice from an attorney who specializes in the FCRA. Again, the best places to find FCRA attorneys are at two groups: the National Association of Consumer Advocates (NACA) www.naca.net and the National Consumer Law Center (NCLC) www.nclc.org.

As a practical matter, however, it's not always possible or affordable for many consumers to find an attorney who will represent them at such an early stage in the credit dispute process. If you are determined to clear your credit report, but it's not practical for you to find legal representation, let's look at the next steps you can take on your own.

Escalation Letter—More Demanding

Since the resolution of your dispute now necessitates some escalation, your letter to the credit bureaus and/or credit grantors will require a more stern and demanding tone. Here are some points that might help you communicate your seriousness. Of course, you should only state things that are true.

- Ask the credit bureau to describe the accuracy and completeness of the disputed data, including the business name, address and phone number of any furnisher that was contacted. This is an important right under the FCRA that is often overlooked.[65]

- List all ways that the bureau's failure to honor your dispute has damaged you. Has it caused credit denials or discouraged you from applying for credit? Is it causing you frustration, aggravation or other emotional distress? If so, is the distress interfering with your work performance, relationships, or daily life?

- Write to the FTC,[66] which under the new FACT Act will forward your complaint to the credit bureau; also, write your Member of Congress[67] and/or the news media.

- Complain to a state authority, like a State Attorney General,[68] or banking department or consumer protection department. In some cases, these offices will contact the bureaus about your complaint. Sometimes that suffices to make the bureaus respond. Some county governments have helpful consumer affairs offices.[69]

- You can also place a 100-word "statement of dispute" on your report, but generally this has not proven to accomplish much.

Taking It To Court

If none of these actions are successful in convincing the CRAs to delete or correct inaccurate information, the

---

[65] 15 U.S.C. 1681i(a)(6)(B)(iii)

[66] www.ftc.gov

[67] www.house.gov and www.senate.gov

[68] Go to www.naag.org. Web site for the National Association of Attorneys General to obtain an address for your State Attorney General

[69] See www.nacaanet.org/about/members.ahtml, the National Association of Consumer Agency Administrators

FCRA gives you the right to go to court and file suit. The merits of such a suit can only be judged on a case-by-case basis. Like any other area, it is preferable to seek the advice of an attorney who specializes in the FCRA. If you are unable to find a specialist, any attorney can obtain valuable information about the FCRA in a manual published by the National Consumer Law Center (www.nclc.org).

Making Your Dispute A Priority

In deposition testimony, CRA employees have acknowledged that their dispute handling departments treat certain cases as "priorities." They generally have identified the priority categories as:

- **A Person or Attorney Threatening To Sue.** You actually have to be careful here. Credit bureaus have been known to treat letters from attorneys as credit repair operators. Thus, invoking your right to sue or having an attorney write the letter could backfire in the sense that it would delay correction of errors rather than expedite them. On the other hand, you have every right to an attorney and to pursue your rights under law. The credit bureau has no right to dismiss a legitimate reference to an attorney or to legal rights as a credit repair tactic. The manner and tone in which you dispute errors call for good judgment, based upon the particular circumstances. If the matter is urgent and there is a lot at stake, involvement of an attorney would seem warranted, particularly if the credit bureaus have not satisfactorily responded to your previous requests for correction. When an actual lawsuit is pending over a credit bureau's failure to correct errors, the bureaus have been known to more quickly make long sought after corrections. The National Association of Consumer Advocates (NACA) (www.naca.net) and the National Consumer Law Center (NCLC) (www.nclc.org) both sponsors conferences to educate attorneys about the FCRA.

- **Some credit repair organizations** may imply that an attorney will handle your case, but from the volume of business that they claim to do, be suspicious. An attorney who will go to bat for you in court cannot effectively do the type of large volume business that some credit repair "law firms" claim they do.

- **An Enforcement Official From the FTC or State Attorney General.** These officials have the authority to trigger wider investigations of credit bureau practices and have done so over the years. In fact, reference to a particular consumer's case before a Congressional hearing or FTC workshop can expedite resolution of disputes.

- **A Celebrity.** Movie and television stars, recording artists, and even athletes are capable of doing testimonials as to how wonderfully the credit bureau performed in their case.

Chapter 7

Identity Theft Basics

Who steals my purse steals trash:
'Tis something, nothing;
Twas mine 'tis his
and has been slave to thousands.
But he that filches from me my good name
Robs me of that which not enriches him,
And makes me poor indeed.

– Othello, III, iii, 157-61 (Iago)

Studies released between 2003 and 2006 supported what experts had been warning for some time: identity theft had reached epidemic proportions. For instance, a Federal Trade Commission survey estimated in 2003 there were 9.9 million victims of identity theft, up from an estimated 6.9 million victims in 2002 and 3.4 million victims in 2001.[70]

(For more details on these and other surveys, see Chapter 10).

---

[70] www.ftc.gov/os/2003/09/synovatereport.pdf

This chapter is designed first and foremost to help those who have become, or fear they have become, victims of identity theft. Later, we'll examine the nature of the crime and a few individual cases.

For the vast majority of people who are not victims of identity theft, the best thing to do is to check your credit report regularly, focusing on two categories:

- **Unfamiliar Accounts (tradelines).** Is there a new credit card or debt listed on your report that you've never heard of?

- **Inquiries From Unfamiliar Entities.** Here, we are talking about "hard" inquiries, meaning those showing you supposedly applied for credit (as opposed to pre-approved credit promotions or account review inquiries). If you live in Ohio and there's an inquiry from a car dealer in Arizona, or an electronics store in Florida, chances are something is wrong; you should investigate immediately, following the steps listed below.

In addition, the three major credit bureaus sell subscription services that are supposed to alert you via e-mail if there is significant new activity on your credit report that could signal identity theft. These services range from $10.95 per month to $119 per year. Provided these services perform as described, they should serve as an effective – though a bit pricey – method of learning of a threat to your personal data *before* the damages begin to compound (see pages 85-88).

Another service specifically designed to guard against identity theft is offered by a Colorado firm, I.D. Watchdog.[71] It monitors a consumer's identity and personal data in 13 different critical areas, including credit, criminal, medical and Social Security records, and resolves breaches.

---

[71] www.IDwatchdog.com; the author is a shareholder and consultant. The firm also provides fee-based identity theft resolution services.

What To Do If The Nightmare Happens To You

Several groups, including the Privacy Rights Clearinghouse, Identity Theft Resource Center, Identity Theft 911, and the Mari Frank Law Office, have done an excellent job of listing the steps that victims should take to contain the damage from identity theft. (See Footnote 73 below for their Web site addresses).[72]

Activity Log/Recordkeeping. In Chapter 6, we told you to keep an activity log and folders to track progress on your disputes to the credit bureaus. This becomes even more important when fighting off identity theft, for several reasons. First, you typically must deal with three credit bureaus, several creditors, and a law enforcement official (local police, detective, Secret Service, etc.). You will want to document your communications with these and any other entities. Second, you need to *keep track of the time* you spend on these chores, as well as any out-of-pocket expenses (folders, certified postage, long-distance phone calls, etc.). If some entity does not meet its legal obligations, you will want to be able to quantify your damages. Accordingly, you might also want to keep a diary, noting when and how your identity theft-related chores are causing you emotional distress or affecting your work performance or personal relationships. In addition, your time and expenses might be tax-deductible in certain circumstances (consult an accountant).

Law Enforcement. Here are the authorities you should notify in order to file a formal report. Remember to **include all fraudulent accounts in the report**, as the credit bureaus say that enables them to promptly remove the

---

[72] Privacy Rights Clearinghouse, www.privacyrights.org, has excellent fact sheets for identity theft, credit reports, and a myriad of other privacy issues. Mari Frank, www.identitytheft.org, is an attorney and author of the quite helpful *Identity Theft Survival Kit, From Victim To Victor, and Safeguarding Your Identity.* The leading group is the ID Theft Resource Center: www.idtheftcenter.org; also see www.identitytheft911.com and www.IDwatchdog.com.

disputed accounts from your credit report. Keep a copy and the report number. Contact:

- Your local police department
- FTC (800) 438-4338 – (800) ID THEFT; www.consumer.gov/idtheft;
- For the FTC uniform affidavit: www.ftc.gov/bcp/conline/pubs/credit/affidavit.pdf

Credit Bureaus (CRAs). Here's the checklist of immediate steps to take with the credit bureaus.

- Put a **"security freeze"** on your credit report so nobody can access your account unless you lift the freeze, a right that exists is some 36 states as of 2007.[73]
- **Notify** at least one of the CRA's **fraud units** that you are a victim of identity theft. They are responsible for notifying the other two CRAs. (Experian: 888-397-3742; Equifax: 800-525-6285; Trans Union: 800-680-7289)
- Ask the CRAs to flag your file with a **fraud alert** (lasts 3-6 months). When you receive your credit report, follow the instructions to extend the fraud alert for 7 years. You can cancel at any time.
- Ask the CRAs to send you a **free copy** of your credit report. (In California, state law entitles you to one free report per month for 12 months.)
- Once you read the report, send a dispute letter, accompanied by police report and/or FTC fraud affidavit specifying which accounts are fraudulent
- Consider subscribing to the CRAs' monitoring-alert services (see CRA Web sites)
- Ask CRAs for **contact info of creditors** with whom fraudulent accounts have been opened.

---

[73] For more on state freeze laws, see: www.pirg.org/consumer/ or www.consumersunion.org/campaigns/learn_more/003484indiv.html

Creditors (New & Existing Accounts). The identity thief has opened up new accounts in your name. You must contact these creditors immediately, by phone and in writing. Their contact data should be listed on your credit report.

- Notify each creditor of the identity theft, specifying the fraudulent account. They will ask you to send a fraud affidavit. (Note everything in your activity log.)

- Fill out and send the FTC uniform fraud affidavit, which most creditors accept.
  www.ftc.gov/bcp/conline/pubs/credit/affidavit.pdf

- Ask them to send any application, transaction, or other records documenting the fraudulent activity that occurred in your name.[74]

- If the thief committed fraud using your existing credit cards or checks, get replacement cards and numbers and specify that you want the "accounts closed at customer's request," as opposed to "card lost or stolen," which some could construe to be your fault.

- Add passwords to all accounts. (Store passwords so you can find them when you forget them later.)

Debt Collectors. Debt Collectors may come after you for unpaid bills generated by the identity thief. If they call you:

- Ask the debt collector for his or her name, company's name, address, and phone number. Advise him that you are noting the time and date of the conversation in your activity log.

---

[74] Required first by California Penal Code 530.8, and later by the 2003 Amendments to the FCRA (FACT Act)

- Inform him that you are a victim of identity theft and not responsible for the debt.
- Ask for the name and contact information of the referring credit issuer.
- Be ready to provide the FTC uniform fraud affidavit.
- Follow up with a letter to the collector, stating that you do not owe this debt and that the account has been closed.
- Request in writing confirmation that the account is being closed and noted as fraudulent, and that any and all reference to the debt in your credit files will be removed.

Checks. If the thief used your checks, put stop payments on all remaining checks, cancel your checking and savings account, and obtain new account numbers. Put a password on your account. Notify the following check verification companies (remember, keep track of your time.)

- CheckRite: (800) 766-2748
- Chexsystems: (800) 428-9623
- CheckCenter/CrossCheck: (800) 843-0760
- Certigy/Equifax: (800) 437-5120
- International Check Services: (800) 526-5380
- SCAN: (800) 262-7771
- TeleCheck: (800) 710-9898

Other Things To Watch For
- ATM Cards (cancel and change PIN)
- Fraudulent change of address – Postal Inspector www.usps.gov/websites/depart/inspector
- Local or cellular phone service
- Social Security number misuse www.ssa.gov
- Drivers license number misuse
- Passports www.travel.state.gov/passport_services.html

Why Has Identity Theft Increased?

Identity theft is:
   (1) a relatively low-risk crime,
   (2) with a potentially very high payoff,
   (3) that can be relatively easy to pull off,
   (4) while enforcement is uneven, at best, despite
   (5) the potentially devastating impact on the victim.

It wasn't officially declared a crime until 1998 when Congress and some states began passing laws to that effect. (For more on the history and evolution of identity theft, see Chapter 10.)

Throughout much of the 1990s, many victims of identity theft had trouble convincing the police that they were victims of a crime at all. The police often would say that the credit card company or bank was the victim because they, and not the consumer, lost money to the thief. Some victims could not even convince authorities to write a police report. Other victims faced jurisdictional problems because the thief resided in a different city or state.

In the early days, identity theft was more of a one-person-at-a-time crime. But in recent years, it's gone "wholesale." Thieves target organizations where they can filch personal data on dozens, if not hundreds or even thousands of people at a time. Methods of attack include bribing or placing a "mole" in auto dealerships, corporate personnel departments, or government agencies, or hitting multiple mailboxes at large apartment or housing complexes. The document that the identity thief covets most is the credit report. It's the best roadmap for committing the crime or invading privacy in other ways.

One notable case involved Philip Cummings, a 10-month employee of Teledata Communications Inc (TCI), a company that facilitates large companies' use of credit reports. From 1999-2002, Cummings allegedly was able to electronically masquerade as the Ford Motor Company and other major companies, pull credit reports in their names, and sell the data to a Nigerian fraud ring. Even after Cummings left TCI and moved out of state, he was able to continue using passwords that allowed him, from February to May 2002, to pull 6,000 reports, 100 at a time, in the name of Washington Mutual Bank. In September 2002, long after the Ford Motor Company incident had been well publicized, the Cummings ring ordered 4,500 credit reports through Central Texas Energy Supply. When a company changed its password, it temporarily stumped the ring's access. But after being arrested, the ring member later cooperated with prosecutors and told them that Cummings had an ample list of active passwords.

The result was that some 30,000 individuals had their good names used for fraud – with initial losses pegged at $2.7 million, but rising well beyond that.[75]

The Key Moment

Of course, identity theft is profitable because the thief is able to get credit in someone else's name. That's where the credit report comes into play. The key moment occurs when the credit reporting agency (CRA) discloses the innocent victim's credit report in response to a thief's fraudulent application for credit. The credit report "validates" the thief and starts him on his "credit joyride." As we explore in greater detail in the next chapter, the CRAs' rather loose algorithms have benefited identity thieves by allowing for disclosure of victims' credit reports even when the imposters' applications are filled with discrepancies.

---

[75] TCI and other breaches were the subject of April 3, 2003 hearing of the House Financial Services Subcommittees on Financial Institutions & Consumer Credit, and Oversight and Investigations, "Fighting Fraud: Improving Information Security," at which this author testified. http://financialservices.house.gov/hearings.asp?formmode=detail&hearing=202. Also see the excellent reporting on security breaches and identity theft, by MSNBC's Bob Sullivan www.msnbc.com/news/839678.asp.

Victims

A book could be filled with the horrifying stories of identity theft victims. To help illustrate their plight, we will offer only a few.

On November 5, 2001, retired Army Captain John Harrison, a Connecticut resident, received a call from a detective in Beaumont, Texas who was investigating a Harley-Davidson motorcycle that had been purchased using Harrison's name and SSN. The detective tracked Harrison down through his credit report. Harrison took all the steps that were recommended by experts (and the above pages in this chapter): He ordered his three credit reports, initiated fraud alerts, contacted creditors immediately, received and reviewed his credit reports, and filed a police report with the Army's Criminal Investigation Division.[76]

The crook, Jerry Wayne Phillips, was caught on his Harley in North Carolina about a month later. Phillips said it was easy to convince Army officials at Fort Bragg, N.C. to issue him identification in Harrison's name and SSN.

'Joyriding'

From July to December 2001, Phillips used Harrison's identity to acquire goods, services, and cash in his name. The acquired items were valued at over $260,000. Staying away from Harrison's home state of Connecticut, Phillips bounced from Florida to Virginia, and on to Texas, opening at least 60 fraudulent accounts: credit accounts, personal and auto loans, checking and savings accounts, and

---

[76] Statement of Capt. John C. Harrison, U.S. Senate Committee on Banking, Housing and Urban Affairs, "The Growing Problem of Identity Theft and Its Relationship to the Fair Credit Reporting Act," June 19, 2003. Harrison filed suit under the FCRA. He was represented by Chris Kittell, of Webster Gresham & Kittell, Clarksdale, Miss. http://banking.senate.gov/index.cfm?Fuseaction=Hearings.Testimony&HearingID=43&WitnessID=177

utility accounts. He purchased two trucks through Ford Credit valued at over $85,000, and a Harley-Davidson motorcycle for $25,000. He rented a house in Virginia and purchased a time-share in Hilton Head, South Carolina. He bounced over 100 checks on his Army and Air Force Exchange Service (AAFES) checking account. Phillips was indicted on federal charges in Texas, pled guilty to one count of identity theft, and was sentenced to 41 months in a Minnesota federal prison.

But that did not end the damage to Harrison. One of the more difficult aspects was the 20-month struggle with credit bureaus and creditors. While Experian and Trans Union did a "fair job," he charged that Equifax failed to obey the FCRA.

"It took eleven months and three dispute letters to get a second report from Equifax. Further, I found the report they sent to me was not the same report they were sending to creditors. Both reports that Equifax has in their system still contain as many as fifteen fraudulent accounts," Harrison told Congress in June 2003. On his credit report, he had 17 different addresses, six different phone numbers, and a changing date of birth, he said.

"Credit bureaus hide behind the fact that they are only reporting what creditors tell them, while at the same time, victims are repeatedly sending affidavits, police reports, and detailed dispute letters proving the creditors are wrong. That is why it takes identity theft victims years instead of months to recover from this crime."

"I've invested over 1,100 hours of my time defending myself and working to restore my credit and banking histories. I've filled eight notebooks with over 1,500 pages of documentation. I can account for about $1,500 in out-of-pocket expenses directly related to my identity theft. Higher interest rates have cost me over $4,000. I've been unknowingly sued by at least one of the creditors. I've had my military retirement garnished. I'm not credit worthy enough to open any new accounts and bad checks reported in my name prevent me from opening any deposit accounts with banks."

Harrison said the toughest part might be the emotional distress he suffered. He was diagnosed with Post Traumatic Stress Disorder (PTSD) and given medication. He lost his job. Harrison ultimately filed an FCRA lawsuit, which settle for a confidential sum.

"Sadly, even as I look back over the last twenty months and retrace my steps, I can't identify a single thing I could have done differently that may have prevented the situation I'm currently in," Harrison said.

Once Again, With Feeling

Malcolm O. Radcliffe, Jr. also filed suit against three credit bureaus after he became a victim of identity theft in 1997. In November of that year, Radcliffe, an Indiana resident, received a phone call from a man who said he would soon be at Radcliffe's house to repossess his Toyota. Problem was, Radcliffe didn't own a Toyota.

When he got his credit report, Radcliffe discovered that numerous accounts, totaling $57,000, had been opened in his name by an imposter. Radcliffe spent hours writing and calling credit bureaus and creditors to dispute the fraudulent trade lines, but his credit report remained marred by inaccuracies not of his making. In some cases, the credit bureaus would verify the fraudulent data as accurate. In other cases, they would agree to delete it, only to reinsert it later. After at least 65 interactions with the credit bureaus and creditors, Radcliffe filed suit under the FCRA. In November 1999, he reached a confidential settlement with Experian, Trans Union, and CSC Credit Services.[77]

---

[77] Malcolm O. Radcliffe, Jr. v. CSC Credit Services, Inc., et al.: U.S. Dist. Ct. – Southern Dist. of Indiana (Evansville) – No. 3:03-CV-00082. Radcliffe was represented by John Waller, of Wooden & McLaughlin, Indianapolis.

Less than a year later, however, more fraud-generated data had returned to his credit report. Many of the "returns" were collection accounts stemming from the original fraudulent accounts that were removed in the 1997 settlement. So by mid-August, Radcliffe called Experian, which again corrected his report. In late September 2000, Radcliffe informed Experian that his credit report still listed a fraud-related SSN, date of birth, and misspelled name. In October, Experian again corrected the mistakes.

In July of 2002, Radcliffe discovered that fraud-generated data was again on his credit reports. He tried calling Experian's 800-number, but after being on hold for 45 minutes, he grew frustrated and gave up.

In February 2003, because of more bad data on his credit reports, Radcliffe was denied credit after making in-store applications at Banana Republic and in Parisien, a Saks store. One of the accounts on his February 2003 Experian report was a Filene's Basement account, which was first reported in 1999 and removed as part of the settlement.

In May 2003, at the age of 69, Radcliffe sued again, this time adding Equifax as a defendant, along with Experian, Trans Union, and CSC Services Corporation. It's typical for credit industry attorneys to tell a FCRA plaintiff that they really don't "have much in the way of damages." John Waller, Radcliffe's attorney, did not agree with them. But he and Radcliffe knew they had a long road ahead of them to get his case before a jury. In February 2004, the 70-year-old Radcliffe finalized his second settlement. He said he hoped it was his last.

Studies Confirm The Anecdotes

In the next chapter, we will discuss in more detail a series of studies about identity theft. At this point, we will mention only a few of the findings.

A 2003 study by the FTC found that the longer it took to discover the identity theft, the greater the damages.

While 63% had no out-of-pocket losses, victims reported a wide range of problems, including wrongful bank and credit card charges, harassment by collectors, loan or insurance rejection, cut-off of utilities, civil lawsuits, and criminal investigations.[78]

Among those victims who contacted a credit bureau, 58% said they were either "very" or "somewhat" satisfied, while 29% said they were somewhat dissatisfied and 9% said they were very dissatisfied. Of those consumers who contacted all three major credit bureaus, 49% said they were satisfied with all three, 20% said they were satisfied with some of them, and 31% said they were dissatisfied with all three. That reflects a significant level of dissatisfaction.

Also in September 2003, the Identity Theft Resource Center (ITRC) published its survey of 173 victims, showing that the damage suffered by identity theft victims was escalating on all fronts. It found that fraudulent charges averaged more than $90,000 per name used and that the average time spent by victims is about 600 hours, an increase of more than 247% over previous studies. It found that it was taking far longer than before to eliminate negative information from credit reports.[79]

John Harrison, the retired Army Captain and identity theft victim, said an "evaluation system" and other incentives had to be created to get CRAs to fight identity theft.

"I don't want to make unfounded accusations," Harrison said, "but it is my belief through common sense that credit bureaus do not lose money as a result of identity theft; they make money. Over a hundred inquiries have been made to my credit reports as a result of fraudulent accounts. These are inquiries the repositories are paid for what would not otherwise have been made. Additionally, with the public becoming more informed about the serious-

---

[78] Federal Trade Commission – Identity Theft Survey (Sept. 2003) www.ftc.gov/os/2003/09/synovatereport.pdf
[79] "Identity Theft: The Aftermath 2003," Identity Theft Resource Center (Sept. 2003); http://www.idtheftcenter.org/idaftermath.pdf

ness and growth of identity theft, I'm certain that sales of credit monitoring systems are doing quite well also. Monetarily speaking, there is not much incentive for the repositories to be aggressive about preventing identity theft or correcting inaccurate reports resulting from identity theft."[80]

No Sign of Real Change

What if three federal juries each found a credit bureau violated the FCRA and each jury awarded hundreds of thousands of dollars in damages? Would that bring change? Maybe not.

In January 2000, Matthew S. Kirkpatrick, a Portland finish carpenter and father of two young children, was surprised to learn that he had been denied a mortgage loan. He understood the importance of good credit and maintained a FICO score around 750. But it turned out that someone in Coeur d'Alene, Idaho, had stolen his name and SSN to take out credit in his name, thereby polluting his credit report with late payments and collection accounts. Kirkpatrick began the arduous task of notifying those who had been defrauded he was not responsible. He specifically recalled Equifax advising him to have the defrauded creditors notify Equifax directly. In fact, by the fall of 2000, two of creditors had done so. Kirkpatrick thought the problem had been resolved and that his FICO score would be restored to 750. He also put a "fraud alert" on his credit report.

Soon thereafter, Kirkpatrick's wife, Lisa, became pregnant with their third child. He quickly made plans to construct a new bedroom, and would do most of the work himself. Wishing to get started right away, he borrowed money from Lisa's retirement account – knowing there would be no penalty as long as the money was repaid by April 15, 2001, still several months away.

---

[80] Harrison, op. cit.

In February 2001, however, Kirkpatrick discovered that his credit report was polluted with more than a dozen collection accounts stemming from the ongoing activities of the Coeur D'Alene fraudster, including accounts involving creditors who already had informed Equifax that he was not responsible. His FICO score had plummeted to 580, well below sub-prime. Even though the local bank branch was familiar with him, it rejected his home improvement loan application, as the underwriters would never permit credit to be granted to someone with such an abysmal credit history.

You Can't Find It?!

Once he overcame his shock, Kirkpatrick set out to compile a dispute package that would clear up the mess quickly. The package he sent to Equifax in late February 2001 included:

- Coeur d'Alene and Portland police reports confirming that Kirkpatrick was not responsible for the fraud
- Letters from two defrauded creditors confirming that he was not at fault
- A copy of his Social Security card w/ signature
- A copy of his driver's license with his photo and current home address in Portland
- A cover letter explaining that he was a victim of identity theft.

But there was no response. Bank of America told him that his loan had been rejected again, as there had been no changes in his Equifax report. Kirkpatrick called Equifax, but the operator ("Lori") said they didn't have his dispute package. The operator grew impatient with him, essentially telling him to either do an oral dispute with her, or hang up.

Kirkpatrick wondered how Equifax could investigate properly without his supporting documentation, but finally relented, disputing 19 fraudulent accounts on his report. He also re-sent the entire dispute package on March 22, 2001.

The same day, Kirkpatrick received a letter from Equifax (dated March 13), advising him that his dispute package *"had been shredded,"* without explaining why.

Kirkpatrick really started to worry. The deadline for returning the borrowed money to his retirement account was fast approaching, and there was no resolution in sight. He called again, this time talking with "Lynn Hamilton."[81] On March 24, he sent a third dispute package. He called again on April 6, but "Sue" told him the package was nowhere to be found. On April 11, "Julie" and "Patty" reiterated that they could not find the package. Four days later, the bank assessed a penalty against the Kirkpatricks for not repaying the retirement account by the deadline.

Kirkpatrick kept trying. He talked to "Sue" again on April 20. Again, no package. But he followed her advice, sending a fourth package with the U.S. Postal Service's "return receipt requested." On April 30, the Postal Service delivered the signed card proving that Equifax had received his fourth package.

But when he called on May 7, "Marlene" amazingly insisted there was no dispute package. A week later, he spoke with "Dale," and supervisor "Aaron." Aaron essentially told him that if he wanted his credit report corrected, he needed to do it himself by contacting all of the defrauded creditors. This wasn't the first Equifax operator to be rude to him; it wouldn't be the last.

Coincidentally, he received Equifax's response to his March 20 phone dispute. Equifax and the defrauded creditors had "verified" that he was responsible for many of the fraudulent accounts. Accordingly, they would remain on his credit report. Kirkpatrick felt defeated.

---

[81] It was possible that some of the names given to Kirkpatrick were aliases.

Meanwhile, the new addition to Kirkpatrick's house remained unfinished, since he could not get the necessary financing. The unfinished work posed potential safety problems for his young children, as well as fire hazards. The white construction paper known as Tyvek, which typically envelopes unfinished homes, was exposed for so long that it began to come loose. When the late autumn winds blew at night, the Tyvek paper would flap eerily against the walls. When the new baby came, the Kirkpatricks were forced to crowd into a space even smaller than what they had before the remodeling began. The stress compounded as time went by.

Hoping to complete the construction, Kirkpatrick in early 2002 tried to find a lender that used a CRA other than Equifax, as Trans Union and Experian had managed to remove the fraudulent accounts by then. He tried again with Bank of America, but 11 fraudulent accounts – all related to Coeur d'Alene – remained. In addition, information on other unknown consumers was creeping into his credit report.

It was then that Kirkpatrick re-read the "Statement of Consumer Rights Under the FCRA" attached to each of his credit reports. There it was, in black and white: It was Equifax's responsibility to investigate and correct disputed information, not his. He contacted his uncle, an attorney in Washington State, who said he'd try to find a lawyer who knew something about the FCRA.

Kirkpatrick tried applying for credit, but banks and credit unions kept rejecting him, usually citing the Equifax report. Visibly changed and increasingly morose, Kirkpatrick reluctantly accepted a small personal loan from an insistent family friend.

He tried disputing again in April of 2002, but six weeks later, Equifax advised him that it had again "verified" fraudulent accounts – meaning that they would remain on his credit report. Moreover, new fraudulent accounts from collection agencies, phone companies and department stores had appeared on his account.

After yet another round of disputes failed to clear up his credit report, Kirkpatrick in June 2002 filed suit under the Fair Credit Reporting Act in federal court in Portland. Nonetheless, Equifax still did not correct the errors.[82]

In January 2005, Kirkpatrick finally got his day in court. He described years of frustration, as Equifax simply would not respond in any meaningful way to his numerous disputes. Due to time zone differences and his work schedule, Kirkpatrick usually tried to phone Equifax dispute operators at 6 a.m. Because of the difficulty in getting through, this became a stress-inducing, pre-dawn ritual.

"I would have shortness of breath, like it was hard to breathe. That was just the dread that I had of having to call."

'Embarrassed' & 'Sorry'

At trial, Equifax admitted it had failed Kirkpatrick. Alicia Fluellen, head of Equifax's dispute-handling department,[83] said she couldn't explain the breakdowns.

"It appears to me to be the Murphy's law of all dispute handling. I have truly never seen that. Every last opportunity that we had to get it right, we just – it was missed or wasn't taken."

In her pre-trial deposition, Fluellen denied that Equifax had violated even one provision of the FCRA.[84] But at trial, five years after his ordeal began, Kirkpatrick finally got an apology when the soft-spoken Fluellen, facing him from the witness stand, said, "I am completely and utterly embarrassed by the errors, very disappointed that we made so many errors on one particular consumer's credit file. This is my very first time coming into contact with Mr. Kirkpatrick. I really do believe he deserves an apology and I

---

[82] Kirkpatrick was represented by Michael Baxter and Robert Sola of Portland. Equifax's lead counsel was Mara McRae, of Atlanta's Kilpatrick & Stockton. The author was an expert for plaintiff.

[83] Fluellen's title was director of consumer customer care.

[84] That portion of the deposition was read at trial.

really would like to say that I am very, very sorry in the way we handled your disputes. I truly am."

Equifax had reason to show remorse. Under the FCRA, the jury could assess monetary damages to compensate Kirkpatrick for the harm he suffered. Moreover, the jury could hit Equifax with punitive damages to deter it from doing to others what it did to Kirkpatrick. Given the long list of seemingly inexcusable mistakes, Equifax's position was akin to that of actor John Cleese in the movie "A Fish Called Wanda," when he was being dangled upside down from a window by actor Kevin Kline, with Kline demanding an apology.[85]

While Fluellen apologized for the mistakes, she did not apologize for Equifax's system. She insisted that Equifax had good procedures in place, but that its employees failed to follow them.

One of these was the "verified victim policy" – meaning, Fluellen explained, that "if one credit grantor verified that the consumer was a victim of fraud, then regardless of what all the other credit grantors say, (Equifax) will remove all disputed accounts from the credit file."

Another "recurring human error" was the operators' failure to remove addresses that Kirkpatrick had disputed as fraudulent. Fluellen could not explain why the "maintenance reviewers," who oversee the operators, *never* caught any of these failures.

To avoid a repeat of the Kirkpatrick debacle, Fluellen testified that Equifax increased its "refresher training" for all agents. It also implemented some new "prompts," so that "if

---

[85] Cleese's classis apology: "All right, all right, I apologize. I'm really, really sorry. I apologize unreservedly. I offer a complete and utter retraction. The imputation was totally without basis in fact and was in no way fair comment and was motivated purely by malice, and I deeply regret any distress that my comments may have caused you or your family, and I hereby undertake not to repeat any such slander at any time in the future."

a consumer disputes an account as fraud, the system will ask the agent a series of (reminder) questions … so we're not depending on the agent to remember a great deal of information (about policies and procedures)," she said.

In 2001, Fluellen said, Equifax received anywhere from 10,000-30,000 letters a day – mainly consumer disputes and consumer requests for their own credit reports, but also some credit grantor responses. Most consumer disputes, including those with attachments, were outsourced to lower-paid operators in Jamaica. The exceptions were consumer disputes accompanied by police reports or fraud affidavits; those stayed with Equifax employees in Atlanta, she said.

'Standoff'

Fluellen, along with the rest of Equifax's defense, apparently convinced the jury that Kirkpatrick's experience was relatively rare, and that Equifax did not need to be punished. The jury awarded Kirkpatrick $210,000 in actual damages to compensate him for the years of misery. But it declined to award punitive damages.

This meant that Equifax likely would not make any substantive changes in its system for investigating consumer disputes. This system involves an automated exchange of messages between it and the credit grantor, and is designed to reduce costs by minimizing the amount of time employees spend on consumer disputes.

Fluellen testified that it wasn't a problem for its experienced operators to process 100 dispute messages, known as Consumer Dispute Verifications (CDVs), *in one hour*. "It's not very difficult," she said. "You're looking at the response from the credit grantor and you're matching up ID (i.e., name, address and SSN), and the more you do it, the faster you become. You're certainly not expected to process 100 CDVs an hour day one. You grow to that."

The problem is that with a complex dispute, like identity theft or a "mixed file," the comparison of identifiers is unlikely to determine the accuracy of the disputed information or the validity of the consumer's dispute. After all, in these kinds of cases, it is the mixing or misuse of identifying data that causes the inaccuracy in the consumer's credit report.

(We provide a more detailed examination of credit bureau and credit grantor "reinvestigations" in Chapter 9.)

When all the attorney's fees were tallied, Equifax's bill for the Kirkpatrick case probably exceeded $1 million.

Suzanne Sloane

In the Spring of 2003, Suzanne Sloane had the joy of giving birth to her second child. But she didn't realize at the time that a hospital employee named Shovana Sloan stole her SSN and took out credit in her name.

It wasn't until February 2004 that Suzanne learned Equifax had created multiple files combining her data with those of fraudster Shovana. She called Equifax, Experian and TransUnion and placed "fraud alerts" on her reports.

But a year later, her Equifax report was still marred by serious, fraud-generated delinquencies. After a March 2005 dispute, Equifax deleted about 22 out of the 24 fraudulent accounts. However, CitiFinancial "verified" that two of the fraudulent accounts belonged to the real Mrs. Sloane. Equifax's bungling worsened the multiple file problem. Sloane disputed again in May, but CitiFinancial "verified" the false data a second time. Equifax simply accepted CitiFinancial's position and did not investigate further. Remember, this was only a few months after Alicia Fluellen's dramatic court apology to Matthew Kirkpatrick.

When the Sloanes' applied for credit with Wachovia in August 2005, the bank received multiple Equifax files for Mrs. Sloane, both of which were smattered with charge-offs and late payments. Moreover, accounts that were previously deleted had been reinserted. The errors were still there in November 2005 when she applied for credit again.

Following a three-day trial, a federal jury in Alexandria, Virg. in July 2006 awarded Mrs. Sloane $351,000 – $106,000 in economic damages and $245,000 in emotional distress damages. The jury found that Equifax negligently failed to "follow reasonable procedures" to achieve "maximum possible accuracy," failed to conduct a reasonable investigation, failed to delete information it found to be inaccurate, and reinserted information into Sloane's file that previously had been disputed and deleted.

However, the jury declined to award punitive damages, finding that Equifax's conduct was not "willful" as defined by the FCRA.[86]

Experience Did Not Make The Difference

Nicole M. Robinson became an identity theft victim in 2000. That same year she began volunteering for the Identity Theft Resource Center. At first, she helped other victims deal with their ordeals. She quickly rose in prominence, appearing on news shows like CNN, Montel Williams, and Peter Jennings. A resident of Prince Georges County, Maryland, she testified before Congressional Committees, State Legislatures and was even invited to a White House identity theft event. *But she couldn't convince Equifax to remove obvious errors from her credit report.*

Robinson's case was so bad that at one point, Experian sent her a 45-page report filled with fraudulent accounts generated by her Texas-based perpetrator. She spent several hours on the phone with a conscientious Experian operator, going though each page, account-by-account. It was grueling, but her Experian report was mostly accurate from then on.

---

[86] Suzanne Sloane vs. Equifax Information Services, LLC, et al., U.S. District Court for the Eastern District of Virginia (Alexandria Div.), Case No. CIV 1:05 cv 1272. Mrs. Sloane was represented by A. Hugo Blankingship III. Equifax is appealing to U.S. Court of Appeals for the Fourth Circuit, challenging the damages as excessive.

Equifax was a different story. Fraud alerts and repeated disputes did not prevent an avalanche of new errors from marring her reports.

Then she got a break. John Harrison, another victim mentioned earlier in this chapter, had to sue to persuade Equifax to finally fix his report. As part of the settlement, he was given the direct phone line to Alicia Fluellen, head of Equifax's dispute department. He gave Fluellen's phone number to Ms. Robinson.

Between 2003–2005, Robinson or a colleague, either by phone or e-mail, communicated directly with Fluellen, her assistant Vickie Banks, or Equifax Vice President Chris Jarrard. Fluellen and Banks said they saw the problem and indicated they would fix it, according to Robinson.

Moreover, after her 2006 appearance before a House Committee, a Hill staffer more than once asked still another Equifax vice president if Robinson's file had been fixed.

None of this was enough. In fact, the inaccuracies worsened because Equifax agents, including one in The Philippines, further mixed her identifiers with the perpetrator, resulting in a never-ending array of multiple files.

Six years after her ordeal began, she filed suit under the FCRA. This time, U.S. District Judge Gerald Bruce Lee ruled that there was not enough evidence to let the jury decide whether Equifax's conduct was "willful," and subject to punitive damages. The standard, clarified by the U.S. Supreme Court, was "reckless disregard" of the consumer's rights. But Judge Lee concluded that Equifax merely made "mistakes." In August 2007, the jury awarded Robinson $200,000 in actual damages.[87] Sadly, six-figure jury verdicts did not appear to be enough to effectuate change at Equifax.

---

[87] Nicole M. Robinson vs. Equifax Information Services, LLC, et al., U.S. District Court for the Eastern District of Virginia (Alexandria Div.), Case No. 06-CV-1336. Ms. Robinson was represented by A. Hugo Blankingship III.

Theft of Choice

A notable case of identity theft surfaced in February 2005. ChoicePoint, a Georgia-based database company and spin-off of Equifax, became a tool of a fraud ring that was able to filch SSNs, identifiers, and sensitive credit data of at least 145,000 people across the nation. About 750 individuals were confirmed as identity theft victims.

The perpetrators were part of a sophisticated Nigerian fraud ring. They certainly knew how to select a target. ChoicePoint was reported to have some 19 billion records on virtually every American adult. It collected information from a wide range of taxpayer-subsidized sources, beginning with local property records showing home ownership and home value, and driver records.

ChoicePoint's Web site offered a long list: boating, pilot and professional licenses, telephone directories, including "reverse directories," credit header data, bankruptcies, liens and judgments, and "physician reports."[88] (For information on ChoicePoint's auto and home ownership databases, see Chapters 13 & 14.)

According to news reports, the fraud ring created up to 50 fake businesses, including debt collection and check cashing firms, which signed up as ChoicePoint "customers." That enabled the ring to used ChoicePoint as a portal for obtaining victims' credit report data. This might have enabled the fraudsters to identify those with higher credit scores, and thus, the most productive identities to steal.

Equifax said about 8,000 credit reports it sold to ChoicePoint may have been accessed illegally, according to the *Atlanta Journal-Constitution*. But Equifax said it had no plans to alter its security system.

"It was not a breach on the Equifax system; therefore we don't feel it is necessary to make any changes," Karen

---

[88] Perault Pale, "ChoicePoint Woes Help Competitors," Feb. 26, 2005; www.choicepoint.com/business/public/prds_1.html

Gaston, Equifax's chief administrative officer, told the Atlanta newspaper. What those reports contained remains unclear, Gaston said. The reports would not have included credit card numbers or salary information on individuals, but could have disclosed what credit cards and loans individuals had and provided other information.[89]

The company said it sells data to 40 percent of the nation's top 1,000 companies and has contracts with 35 government agencies, including several law enforcement agencies. In 2004, the company earned $148 million on revenue of $919 million.

One irony of the episode was that ChoicePoint billed self as an expert in authenticating individuals for businesses and government agencies so as to help avoid fraud.[90]

Over There, Over Here

A disturbing trend in identity theft was the increased number of service men and women who had become victims. Those stationed in Iraq, Afghanistan and elsewhere overseas were particularly vulnerable, as they often did not discover they were victims until they returned from a tour of duty.

Theft of service members' identities came in many forms. Enlisted men on a U.S. Navy vessel in the Indian Ocean had their identities stolen by shipmates, who transferred their data to a ring back in the States that committed the fraud. Another ring apparently planted a member inside a credit union at a military base in the United States. This was very strategic positioning, as the ring would know who was stationed overseas and therefore unlikely to discover the identity theft until long after fraudulent credit

---

[89] Robert Luke and Matt Kempner, "ChoicePoint Execs Defend Selling Stock," Feb. 25, 2005.
www.ajc.com/business/content/business/0205/26credit.html
[90] For more on ChoicePoint, read two excellent books: Robert O'Harrow Jr.'s No Place To Hide (Free Press 2004); and Daniel Solove's The Digital Person (NYU Press)

purchases were made.

After struggling to overcome the theft of his own identity, Naval Commander Franklin D. Mellott became the Military Victim Assistance Coordinator for the San Diego-based Identity Theft Resource Center.

Testifying before a House Subcommittee in June 2003, Mellott described his experience.

"I found myself fighting for my financial future and my Naval career. There was jurisdictional finger-pointing just trying to get someone to take a police report. There were countless telephone calls and letters to credit reporting agencies. I spent more than 100 hours working with the IRS and two companies in California trying to resolve income wrongly reported against my taxpayer ID number. Generally speaking, I wasted my valuable time off from the rigors of combat duty fighting with a system that makes it all too easy for a criminal to get credit in someone else's name. The mess was entirely mine to clean up. Unfortunately, it got worse."[91]

"In February 2002, after I placed fraud alerts on my accounts with all three reporting agencies, my half-brother was able to use my SSN yet again – this time establishing cellular service with AT&T Wireless. To add insult to injury, after I filed my initial fraud notifications, Experian merged my credit history with that of the criminal! They listed his wife's name as my wife, put most of his previous addresses in my file, listed his name as an alias of mine, listed his SSN as an alternate SSN of mine, and listed numerous collection actions from his past on my otherwise spotless file. When I asked how it happened, I was told, 'the computer did it.' I wish I could say this was a singular event, but it was not. I also found the reporting agencies unresponsive. Just a few months ago, after my case was featured in *SmartMoney*

---

[91] Statement of Commander Franklin D. Mellott, Financial Institutions and Consumer Credit Subcommittee, U.S. House Committee on Financial Services, "Fighting Identity Theft – The Role of the Fair Credit Reporting Act," June 24, 2003.

Magazine, I sent all three credit reporting agencies a certified return-receipt letter asking them to incorporate specific wording in my fraud alert. I asked that if they could not (or would not), to inform me why. Not a single one of them incorporated the language. None of them even bothered to reply."

As bad as his experience was, Mellott predicted worse for other service members.

"I am even more concerned for those 19-year-old soldiers, sailors, and their families that are so easily victimized by this crime. Imagine their spouses, new to the ways of the military, trying to balance the day-to-day challenges of a young family with the crippling effects of identity theft and mistakes by the credit industry. Furthermore, I am concerned because I can see how it could be nearly impossible to fight these problems from overseas."

Private Services

The market responded to the need for identity theft resolution services in various ways:

- In 2007, I.D. Watchdog, a Denver-based company, unveiled both resolution services for victims, and a more extensive file-monitoring service for prevention. www.IDwathdog.com
- Credit unions, insurers and other companies contracted with Identity Theft 911 to provide resolution services. www.IdentityTheft911.com
- Citi Identity Theft Solutions, a unit of Citigroup Inc., provides free identity-theft support for Citi Cards and Citibank customers to recover their identity and to re-establish credit history.

Chapter 8

Making & Mixing Credit Reports

> *Rumor travels faster, but it don't stay put as long as truth.*
> – Will Rogers
> "Politics Getting Ready to Jell"
> The Illiterate Digest (1924)

Like many caring sons, David Jokinen grew closer to his mother in her final years. Throughout his 40s and 50s, Jokinen had spent a great deal of time traveling to Europe and Canada as a consultant and author on urban affairs, engineering, and architecture.

But as his mother entered her 90s, Jokinen, a self-employed businessman, spent more and more time looking after her affairs. He was a co-signer on her three credit cards. When she died at the age of 95 in April 2001, Jokinen immediately sent his mother's death certificate to the three credit card issuers, one of which was Chase Bank. All three said it was "fine" for Jokinen to now use the card in his own name. A month later, Chase contacted Jokinen and asked for another copy of the death certificate. Jokinen asked what had happened to the copies he had mailed and faxed. The Chase representative said he didn't know, and surmised that it probably was misplaced or lost.[92]

Several months later, he learned that Equifax and Experian could not calculate a FICO score because – according to their records – Jokinen was "dead." The incident prevented Jokinen from obtaining a mortgage for which he had applied. After some digging, he discovered that Chase had confused his Social Security number with his mother's death.[93] In a figurative sense, the linkage was fatal. He had now become the victim of a "mixed file."

Thus began a two-year nightmare in which the credit bureaus were either unable or unwilling to correct an obvious error. Chase Bank employees suggested to Jokinen that it wasn't worth the bank's time to fix such "little" mistakes.

Please, Tell Them I'm Alive

In a scene out of a science fiction movie, Jokinen, after some cajoling, persuaded managers in the Houston office of the U.S. Social Security Administration to write a letter declaring that he was in fact alive, and not dead. As he awaited the all-important letter, word quickly spread through the staff offices and the waiting room. Jokinen's strange request was translated into Spanish, Vietnamese and Chinese for curious onlookers. When SSA officials finally handed him the letter, Jokinen held it high in triumph. All those in the waiting room stood and applauded.[94]

Meanwhile, Jokinen said that because of credit report errors, he was spending a minimum of seven hours a week, paying thousands of dollars in higher interest rates, and had

---

[92] Testimony of David Jokinen, "The Accuracy of Credit Report Information and the Fair Credit Reporting Act," U.S. Senate Committee on Banking, Housing, and Urban Development, July 10, 2003

[93] In fact, this can happen even without the reversal of SSNs. If one account holder dies and the *account* is coded as "deceased," (which sends it to the estate claims division of any credit card operation) the account will report on all account holders as "deceased."

[94] *Id.*

lost out on hundreds of thousands in investments from prospective investors who were shocked to see that he was "dead."

Bad as these damages were, he said the worst part was the emotional toll it took on him. As he told the Senate Banking Committee on July 10, 2003:

> "I was my mother's only child. We were quite close. My mother had Tuberculosis during the Second World War. She was confined to a T.B. sanitarium in Detroit for 3 years. My mother left our house when I was five years old. I never saw her in person again until I was 8 years old. In 1943 the T.B. doctors removed half of my mother's lung. During her recovery, the T.B. doctor told my mother she probably only had 2 to 5 more years to live. That's because she was now living on only half a lung, and it would eventually wear out. That was when she was 39 years old. She actually lived to 95. Because of Chase Bank's stupidity I have now relived her last few painful years over and over again – while trying to get this mess cleared up."[95]

Jokinen said he only began to see action after he found a lawyer and filed suit under the FCRA.[96] His appearance before the Senate Banking Committee inspired media coverage that put added pressure on Chase and the credit bureaus to clean up his reports.

---

[95] *Id.*

[96] Jokinen's was initially represented by attorney Russell Van Beustring, of Houston, Texas, and later retained the services of The Tien Law Firm and Williams and Bailey, both of Houston. The case settled for a confidential sum.

The System

Many people believe that the three major consumer reporting agencies (CRAs)—Equifax, Experian, and Trans Union—maintain an electronic folder on us, similar to the folders in which we store our documents on our personal computers. As we open and close our accounts and credit grantors furnish monthly updates on our payment performance, the CRAs simply add the updated information to our folders.

In fact, there are notable distinctions among the three. Equifax and Trans Union tend to follow the file-building model, while Experian is said to store information in a more dynamic database. Perhaps most important, the CRAs only pull together an actual credit report or calculate a credit score when either a credit grantor, employer, or some other user asks for your report, or when you ask for your own report. In this sense, it is more accurate to say that credit reports and credit scores are made "on the fly." And, the content of the credit report often depends on what identifying information the credit grantor provides when asking for it.

The credit grantors, or "furnishers," each month provide the CRAs with millions of bits of data on consumers' payment histories. Some major creditors are connected to the bureaus and can report to them online. Many others submit a monthly magnetic tape. An important issue is whether the creditor reports to the bureau using the more modern "Metro 2" format. This format permits the creditor to fill in data fields corresponding to the identifying "Credit Header" and the "Account Column Title Description" we listed in Chapter 5 (e.g., balance, credit limit, account number, type, and status). But many creditors still use the old, less precise Metro I format.[97]

---

[97] Trans Union announced that all customers must report using the Metro 2 format by December 31st 2003. According to the Web site of The Service Bureau, "all bureaus will require the Metro 2 format in the near future." http://www.servbur.com/index.html

The three CRAs each store this information in their own massive database. The CRA databases include data on virtually all American adult users of credit—an estimated 205 million people.[98]

A credit report is not fully assembled until the CRAs have a reason to assemble one. For instance, when a consumer applies for credit, the credit grantor or "subscriber" relays to the CRA identifying data from the consumer's credit application, at a minimum, name and address, often the SSN, and sometimes date of birth. (It's worth noting that the CRA can return a credit report to the credit grantor without an SSN.)

This is when the key moment occurs. Applying this identifying or "indicative" data, the CRA's algorithm then decides which information in the database relates to or "matches" that consumer, and then "returns" to the credit grantor (subscriber) a consumer credit report consisting of this information. Thus, it is the algorithm, or "business rule," that decides which data go into your credit report.

The Search Logic/Algorithm

In the Matthew Kirkpatrick trial cited in the previous chapter, Equifax Vice President Phyllis Dorman said that when "building a file" after receiving data from a creditor, or when deciding what data to include on a credit report that will be disclosed to the creditor, the first factor considered by the Equifax system is geographic region.

Then its "matching algorithm," known as L90, relies on 13 matching elements. Two of the elements that constitute a distinct category are: (1) exact Social Security number (SSN) and (2) partial SSN (meaning that most, but not all digits are the same).[99]

---

[98] www.experian.com/small_business/knowledge.html, visited 9/14/07.
[99] Testimony of Phyllis Dorman, Matthew Kirkpatrick v. Equifax Credit Information Services, U.S. Dist. Ct., Oregon, CV-02-1197-MO; 1/20/05

The remaining elements are (3) last name, (4) first name, (5) middle name, (6) suffix, (7) age, (8) gender, (9) street number, (10) street name, [100] (11) apartment number, (12) City, state and zip, and (13) trade account number.

There is a very important difference in how the system works when you ask to see a copy of your own credit report as opposed to how it works when a subscriber asks the CRA for your credit report. One reason for this is that the CRAs have a duty to ensure that they do not give your credit report to anyone who does not have a permissible purpose to see it—particularly someone who is trying to impersonate you or otherwise do you harm. Accordingly, when you ask for your own report, you are required to give extensive identifying information to authenticate yourself—to prove that you are really you. This also enables the CRA's algorithm to more concisely assign the proper accounts to your credit report.

However, it can be a very different story when a credit grantor or other subscriber asks for your credit report. For starters, the setting is different. To have instant access to credit reports, subscribers must sign contracts pledging to only use credit reports for permissible purposes, to abide by other restrictions, and comply with the FCRA. CRAs look at their subscribers as members of a trusted circle who know and play by the rules.

More importantly, the priorities are different. Since the subscriber is buying the credit report in order to decide whether or not to grant you credit, the CRA wants to ensure that it does not leave out anything that *could* be relevant to that decision. After all, if the CRA failed to include evidence of late payments in your credit report, and you default, the credit grantor is going to blame the CRA. Another factor is the credit grantor might only have limited information about the consumer, like name and address, and no SSN, or its

---

[100] Some algorithms may only use the first 4-to-6 characters of the number-address field, which would mean that "123 Main Street" would match "123 Mainwright Street."

employee might have written down the SSN incorrectly. Therefore, the CRA seeks to maximize disclosure of any *possible* information that might relate to the consumer about whom a subscriber inquires. This becomes trickier when the CRA conducts the search based upon very limited, or even imperfect, identification information.

To accomplish this, the CRAs' algorithms are designed to accommodate such errors as transposed digits within SSNs, misspellings, nick names, and changed last names (women who marry), and different addresses (people who move), by accepting "partial matches" of SSNs and first names, and in some circumstances, assigning less importance to last names.

Thus, while you must provide an exact match of your SSN to obtain your own credit report, a subscriber can still obtain your credit report even if there is a match of only seven of the nine digits in your SSN. What's more: if the SSN on the credit application exactly matches yours, the CRAs' algorithms often will tolerate major discrepancies in last name, street address, city, and state.

Accordingly, it's quite possible that the "subscriber" credit report sent to the company holding your credit application will have more data than the credit report you obtained directly from the credit bureau. There have been occasions when a subscriber will reject an application for credit based on information in a credit report, but when the consumer gets her own report, the information isn't there. It was only in the subscriber report.

In their defense, credit bureaus argue their systems, more often than not, properly mix data into one consumer's report, thereby increasing accuracy. For example, sometimes Joseph A. Smith applies for credit in his full name, but sometimes he leaves out his middle initial. Other times he only uses "Joe." Then he moves to another state. These cases are common, and the current approach maximizes the likelihood that the full credit history will be passed on to credit grantors.

Multiple Files

Another result of this approach is "multiple files," meaning that the request for one consumer's credit report results in the return to the credit grantor of more than one report. These multiple files, also referred to as fragmented, or "frag" files, often pertain to more than one person; each multiple file receives its own credit score. The credit grantor can specify whether he wants the credit bureau to return "multiple files," or just the "best," or most likely, single file. Remember, in their December 2002 study, the Consumer Federation of America and National Credit Reporting Association found that in 10% of the cases, instead of there being three credit reports for each individual (one each for Equifax, Experian and Trans Union), a fourth, or fifth, or even sixth credit report would be returned, most of which had separate credit scores. In litigation, Equifax admitted it sent creditors multiple files about 4% of the time.

These were not duplicates. In some cases, the "extra" reports clearly included the credit activity of an entirely separate person, as none of the accounts matched with those on the three primary reports. But it was very common for the additional report to contain a mixture of credit data, some belonging to the applicant, some not. In still other cases, applicants had split files that appeared to be the result of applying for credit under variations of their name.

Partial Matches

In addition to multiple files, the acceptance of "partial matches" by CRA algorithms is known to cause "mixed files"—the mixing of one consumer's credit history into the credit report of another—as well as other inaccuracies. Such problems became the leading cause of consumer complaints to the FTC in the early 1990s, prompting formal investigations, consent agreements with all three CRAs, and Congressional reform in 1996 and 2003 (see Chapter 10).

Some individual examples help highlight how a consumer's credit report can become mixed with that of a total stranger. Myra Coleman was a longtime resident of Itta Bene, Mississippi. But unbeknownst to her, a woman in Madera, California, named Maria Gaytan, applied for credit, apparently using Ms. Coleman's SSN. Because the use of Ms. Coleman's SSN created an "exact match," TransUnion's algorithm proceeded to disregard virtually all other identifying data. It "concluded" that Ms. Gaytan was in fact Ms. Coleman and allowed Ms. Coleman's credit report to be disclosed in response to the application, thereby enabling Ms. Gaytan to obtain credit. Ms. Gaytan's unpaid bills were then included in Ms. Coleman's credit report.

In pre-trial discovery, Ms. Coleman's attorney, Sylvia Antalis Goldsmith, was able to uncover how the TransUnion algorithm worked in this instance. TransUnion's (TU) officials testified that because of the exact match of the SSN, the algorithm only needed to find enough common letters in the *first name* to conclude that the two people were the same. Thus, "Myra" and "Maria" both have the letters "M," "R" and "A." TU believed its algorithm needed to accommodate what it considered a common occurrence: women marry and change their last name, and change residences.[101]

Another example was Jason Turner, a 19-year-old resident of Birmingham, Alabama. He was disappointed when he was rejected by Capital One after applying for his first credit card. When he obtained his Equifax report, Turner, who was born in 1982, was surprised to see that there were several accounts paid late, including one that dated back to when he was 14-years-old. Turns out that Equifax had merged him with another Jason Turner, born several years earlier, who at one point lived in Florida. A key factor was

---

[101] Coleman v. Trans Union (U.S. Dist. Ct. Mississippi). Ms. Coleman won a small jury award. Goldsmith was with the firm of Murray and Murray in Sandusky, Ohio until March 2005.

that there were only two digits different in their SSNs. Thus, it appeared that the seven-out-of-nine digit SSN match, coupled with the identical name and possibly a regional commonality, was sufficient for the Equifax algorithm to disregard date-of-birth and location of residence. Because young Jason Turner was a "newcomer" to Equifax and "didn't have a file," its system kept assuming that the two Jason Turners were one and the same, and repeatedly dumped the older Turner's negative history onto the younger Jason's credit report.[102]

A Never-Ending Mix

Judy Thomas was a realtor in Klamath Falls, Oregon, who, upon discovering errors in her credit report in 1996, sent a dispute letter to TransUnion. TransUnion said it would correct the mistakes. But after applying for a mortgage in 1999, Thomas learned that the 1996 errors, plus new ones, were back on her credit report, delaying approval of her mortgage. Through litigation, Thomas learned that her credit report was polluted with negative information from the credit history of Judith Upton, of Stevenson, Washington, whose SSN was only different by one digit. It appeared the similarity in the SSNs and the first names, (and possibly regions), were enough for the TU algorithm to override all other discrepancies.[103]

These are only four of the thousands upon thousands of mixed file cases that have occurred since the early 1990s. They illustrate how the use of algorithms that tolerate "partial matches" contributes to the regular mis-merging of data.

---

[102] Jason Turner was represented by Christopher Kittell, of Webster Gresham & Kittell, Clarksdale, Miss., and Penny Hays, Birmingham, Ala. The case settled for a confidential sum.

[103] In 2002, a federal jury in Oregon awarded Thomas $5 million in punitive damages and $350,000 in compensatory damages. The punitive award was reduced to $1 million. Trans Union paid. Thomas was represented by Portland attorneys Robert Sola and Michael Baxter.

In all of these cases, the victims only learned about the errors after they had been rejected for credit.

How The Algorithm Helps Identity Thieves

In important ways, the CRAs algorithms have helped identity thieves. In "true-name fraud," the key moment occurs when the CRA discloses the innocent victim's credit report to a subscriber holding the identity thief's application for credit. This disclosure enables the fraudster to obtain credit in the name of the innocent victim.

Identity thieves often enter mistaken data when they fraudulently apply for credit. But if they have obtained the victim's SSN, it will help override other discrepancies in the application and convince the CRA algorithm to disclose the victim's credit report. Even if there are mistakes in the SSN, the "partial match" tolerance within the algorithm still gives the fraudster a chance of triggering release of the credit report.

The State of California, a pioneer in identity theft prevention, tried to combat this problem by passing a law that required credit grantors to match at least three identifiers before being allowed to receive the credit report. In 2003, a few years after the law was enacted, at least one CRA complained that the new law was interfering with the granting of instant credit in about 12 percent of the cases. But the CRA had no data indicating what percentage of these might have been identity theft. Some privacy experts felt the law might be accomplishing something positive: even if the applicant was not an identity thief, the incident alerted consumers to possible discrepancies in their credit reports deserving attention.

Reinsertion

Another troubling aspect about these cases is the likelihood that errors will reappear, or be *reinserted* into the credit report, after they are deleted. This often is caused by flaws in the system. In fact, the consent agreements with the FTC and State Attorneys General, as well as the 1996 Amendments to the FCRA, required that CRAs take specific steps to either prevent reinsertion or to notify consumers that it had occurred and justify it.

The CRAs first defense against reinsertion is a process known as "cloaking" or "suppression." If credit grantors are not careful to delete all inaccurate information from their systems, that information could be re-reported to the CRAs in the course of the routine monthly updates.

Anticipating this problem, the CRAs created cloaking so it could flag previously-deleted trade lines and then, if they were re-reported by the credit grantors, they would be "cloaked" so as not to reappear on the consumer's credit report. In other words, under the current system, it appears that a CRA cannot afford to actually delete inaccurate data from its database because it will lose its ability to flag that data when credit grantors mistakenly re-report them.

But the cloaking system is far from perfect. Many of the major credit grantors have more than one "subscriber number" they use to identify themselves to CRA computers. There have been cases in which the cloaking procedure was only pegged to one subscriber number. So if the credit grantor reported the data under a different subscriber number, then the cloaking procedure would not be triggered. Moreover, if there are discrepancies or a change in the subscriber's name, that too will bypass the cloaking procedure.

A second way that information reappears relates to debt collections. Even when some accounts are the result of a mixed file and are deleted, they still sometimes are sent or sold to collection agencies. Once the collection agency acquires an account, it begins reporting it to the CRAs, usually with a different account number, enabling it to bypass the cloaking system.[104]

---

[104] There is some question whether "cloaking" frustrates legitimate re-scoring. Ruth Koontz, of Lenders' Credit Services, Inc., said there have

Archived 'Monthly Snapshots'

If previously deleted information were wrongly reinserted into a credit report or there were other inaccuracies dating back months or even years, one of the challenges facing consumers is finding out when the reinsertion occurred. More generally, consumers on their own have no practical way of knowing what their credit reports looked like in the past. If they were denied credit based upon a "subscriber" version of their report, they cannot be sure what information that version contained unless the credit grantor hands over its copy.[105]

The fact is that Equifax and Trans Union maintain historical archives that allow them to go back and see what your credit report looked like in times past. However, for the most part they have only produced records from these archives after being sued by consumers for alleged FCRA violations. Attorneys representing those consumers were able to obtain them as part of discovery, which requires companies to disclose internal records that are relevant to a lawsuit. However, in some cases, the CRAs have fiercely resisted having to disclose these records or have tried to charge excessively for producing them.

In essence, these archival records are "monthly snapshots" of the information in the database going back as many as 10 years. At Equifax, they are called "Frozen Data Scans;" and at TransUnion, "Name Scans." Experian's system does not keep monthly snapshots in the same way, but instead maintains history of accounts in each consumer's file in the form of a ""Long Administrative Report."

---

been times when the only delinquent account on a credit report was removed during a re-scoring, yet the score did not improve. This raised the question as to whether "cloaked accounts" affect scoring and the CRAs don't realize it.

[105] For many years, CRA contracts prohibited credit grantors from showing their version of the credit report to the consumer about whom it pertained.

Navigating The Monthly Snapshot

The monthly snapshots are difficult to decipher for the untrained eye. They contain dozens upon dozens of lines of raw data and show how the CRA organizes information into "data fields." According to deposition testimony in Carol Fleischer's case, one TransUnion "Name Scan" showed how data on her and Ms. Cassidy were mixed within the TU database. At the top of Trans Union's Name Scan for April 2000 was Carol Cassidy's name and correct address, and then showed Ms. Fleischer's address as Ms. Cassidy's previous address. It also showed that Ms. Fleischer's SSN was listed as Ms. Cassidy's SSN (only the last digit of the nine SSN digits was different). It then showed many of the derogatory trade lines stemming from Ms. Cassidy's activities. It showed TU had maintained data on Ms. Cassidy ("File Since Date") since November 1985.

Farther below in the TU Name Scan, it showed Ms. Fleischer's correct name, address, and SSN, but a "File Since" Date of January 2000. The testimony indicated that the "new" file on Ms. Fleischer was created by an inquiry from a creditor who was checking her TU report after Ms. Fleischer had applied for credit. In other words, whenever Ms. Fleischer applied for credit, it would create a "new file" on her (hence the new "File Since Date"). But then the system would proceed to merge all of Ms. Cassidy's and Ms. Fleischer's data together in subsequent months. Despite repeated disputes by Ms. Fleischer, TU's algorithm was unable to see them as different people whose data should be kept apart.

Valuable Snapshots

The monthly scans proved valuable in a class action lawsuit against all three CRAs on behalf of millions of consumers whose credit reports listed an account as "Included in Bankruptcy," even though the consumer never filed for bankruptcy. (The consumer was often the co-signer on an account whose spouse or ex-spouse had filed for bankruptcy.) In that case, the scans enabled the CRAs to identify the number of class members and paved the way for a settlement.[106]

As Thomas C. Harney, a Kilpatrick & Stockton (K&S) attorney representing Equifax, testified in a September 2003 Fairness Hearing, ". . . The only way we could get this information was to go back to these monthly archives or snapshots, also called cuts, that we've talked about before and take this snapshot in time."[107]

As mentioned before, the CRAs sometimes resist disclosing monthly scans, even when they were supposed to be handed over in discovery. In January 2004, U.S. District Judge T. John Ward scolded Lewis Perling, then a K&S attorney representing Equifax, for not producing frozen scans by the court's deadline, and for not producing witnesses and other documents.

Noting that Equifax should have coughed up the evidence months earlier, Judge Ward ordered Perling to produce within 10 days all evidence subpoenaed by plaintiffs, including "those stored by electronic means, . . . all of these screens, frozen screens."[108]

Judge Ward threatened to create special procedures for Kirkpatrick & Stockton's out-of-town attorneys to appear in his court if there was not immediate compliance. Turning to Perling, he added, "Since I have ordered you specifically, and if you fail to comply, I will still have jurisdiction over your person, and I will order you back over here for a contempt hearing, and when I do those kinds of things, I can

---

[106] Franklin E. Clark, et al. v. Experian, et al.: U.S. Dist. Ct. – South Carolina – C.A. No. 8:00-1217-24.

[107] Id., "Fairness Hearing," September 23-24, 2003

[108] "Transcript of Hearing On Plaintiffs' Motion To Compel," January 13, 2004, Deborah Moore v. CSC Credit Services, Inc., et al.: U.S. Dist. Ct. – Eastern Dist. of Texas – Civ. Dock. No. 2:02-CV-303. Moore was represented by David Szwak of Shreveport, Louisiana. In 2007, Perling joined King & Spaulding after Equifax selected it as its new law firm.

assure you, you will need to bring your toothbrush. I do not tolerate your kind of behavior sir."[109]

The 'Do-Not-Confuse' Statement

The FCRA gives all consumers the right to place a statement on their credit report to further explain its contents or to prevent some harm. Carol Fleischer, of Ann Arbor, Mich., thought she was being wrongly confused with another woman, so she placed a "Do Not Confuse Me With Anyone Else" statement in her credit report, which was duly recorded in the Trans Union Name Scan. Some people might think that placing such a statement would alert TU not to mix her file with someone else.

In litigation, however, Ms. Fleischer learned that was not the case. TU's Regina Sorenson testified that the purpose of the "Do Not Confuse" statement was not to prevent further mixing; instead she said, "It's to alert potential creditors that there may be more than one consumer with similar identification in the system."

TU's Lynn Romanowski also testified that Ms. Fleischer's "Do Not Confuse" statement needed to be on both her file and on Ms. Cassidy's file to prevent improper mixing.

> **Romanowski**: A consumer statement present on both files would prevent those two files from being permitted to combine.
> **Szwak**: So if a "do not confuse statement" only appears on one file but not the other, it would still permit the combination of those files?
> **Romanowski**: At this point in time, yes, according to this scan, yes.[110]

---

[109] *Id.*

[110] Deposition of Lynn Romanowski, <u>Fleischer v. Trans Union, et al.</u>: U.S. Dist. Ct. – Eastern Dist. of Michigan – Case No. CV 02-71301

It's safe to say that nobody outside of Trans Union had any idea that to prevent the mixing of files you needed to place the "Do Not Confuse" Statements in your file <u>and</u> the file of a total stranger.

Organizational Structure

Like all major corporations, the CRAs are organized into various departments and divisions. TransUnion's (TU) organizational infrastructure helps illustrate its approach and operations. TU's main credit reporting database is called CHRONUS. Within TU, there are at least three major departments or divisions that interact with CHRONUS. One department, headed by William Stockdale, is responsible for the manner in which CHRONUS receives consumer data from furnishers and integrates those data. Another department is responsible for the "rules" or algorithms by which CHRONUS assembles and returns credit reports in response to subscriber inquiries. A third department, consumer relations, responds to consumer request for copies of their credit reports (disclosure), handles consumer disputes, and conducts reinvestigations.[111]

As we will see in the next chapter on "reinvestigations," when a consumer discovers inaccuracies in her credit report, the responses of all three departments likely will determine whether the inaccuracies are corrected and/or deleted, and whether they will reoccur (re-mixing and/or reinsertion).

There have been instances when each of these three departments were not sufficiently familiar with each other's practices and procedures to ensure that corrections were not undone.

For instance, let's say TU's consumer affairs department corrects a consumer's mixed file, removing all of the data generated by the "other" person. However, if the

---

[111] From depositions in <u>Fleischer</u> and <u>Thomas</u>, op. cit.

consumer affairs department does not know that the "partial match" algorithms created by the other department will continue to cause mixed files in the future, then they are not prepared to do all that is necessary to ensure that a consumer's credit report remains accurate.

Bad Mix, Good Decision

Victoria Apodaca, a Moriarty, New Mexico school teacher, had excellent credit. She planned to use it to help her son buy his first house. But she discovered her Equifax report contained a recent bankruptcy that truly belonged to Vickie Apodaca of Las Cruces, N.M. Their SSNs were nearly identical – only one digit was different. Victoria Apodaca repeatedly disputed the error, often trudging down the long hall to the school office in order to refax supporting material to Equifax. She even drove 60 miles to the bankruptcy court in Los Cruces for a copy of the other Apodaca's certified bankruptcy papers, and provided them to Equifax as well – all to no avail. She finally filed an FCRA lawsuit.[112]

In rejecting Equifax's motion to throw out punitive damages, Judge M. Christina Armijo said a jury could reasonably conclude that Equifax needed to adjust its partial matching practices once it knew that partial matching was causing inaccuracies.

"The real question in this case is not whether to operate a system that defaults to an over-inclusive procedure instead of an under-inclusive procedure, but what additional steps, if any, are required to override or correct the standard procedures to which a credit-reporting agency defaults when those procedures are not functioning properly," she wrote.

---

[112] Apodaca was represented by Richard Feferman and Rob Treinen, of Feferman & Warren, Albuquerque, N.M.

"In other words, I do not understand Plaintiff to be claiming punitive damages merely because Equifax's credit-reporting system initially defaulted to an over-inclusive procedure that mistakenly included information belonging to another consumer on her credit report and relied on the furnisher of that information to determine its accuracy or applicability. Rather, I understand Plaintiff to be making the argument that punitive damages are warranted because Equifax consciously and recklessly decided not to make available any additional steps which would have overridden or supplemented the standard procedures to which it initially defaulted in Plaintiff's case, even though the company knew that those procedures were so over-inclusive they would result in violations of consumer rights without such additional steps," she wrote.[113]

Not long after Judge Armijo's opinion, Equifax settled Victoria Apodaca's lawsuit for a confidential sum.

---

113 <u>Apodaca v. Discover Financial Services, et al.</u>, 417 F.Supp.2d 1220 (D.N.M. 2006)

Chapter 9

Reinvestigations (or not)

> *Investigate – v. To observe or study by close examination and systematic inquiry. Systematic—adj. Marked by thoroughness and regularity.*
>
> -- Webster's New Collegiate Dictionary

For the past several years, a tension has been building over the adequacy of reinvestigations being performed both by consumer reporting agencies (CRAs) and credit grantors in response to consumer disputes.

During the 2003 Congressional debate over the FCRA Amendments, privacy experts and consumer advocates repeatedly criticized both CRAs and credit grantors for failing to live up to their duties to reinvestigate. Rather than truly investigate, critics charged, CRAs and credit grantors, upon receiving a dispute, prefer only to *compare* the disputed information to what they previously reported. If the disputed information essentially matched what the credit grantor found in its files, then it would "verify" it.

This process has caused many a maddening moment for consumers who dispute what they know to be inaccurate information, but are told by the CRA the information has been "verified." It also has drawn the attention of the law's overseers, the FTC and State Attorneys General (AGs), and its creator, Congress. Between 1991-92, either the FTC or State AGs reached agreements with each of the three major CRAs that included requirements to improve reinvestigations. In 1996, Congress likewise amended the FCRA to put a greater duty on CRAs and on credit grantors to conduct reasonable reinvestigations, and to strengthen consumers' rights if they failed to do so. (See Chapter 10)

Despite these new requirements, the 2003 Congressional hearings confirmed that the CRAs and credit grantors continued to run an automated system of data-comparison which did not comport with the normal definition of "reinvestigate." Many critics argued that CRAs and credit grantors were not complying with the law. A few courts have agreed in individual cases.

In the 2003 Amendments (FACT Act) to the FCRA, Congress again sought to bolster consumers' rights to accuracy. It gave consumers the right to dispute errors directly to the credit grantor when they were the source of the error. (However, consumers should still file disputes with the CRAs to maximize legal options). Congress also enhanced the accuracy standards for credit grantors, requiring that they not report inaccurate data that they *"know or reasonably should know"* as opposed to the old, weaker standard, of "knows or *consciously avoids* knowing." Congress directed the federal banking regulatory agencies to publish rules and guidance to improve furnisher accuracy by December 1, 2004. (They missed the deadline.) The FTC must conduct its own multi-year study on accuracy.

It will take some time to determine what impact these changes will have, and whether they will prompt CRAs and credit grantors to conduct true reinvestigations upon receiving disputes.

To understand how far they have to go, it is necessary to examine the systems that have been in place in the years leading up to the 2003 Amendments. Let's begin by looking at the situation from what might be the perspectives of CRAs.

Rising Volume

For starters, the volume of disputes has risen dramatically. Various depositions of CRA representatives have produced estimates that CRAs can receive 5,000 to 25,000 consumer disputes per day, with 7,000-10,000 being the more typical range. The CRAs staff their dispute departments at levels where dispute handlers are expected to handle between 10-12 consumer disputes per hour. Because each consumer dispute averages three disputed items, this means that the CRA employee only has a few minutes to handle each disputed item. (Do the math: 12 consumer disputes with three items on each dispute, or 12 x 3 = 36 disputed items; divide the 36 disputed items by 60 minutes = 1.66 minutes to handle each dispute item.)

This volume naturally poses tremendous challenges for CRAs and credit grantors. An important factor is that CRAs can lower their costs to the extent they can reduce the amount they pay employees. Thus, they strive to automate and minimize the need for human involvement. Possibly the greatest risk to handling disputes too cheaply, and not adequately, is that the CRA or credit grantor could get hit with a large fine or jury award for non-compliance with the FCRA. But since such fines or jury awards have been few and far between, the risk, from the CRAs' and credit grantors' viewpoints, probably does not seem that great.

Credit Repair Volume

Another factor is that a significant percentage of disputes come from credit repair agencies, some of which attempt to get accurate-but-negative information removed from consumers' credit reports by flooding the system with disputes. There have been no independent studies that provide reliable numbers about credit repair volume. In his 2003 testimony before Congress, TransUnion CEO Harry Gambill estimated that 35 percent of disputes came from credit repair agencies. A second industry source placed it closer to 25 percent. Even if that range is accurate, it means that about 65-75 percent of disputes are from individual consumers and are presumably legitimate. It is difficult to believe that CRAs and credit grantors can adequately investigate thousands of legitimate disputes a day using the current system.

To handle the volume, the CRAs created "E-OSCAR," an automated system for exchanging messages when consumers dispute inaccuracies. Remarkably, the CRAs found a way to profit from disputes as well. For example, Equifax pays its outsource vendor in the Philippines between $.41 and $.57 to process each consumer dispute letter. But Equifax charges creditors at least $.25 for each account dispute (ACDV) processed through E-OSCAR. Thus, for a letter disputing five accounts, Equifax would charge creditors at least $1.25, but would only have to pay its vendor about $.57.   Accordingly, in 2005 E-OSCAR was transferred from its creator, the Consumer Data Industry Assoc. (CDIA), a non-profit industry lobbying group, to a new for-profit company, Online Data Exchange, L.L.C.[114]

The CRAs naturally have reduced costs by outsourcing dispute handling to call centers in low-wage countries like the Philippines, India, Jamaica and Costa Rica.[115]

Exchanging Codes

As we saw in Chapter 5, "How To Dispute Errors," the dispute form urges consumers to categorize their dispute, e.g., "Not Mine," or "Paid In Full."   The CRAs typically have a two-digit code for each category. [116]

---

[114] Prepared statement of Leonard Bennett, "Fair Credit Reporting Act: How it Functions for Consumers and the Economy," before the House Committee on Financial Services, June 19, 2007; www.house.gov/apps/list/hearing/financialsvcs_dem/ht061907.shtml

[115] *Privacy Times*, Sept. 12, 2003 Volume 23 No. 17; also see Lazarus, David, "Credit Agencies Sending Our Files Abroad," *San Francisco Chronicle*, Nov. 7, 2003.

[116] Or, a two-symbol, alpha-numeric code, i.e., "A4" means "not mine"

When a consumer writes to the CRA to dispute inaccurate information in his or her credit report, the CRA typically reduces the consumer's dispute to the corresponding two-digit code and transmits it to the creditor in the form of an Automated Consumer Dispute Verification (ACDV). The creditor typically only checks to see if the data it has on file is roughly the same as that which it furnished previously, or if two of the consumer's identifiers in its file match those on the ACDV. If they do, then the creditor "verifies" the disputed data.

It's conceivable that this system might be an appropriate and effective response to the tactics of credit repair agencies. Some credit repair specialists advertise that they can "remove" negative information from consumers' credit reports (even if that negative information is accurate). They typically try to flood the system with disputes in the hope that CRAs and credit grantors won't meet the 30-day deadline reinvestigation deadline, thereby forcing them to delete negative data that they didn't have time to verify.

But again, it is difficult to believe that CRAs and credit grantors can adequately investigate thousands of legitimate disputes a day using the current system. According to the CRAs' trade group CDIA, 46% of disputes were verified as reported; 27% were modified or updated per furnisher's instructions; 10.5% had data deleted per furnisher's instructions; 16% had data deleted due to legal time limits.[117]

Not True, But 'Verified'

This process is particularly frustrating for consumers who are victims of mixed files and/or identity theft. For instance, Judy Thomas, a Klamath Falls, Oregon realtor in 1996 first disputed information in her credit report that actually related to the credit problems of Judith Upton, of

---

[117] Statement of Richard J. Hillman Director, Financial Markets, General Accounting Office, Before the Senate Committee on Banking, Housing, and Urban Affairs, July 31, 2003 www.gao.gov/new.items/d031036t.pdf

Stevenson, Washington. TransUnion said it would be removed. But in 1999, Ms. Thomas discovered the information had been reinserted, so she disputed it again. This time, the furnishers "verified" because the information disputed by Thomas was precisely the same information *about Ms. Upton* that the credit grantors had furnished before. In other words, their automated comparison about "then-and-now" showed no discrepancy, so neither the credit grantor nor TransUnion saw any reason to change it.

Carol Fleischer was a Michigan resident who sued after TransUnion failed to unmix her file, which included a negative Capital One account that was not hers.

Regina Sorenson, a TransUnion consumer affairs manager, testified that this two-dimensional exchange of messages between itself and Capital One was the extent of TU's "investigation." Here's how she described it when questioned by Fleischer's co-counsel, David Szwak:

> **Szwak** - Now you sent [Capital One] a CDV (consumer dispute verification) and the response came back verified as to the name and the Social Security number; is that true?
>
> **Sorenson** - Verified means the account information was accurately reported and they also verified name and Social Security number.
>
> **Szwak** - And as a result, you all completed your investigation by updating it to show it had been verified by Capital One and leaving Capital One on Ms. Fleischer's credit report; is that true?
>
> **Sorenson** - Yes, it is.
>
> **Szwak** - Other than sending the CDV to the six furnishers, what else did Trans Union do to investigate Ms. Fleischer's complaints?
>
> **Sorenson - Nothing else.**[118]

---

[118] Deposition of Regina Sorenson, in <u>Carol Fleischer v. TransUnion, et al.</u> U.S. District Court for the Eastern District of Michigan (Southern Div); Case No. CV 02-71301.

As an 18-year-old, Jason Turner, of Alabama, did not think Equifax had a file on him. But when he applied for his first Capital One card, Equifax returned a credit report showing he had several delinquent accounts, one of which went bad supposedly when Jason was 14 years old. Naturally, he was rejected for the credit card. He was also rejected for an auto loan.

Young Jason eventually learned that every time he applied for credit, Equifax would create a report that included the bad history of a much older Jason Turner. This happened because the names were identical, and because 7-out-of-the-9 digits of their SSNs were identical. (The older Jason never lived in Alabama.) The Equifax algorithm assumed the two Jasons were the same person, and disregarded major discrepancies in ages, as well as dates of birth and addresses.

Both Jason and his mother tried to convince Equifax that the derogatory accounts did not belong to young Jason. But they ran into a wall. First, the Equifax dispute handlers apparently did not know that the partial match of the two Jason Turners' SSNs kept causing the older Jason's bad payment history to be dumped onto young Jason's report when he applied for credit.

In response to the dispute, Equifax's Celestina Spencer queried the system using young Jason's SSN. But this query used a "search logic" requiring an exact match of all nine digits of the SSN. Ironically, Spencer was unable to find any accounts that belonged to young Jason: by using the stricter, 9-for-9 digit SSN match, Spencer ensured that the older Jason Turner's derogatory information was not mixed into Young Jason's credit report. Thus, Spencer told Jason's mother that Jason "did not have a file." [119]

---

[119] Deposition of Celestina Spencer, <u>Jason Turner v. Equifax Credit Information Services, Inc.</u>: U.S. District Court for the Northern District of Alabama (Southern Div); Case No. CV 02-J-0787-S.

Mrs. Turner tried to explain that Equifax disclosed an inaccurate file to Capital One and to the auto dealer, and that it needed to be corrected. But as Ms. Spencer later said in a deposition, "Nothing was being done because there was nothing to do . . .. I wanted her [Mrs. Turner] to understand that it was not his credit file for me to do anything to."

In other words, Equifax was telling Capital One that Jason was a deadbeat, but telling his mother that it "did not have a file" on him. When confronted with this discrepancy, Ms. Spencer, the Equifax dispute handler, said:

> There should not have been a file, but there could have been because his addresses are here [and] because they would have keyed in his name and his addresses. Our system -- I don't know how to answer that question. He is there, but he is not there.

After months of trying, Jason's mother finally convinced Ms. Spencer to conduct a reinvestigation. So what did she do? Ms. Spencer sent a standard "CDV," or Consumer Dispute Verification, to Capital One. But the CDV listed the older Jason Turner's SSN, date-of-birth, and derogatory trade lines, with the younger Jason's address. Capital One then "verified" the information.

An exchange between Christopher Kittell, a Mississippi attorney who represented young Jason Turner, and Alicia Fluellen, senior manager for Equifax's Office of Consumer Affairs, confirmed that the CDV exchange *was* the Equifax investigation

> **Kittell**: Are there are other methods of investigation despite the CDV or other than the CDV?
> **Fluellen**: No, we send out a CDV.
> **Kittell**: That's it. If it comes back one way, good for the consumer, if it comes back agreeing with the

creditor, then not agreeing with the consumer, then it stays?

Fluellen: Correct.

Kittell: Basically, Equifax takes the word of the creditor, whatever the creditor says is what Equifax does?

Fluellen: Yeah.[120]

Of course, many felt this was a huge breakdown in how the system was supposed to work. In the 1996 Amendments, Congress increased duties on CRAs to ensure they would investigate disputes. The amendments required that CRAs forward disputes to creditors within five days, and then complete the reinvestigation within 30 days. If not completed by the 30-day deadline, the law required that the disputed data be deleted. In an effort to add depth to reinvestigations, the Amendments required CRAs to "provide all relevant information" concerning a consumer's dispute to the furnishers. That meant that if a consumer attached payment statements or letters to his dispute, the CRA was supposed to send them to, or otherwise advise the creditor. Moreover, for the first time, the Amendments placed a duty on creditors to reinvestigate, but generally imposed liability for failing to do so after they received consumer disputes from the CRA.

Despite these changes in the law, there was abundant evidence that the old ways continued right up to the point that this book went to press.[121] Many believed this two-dimensional message exchange does not amount to a true reinvestigation. (*Webster's New Collegiate Dictionary* defines "investigate" as "to observe or study by close examination and systematic inquiry." One of the definitions of "systematic" is "marked by thoroughness and regularity.")

---

[120] Deposition of Alicia Fluellen, <u>Jason Turner v. Equifax Credit Info. Serv., Inc.</u>: U.S. Dist. Ct., Northern Dist. of Alabama; Case No. CV 02-J-0787-S. Equifax designated Fluellen as its "30(b)(6)" witness, meaning she was representing the company and describing its policies.

[121] September 2007

Credit Grantors

As noted earlier, major credit card companies have seen their dispute volume rise in recent years. They too generally try to cope with the volume by using an automated message exchange.

Pamela Tuskey, a manager in Capital One's credit report dispute department, confirmed in a deposition with Ian Lyngklip, a Michigan attorney, that in October 2001, Capital One received about 1,000 disputes per day. By May 2002, it had grown to 2,000 disputes per day. By the spring of 2003, the official said the number of disputes had grown to 4,000 per day. Some of the increased volume was attributed to the boom in home buying and mortgage refinancing, when more and more consumers discovered the importance of their credit scores, she said.[122]

Tuskey said her department's job was to "verify" disputed information that Capital One had reported to the CRAs. That meant her personnel would simply check the disputed information against the information in its system. If the two matched up, it was "verified."[123]

She said her department did not have ready access to original credit card applications or other primary documents that might come in handy for affirming that the consumer's dispute was well-founded. The pulling of paper files was considered "in-depth research," and was not handled by her department. Instead, "research" was conducted by a smaller committee in charge of "escalated" disputes. One example of an "escalated" dispute was an irate customer, or attorney, who directly wrote or called Capital One, she said. [124]

When Lyngklip asked Tuskey why her department did not do "in-depth research," she replied that sometime

---

[122] Deposition of Pamela Tuskey, in <u>Carol Fleischer v. Trans Union, et al.</u> U.S. District Court for the Eastern District of Michigan (Southern Div); Case No. CV 02-71301.

[123] *Id.*

[124] *Id.*

around February of 2000, representatives from Trans Union, Experian and Equifax each paid separate visits "to explain to my team how to more properly and more accurately work accounts."[125]

"One of the questions that I had for them, as a manager," Tuskey continued, "was should we verify the accounts – and I even explained to them what my definition of verify is – which is, we pull up our system of record, in this case Unisys or Beast, we look at what the bureau has sent us on the ACDV. If there are any discrepancies, we make sure that what the bureau has mirrors exactly what we, as Capital One, have. That's verifying," Tuskey said.[126]

> **Lyngklip**: That was what you described to the representatives as verifying?
> **Tuskey**: Yes.
> **Lyngklip**: And what did they say in response to that?
> **Tuskey**:   Well, I actually followed that up with, 'Do you want us to do that, or do you want us to do things such as pull statements, etc., actually do the research which would involve CHIA?[127] And in each case, the bureau rep said, 'No, we want you to verify it. We want you to make our system look like your system.' So that's what we've been doing.

However, in a mixed file or identity theft case, having the credit bureau's data "mirror" Capital One's data was not going to establish whether the information was accurate in the first place.

One thing that was missing from this equation was concern for the truth. After all, shouldn't the purpose of an "investigation" be to get to the truth? In fact, both CRA officials and credit grantor personnel have testified that it's

---

[125] *Id.*

[126] *Id.*

[127] CHIA is the system where Capital One stores applications and other primary documents

not their job to arbitrate the truth. Look at this exchange between Lyngklip and Tuskey:

> **Lyngklip**: For purposes of how you administer the FCRA, does the underlying truth of the matter enter into the decision? In other words, if the information in Cap One's system is not, in fact, true, is Cap One going to verify the data as accurate as long as it matches?
>
> **Tuskey**: Not – if we – if we do not – I'm not quite sure if you're – are you – restate that question.
>
> **Lyngklip**: Sure, I can do that. Cap One, as a matter of how it administers to the FCRA . . . and looks at the accuracy requirements, does not equate accuracy with truthfulness, what it does is it measures accuracy in terms of whether or not the data matches between what's in the credit reporting system and what's in Cap One's computer; is that a fair statement? . . .
>
> **Tuskey**: So your, your – the way the question is posed to me makes it sound like I have to choose between whether I'm saying what my associates do is accurate or truthful but not both.
>
> **Lyngklip**: Well, no, what I'm asking is this: Is it possible, is it possible that Cap One will verify information that is not, in fact, truthful?
>
> **Tuskey**: There's a possibility of that. It certainly would not be done intentionally.[128]

Is That All There Is?

Lyngklip asked if Tuskey's department ever did anything but check its own computers. "What about picking up the phone and calling up the person who is disputing the credit report?" Lyngklip asked. "It would seem to me that

---

[128] Deposition of Tuskey, op. cit.

that would be a pretty good source of information to determine whether or not two individuals are the same person."

"No, my team does not have any direct contact with the cardholders," Tuskey replied. "Again, we're not a customer-contact center. That's not within the scope of our job."

Training also did not appear to be a priority.

> **Lyngklip**: How did you find out about the procedures and in terms of how they come to their decision, and how did you find out about the mechanics of the credit dispute process?
>
> **Tuskey**: I found out the way any new associate would find out. I had side-by-side training. At the time that we're looking into here, we had no formal policies or procedures, no written documentation. It was really all on-the-job training, so I became familiar by sitting with a veteran associate as well as a quality associate just like everybody else. . . .
>
> **Lyngklip**: This might sound like a silly question, and I don't mean to be flip at all, but who trained the first staff person? Do we know how those procedures were handed down and where they came from originally?
>
> **Tuskey**: No. My guess, since everything had not been documented at all, my guess is it was just like oral history; you tell me and I'll tell the next person and the next person, and a lot of judgment calls going on.
>
> **Lyngklip**: Now, that describes how the decision-making process is made in terms of whether or not a particular dispute will be resolved in favor of or against a consumer, what about the mechanics of navigating the screens? Is that something that's written down in training manuals or guides?
>
> **Tuskey**: Now it is.
>
> **Lyngklip**: Again, when was that implemented?
>
> **Tuskey**: Three weeks ago.

Tuskey's deposition was taken May 21, 2003, some six years after the FCRA Amendments of 1996 put a duty on Capital One and other creditors to report information accurately, and to investigate consumer disputes. A company source said that in light of the 2003 Amendments to the FCRA, Capital One was reviewing its credit reporting-related procedures.

MBNA

At MBNA, an "investigation" similarly consists of a *comparison* of the disputed data with information in its database, the Customer Information System (CIS). One of the first to delve into its practices was Leonard Bennett, a Newport News, Virginia attorney who represented Linda Johnson.

The lawsuit swirled around an MBNA MasterCard opened by plaintiff Linda Johnson's ex-husband, Edward Slater, in 1987 – four years before he married her. They had since divorced. Johnson said she was only an authorized user, which meant she was not responsible for paying the account. In December 2000, Slater filed for bankruptcy, and MBNA promptly removed his name from the account. That same month, MBNA contacted Johnson and informed her that she was responsible for the approximately $17,000 balance on the account. After obtaining copies of her credit report from Experian, Equifax, and Trans Union, Johnson disputed the MBNA account with each of them. Experian and Trans Union sent automated consumer dispute verifications (ACDVs) to MBNA specifically indicating Johnson's claim that she was not a co-obligor on the account.

MBNA agents responded by comparing the disputed data with the account information contained in MBNA's computerized Customer Information System (CIS). Since the two were identical, MBNA "verified" that the disputed information was correct. In other words, MBNA did nothing more than confirm that it indeed reported the original (inaccurate) data. The CRAs continued to report it on Johnson's credit report.

Tricia Furr, an MBNA credit reporting specialist, confirmed that MBNA's "Desktop Procedure" manual directs specialists to confirm a match of two out of three identifiers – name, address and/or SSN. Once a two-out-of-three match is established, MBNA can inform the CRA that the disputed information is "verified as reported." Ms. Furr said that MBNA's "reinvestigations" did not go beyond the information contained in its own CIS.[129]

> **Furr**: I looked at the balance that we have on CIS and the history of the account as compared to the trade line as opposed to what we had on our Customer Information screen. . .
>
> **Bennett**: In performing the investigation and re-investigation of consumer disputes, once it receives an ACDV[130] from a credit reporting agency, when are MBNA's credit reporting specialists supposed to look beyond the Customer Information System for investigation? . . . I am asking the practices and procedures now.
>
> **Furr**: The Customer Information System is the only thing that we have to use for verification. So, there is no where else to look.
>
> **Bennett**: Do you ever pull documents, like old statements, and check payments and credit card applications?
>
> **Furr**: No, sir.

---

[129] The depositions of MBNA personnel were taken in the case, <u>Linda Johnson v. MBNA America Bank, N.A.</u>, Slip Op. No. 3:02 cv 523, U.S. District Court For The Eastern District of Virginia (Richmond Division).
[130] The dispute form is known as an "ACDV," or Automated Consumer Dispute Verification

Reading from MBNA's internal records, MBNA Vice President Edward Hughes quoted an MBNA employee's communication to a customer's attorney: "It would be up to (c)ard holder to prove MBNA was reporting wrong, not MBNA proving right."

Here Comes The Judge

In this case, Hughes' statement proved to be wrong. Linda Johnson was one of the few consumers who sued and actually had the chance to tell her story to a jury. MBNA argued that its verification methods complied with the FCRA. The jury disagreed, and awarded Johnson $90,300.

Judge Richard Williams affirmed the jury verdict. "According to [MBNA], the duty to investigate means that any investigation is sufficient, no matter how cursory. Such a construction is illogical. There would be no point in having the statute, and the requirement of an investigation, if there was no qualitative component to the investigation. The statute itself does impose a qualitative component to the [MBNA's] negligence" Judge Williams said.[131]

MBNA appealed Judge Williams' decision. But on February 11, 2004, a three-member panel of the U.S. Court of Appeals for the Fourth Circuit affirmed, finding that MBNA's standard response to consumer disputes did not amount to a true "reinvestigation" under the FCRA.

"MBNA argues that the language of § 1681s-2(b)(1)(A), requiring furnishers of credit information to 'conduct an investigation' regarding disputed information, imposes only a minimal duty on creditors to briefly review their records to determine whether the disputed information is correct," the panel wrote, in an opinion authored by Chief Judge William W. Wilkens. "Stated differently, MBNA contends that this provision does not contain any qualitative

---

[131] <u>Johnson v. MBNA</u>, op. cit., bench ruling February 24, 2003

component that would allow courts or juries to assess whether the creditor's investigation was reasonable."[132]

"The key term at issue here, 'investigation,' is defined [by the dictionary] as 'a detailed inquiry or systematic examination.' Thus, the plain meaning of 'investigation' clearly requires some degree of careful inquiry by creditors," he wrote.

Further, he said, the statute "uses the term 'investigation' in the context of articulating a creditor's duties in the consumer dispute process outlined by the FCRA. It would make little sense to conclude that, in creating a system intended to give consumers a means to dispute – and, ultimately, correct – inaccurate information on their credit reports, Congress used the term 'investigation' to include superficial, *un*reasonable inquiries by creditors. We therefore hold that § 1681s-2(b)(1) requires creditors, after receiving notice of a consumer dispute from a credit reporting agency, to conduct a reasonable investigation of their records to determine whether the disputed information can be verified."

MBNA also tried to argue that its investigation in Johnson's case was reasonable. But the court pointed to the specific nature of Johnson's dispute, and the testimony of MBNA agents that their investigation was primarily limited to (1) confirming that the name and address listed on the ACDVs were the same as the name and address contained in the Customer Information System, and (2) noting that the CIS contained a code indicating that Johnson was the sole responsible party on the account.

"The MBNA agents also testified that, in investigating consumer disputes generally, they do not look beyond the information contained in the CIS and never consult underlying documents such as account applications. Based on this evidence, a jury could reasonably conclude that

---

[132] Johnson v. MBNA America Bank: 357 F.3d 426 (4th Cir. 2004).

MBNA acted unreasonably in failing to verify the accuracy of the information contained in the CIS," he wrote.

Richard Rubin, a Santa Fe, New Mexico attorney who argued the case for Johnson before the Fourth Circuit, noted that the panel adopted his position that had MBNA simply told the truth and stated that its investigation was inconclusive, the CRAs would have deleted the tradeline as required by the FCRA, and the litigation never would have occurred.

Chapter 10

History

> *Those who cannot remember the past are condemned to repeat it.*

> -- George Santayana, "Life of Reason, Reason in Common Sense," *Scribner's* (1905)

Credit bureaus had humble beginnings. Local credit bureaus started taking shape in the late 1800s, when merchants who increasingly offered credit needed to keep track of those who failed to repay. One of the first credit bureaus was established in Brooklyn in 1860.[133]

Equifax was founded as the Retail Credit Co. in Atlanta in 1899 by brothers Cator and Guy Woolford, who compiled credit records of the city's citizens in a "Merchants Guide" that they sold to local grocers for $25 a year.[134]

Also in the 1890s, J.E.R. Chilton started to collect information on customers in Dallas, Texas.

In 1906, the first national organization of credit bureaus was founded – the National Association of Retail Credit Agencies. It later became the Associated Credit Bureaus (ACB); it is now known as the Consumer Data Industry Association (CDIA).

---

[133] Cole, R.H. (1992), Consumer and Commercial Credit Management (Irwin, Homewood)
[134] Serwer, Andy, "Street Life: Credit Bureaus Exposed," *Fortune.com*, April 14, 2003

This original organization was set up as a network of six small credit bureaus. The number of credit bureaus increased remarkably in the 1920s as well as the 1950s with the introduction of credit cards and installment credit. During that period, the credit reporting market was homegrown: information was collected from local lenders and distributed locally.[135]

Automation & Consolidation

In the 1970s, however, the industry started to automate on a larger scale. Database concentration led to industry consolidation. The larger market-players began to bring smaller bureaus into their computer systems to benefit from their information collection. Smaller agencies used the computer processing power and network of the larger companies. Local credit bureaus either became affiliates of one of the bigger players, or remained independent as resellers of credit reports.

In the 1970s, there were 2,250 credit bureaus in the market. This number has been reduced to 1,833 bureaus in 1997. Currently, it is estimated there are only 220 independent resellers.

In the 1980s, there were five national credit reporting agencies: Trans Union, TRW, Equifax, Chilton Corporation and Pinger Systems. The Chilton Corporation eventually merged with TRW, whereas Pinger was sold to the Computer Science Corporation (CSC). CSC is a separate company, but for credit-reporting and operational purposes, it is now an affiliate of Equifax.

Credit reporting was only one division of TRW. Other divisions were devoted to aerospace and automotive parts. TRW later purchased Chilton. In the mid-1990s, TRW

---

[135]Jentzsch, Nicola, The Regulation of Financial Privacy: U.S. vs. Europe, European Credit Research Institute (ECRI Report No. 5 – June 2003)

sold its credit reporting division, renamed Experian, to an intermediary. Experian was later bought by Grand Universal Stores, a United Kingdom company that continues as owner.

The Marmon Group is a Chicago-based company, privately owned by the Pritzkers of Chicago, one of America's wealthiest families. The Pritzkers also own the Hyatt Hotel chain. In 1981, the Marmon Group bought a large, failing amalgamation of businesses called Trans Union, which was into railcar and equipment leasing, water treatment, and international trade. It also had a credit bureau, a business that grew from a company called the Credit Bureau of Cook County.

So, by the end of the 1980s there were three national consumer credit reporting agencies (CRAs) – Equifax, TRW (Experian) and Trans Union.

Congress, Consumers 'Discover' Credit Reporting

The growth and consolidation in the credit reporting system was felt by the public and by Congress. By the late 1960s, Congress increasingly was concerned with a broad range of consumer protection issues. It was during this period that Congress enacted the Truth in Lending Act, requiring disclosure of credit terms.

There was also growing concern about privacy. For the first time, the specter of huge computerized databanks containing personal information on millions of Americans spurred debate over the need to protect citizens from "Big Brother." In 1967, Prof. Alan Westin of Columbia University published Privacy and Freedom, one of the first books to explore the need for a code of "fair information practices" to ensure Americans' privacy in the computer age.[136]

The Fair Credit Reporting Act has a rather odd sort of history. While the legislation was supposed to protect consumers, initial support for the bill among consumer

---

[136] Westin, Alan, Privacy and Freedom (New York: Atheneum, 1967)

groups turned to opposition, while the credit reporting industry came to embrace it. While the House held most of the public hearings and debate, the bill was drafted largely in secret by Senate Banking Committee members and representatives of the credit reporting industry.[137]

In 1969, the proposal's leading proponent was Senator William Proxmire (D-WI). Proxmire believed that inaccuracy and misleading data were the most serious of several problems plaguing the credit reporting system. The other problems were maintaining confidentiality, and the volume of untimely or irrelevant data.

"Although a number of Congressional committees have recently begun to investigate the activities of credit reporting agencies, most Americans still do not realize the vast size and scope of today's credit reporting industry or the tremendous amount of information which these agencies maintain and distribute," Proxmire said on the Senate Floor.[138]

A Legislative Coup

Unfortunately for Proxmire, he was outnumbered by pro-industry Senators. They undertook their own negotiations with the credit-granting and credit-reporting industries and produced a bill that was quietly attached to a separate Senate bill. The legislative maneuvering allowed the pro-industry Senators to get their version into a final House-Senate conference even before the House could start moving a more pro-consumer bill. Proxmire was forced to compromise.

---

[137] This history is largely from the leading manual used by FCRA practitioners: The Fair Credit Reporting Act (Fourth Edition) National Consumer Law Center. Historically authored by Willard P. Ogburn, Joanne S. Faulkner and Jonathan Sheldon, and most recently, by Anthony Rodriguez, the FCRA Manual is a "must-read" for anyone who is serious about FCRA law and litigation. www.nclc.org
[138] 115 Cong. Rec. 2410 (January 31, 1969)

"It is an industry bill," crowed John L. Spafford, President of the Associated Credit Bureaus, the industry trade group and forerunner of the CDIA.[139]

Anthony Roisman, of the Consumer Federation of America, said, "If the choice is the Senate Bill or no bill, then I think it has to be no bill."[140]

Professor Arthur Miller, then at University of Michigan, added, "I have the feeling about S. 823 that it really is an Act to protect and immunize the credit bureaus rather than an act to protect the individual who has been abused by credit information flow created by the bureaus."

Miller put his finger on a central attraction to industry. The Act granted CRAs and furnishers substantial immunity from liability under many state defamation and other tort laws. This was contrary to Proxmire's original intent, which was to create new federal liability while preserving state liability.

Another striking aspect about the original statute was the absence of specific standards. For starters, it did not give consumers the *right to obtain actual copies* of their credit reports. Instead, it only gave them the right to *know the substance* of what was in their reports. It said credit bureaus must complete reinvestigations within a "reasonable" period of time, but it did not set any firm deadlines. It put no duty on credit grantors, the main source of data in credit reports, to report accurate information or to reinvestigate upon receiving disputes.

Proxmire sought to strengthen the FCRA in the next Congress in 1973. He proposed direct consumer access to their files, and disclosure to consumers by creditors of reports that were the basis for an adverse action. He also proposed repealing the industry's immunity under various

---

[139] Hearings Before Subcommittee on Consumer Affairs of House Committee on Banking and Currency on HR 16340, 91st Cong., 2d Sess. 108 (1970)

[140] *Id.*

state defamation and tort laws. The bill never made it out of committee.

The FTC's First Enforcement Effort

In the mid-1970s, the FTC launched what would become a multi-year enforcement action against Retail Credit (later to be named Equifax). The investigation and hearings opened a window into previously unknown practices. These included its policy of ranking various offices according to which one collected the greatest amount of negative information, and the use of production quotas that encouraged employees to cut corners. In 1980, the FTC found that these and a host of other practices were illegal.[141] But in 1982, the findings were set aside by the U.S. Court of Appeals for the 11th Circuit.[142]

The Privacy Protection Study Commission

In 1975, the FCRA became a major focus of the Privacy Protection Study Commission (PPSC), which was created by the Privacy Act of 1974.[143] The Commission's charge was to study private sector information practices and recommend to Congress whether new privacy laws were needed, or whether existing privacy laws, like the FCRA, needed to be improved.[144] The Commission's members were

---

[141] 96 FTC 1045 (1980)

[142] Equifax Inc. v. FTC, 678 F.2d 1047 (11th Cir. 1982)

[143] 5 U.S.C. 552a

[144] The charge of the PPSC was to make a "study of the data banks, automatic data processing programs, and information systems of governmental, regional, and private organizations, In order to determine the standards and procedures in force for the protection of personal information." The President and Congress also asked the PPSC to recommend to "the extent, if any, to which the principles and requirements of the Privacy Act of 1974 should be applied to organizations other than agencies of the Federal Executive branch and to make such other legislative recommendations as the Commission deems

appointed by the President and Congress.[145] The report, released in July 1977, was entitled <u>Personal Privacy In The Information Age</u>.[146]

The report's introduction articulated three objectives[147] that endorsed Fair Information Act Principles. "These three objectives both subsume and conceptually augment the principles of the Privacy Act of 1974 and the five fair information practices principles[148] set forth in the 1973 report of the [HEW] Secretary's Advisory Committee On Automated Personal Data Systems."[149]

---

necessary to protect the privacy of individuals while meeting the legitimate needs of government and society for information."

[145] The members were: David F. Linowes, Boeschenstein Professor of Political Economy and Public Policy, Univ of Illinois (Chairman); Dr. Willis H. Ware, The Rand Corp. (Vice Chairman); William O. Bailey, President, Aetna Life & Casualty Co.; William B. Dickinson, Retired Managing Editor, *Philadelphia Evening Bulletin*; Congressman Barry M. Goldwater, Jr. of California; Congressman Edward I. Koch of New York; State Senator Robert J. Tennessen, of Minnesota. The PPSC had over 50 full-time staffers or consultants.

[146] *Personal Privacy In The Information Age: The Report of the Privacy Protection Study Commission,* (July 1977; GPO Stock No. 052-003-00395) Herein referred to as the PPSC Report.

[147] The three general principles were: (1) minimize intrusiveness; (2) open up record-keeping operations in ways that will minimize the extent to which recorded information about an individual is itself a source of unfairness in any decision about him made on the basis of it (maximize fairness); and (3) create legitimate enforceable expectations of confidentiality

[148] The five FIP principles of the HEW task force were: (1) there must be no personal data recordkeeping systems whose very existence is secret; (2) there must be a way for an individual to find out what information about him is in a record and how it is used; (3) there must be a way for an individual to prevent information about him obtained for one purpose from being used or made available for other purposes without his consent; (4) there must be a way for an individual to correct or amend a record of identifiable information about him; and (5) any organization creating, maintaining, using, or disseminating records of identifiable personal data must assure the reliability of the data for their intended use and must take reasonable precautions to prevent misuse of the data.

[149] PPSC Report, Pg. 15.

After the introduction, the first substantive chapter, Chapter 2, "The Consumer-Credit Relationship," focused on the FCRA. "Although their scope and particular requirements differ, the FCRA and the Privacy Act of 1974 share a common aim: that the policies and practices of record-keeping institutions minimize unfairness to individuals in the collection, maintenance, use and disclosure of records about them," the report stated.[150] In that chapter, the commission recommended 18 changes to strengthen the FCRA so it would more effectively realize these goals.[151] Some of the recommendations became law with the enactment of the 1996 FCRA amendments. Other recommendations became "industry best practices."[152]

The PPSC report set the foundation for analyzing and evaluating law, policy and organizational practices relating to the collection, use and disclosure of personal data. Its *methodology* was to *identify the principles of Fair Information Practice* and *then apply them* to the issue at hand, whether it be a standard industry practice or the statute governing that industry.

Despite the PPSC's extensive hearings and recommendations regarding the FCRA, Congress made no serious effort to improve the FCRA throughout the 1970s and most of the 1980s.

By the mid-1980s, the national credit reporting agencies had to be feeling nearly untouchable. They had overtaken the legislative process in 1970 and re-wrote what was supposed to be a consumer protection law so it instead

---

[150] Ibid, Pg. 67

[151] Ibid, "Chapter 2: The Consumer-Credit Relationship," pgs. 41-100

[152] The remaining 14 chapters address personal data held by banks, insurers, employers, health care providers, direct marketers, government agencies, the Privacy Act, and Social Security numbers. In nearly all the chapters, the PPSC made extensive recommendations to enact new privacy laws or strengthen existing ones. From a policy point of view, the commission defined "information privacy" in terms of Fair Information Practices, and explained that the FCRA was based on FIPs and therefore was an "information privacy" law.

provided them with valuable tort immunity and other benefits. Proxmire's bid to strengthen the law in favor of consumers went nowhere. Similarly, the recommendations of the Privacy Protection Study Commission just gathered dust on a shelf. And the FTC's first major enforcement effort was set aside by a federal appeals court.

Meanwhile, mergers and acquisition had allowed the national CRAs to consolidate their control over the market. Fast-improving information technology enabled them to gather, store and sell more personal data – "faster, better, cheaper." Yes, for the CRAs in the 1980s, life was good.

The Complaints Just Kept On Coming

By the late 1980s, complaints were rising about credit report inaccuracies. The first person to attempt to assess the extent of the inaccuracy was a mortgage broker, reflecting the fact that error-prone credit reports were hampering the home-buying process. On August 7, 1989, James Williams of Consolidated Information Service, a New York-area mortgage reporting firm, released a report analyzing 1,500 reports from TRW, Equifax, and Trans Union, and found a serious error rate of 42% to 47%.[153]

The Williams study and subsequent legislative proposals set off a debate over credit report accuracy that continued into the 21st Century proved a dominant theme in the 2003 legislative proceedings in Congress.

In the October 3, 1989 issue of *Privacy Times*, this author co-wrote an article on consumer complaints to the FTC about their credit reports. (The complaints were obtained through a Freedom of Information Act request, with the names redacted.) The story found that several consumers complained about inaccuracies, and a common cause of inaccuracy was the mixing of files of two consumers with

---

[153] James Williams, Consolidated Information Services, *Credit File Errors, A Report*, August 1989

similar names or SSNs.   Another theme was the credit bureaus' callous attitude toward consumers.

One consumer, in reference to his credit report, wrote to the credit agency, "How is it possible to get files so mixed up? It contained five different Social Security numbers other than my own!"   Another consumer said, "TRW had corrected the original errors, but now they have added someone else's credit profile to mine." When the consumer complained to a TRW agent about the cost of all the long distance phone calls to correct the mistakes, the agent told her to "speak to an attorney."[154]

On June 12, 1990, as the FCRA legislative debate picked up steam, the U.S. Public Interest Research Group (U.S. PIRG) released its first study on the issue, entitled "Nightmare On Credit Street, Or, How The Credit Bureau Ruined My Life." U.S. PIRG was a fierce advocate for consumer rights, with independent PIRGs in several key states. "Nightmare On Credit Street" was a series of case studies. The first case study was entitled "Paul Rosenzweig: Credit Bureaus Commonly Include Credit Information Mixed With Someone Else's Information." It quoted Mr. Rosenzweig's letter to CALPIRG:

"To sum up the situation, there is another Paul Rosenzweig in L.A., he has a different Social Security number and birth date so it is beyond me that his bad credit keeps ruining mine. . . I have spent every moment of my free time trying to fix this mistake which I did not make and it has made my life a living hell. I really feel sorry for the Bob Smiths out there."

Another case study in the 1990 U.S. PIRG report focused on the failure to correct inaccuracies.   The New Jersey Dept. of the Public Advocate found similar problems in an April 1990 report, "Credit Reporting Complaints," by Pat Donahue.

---

[154] *Privacy Times*, October 3, 1989

In April 29, 1991, Consumers Union released its first report, "What Are They Saying About Me? The Results of A Review of 161 Credit Reports From The Three Major Credit Bureaus." The rather unscientific survey found that 48% of the credit reports examined contained "serious errors," defined as those that could, or did, cause the denial of credit, employment or insurance.

In 1991, U.S. PIRG released its second study, "Don't Write, Don't Call, We Don't Care." It highlighted several examples of credit bureaus failing to respond to consumers seeking correction of errors.

In October 1993, U.S. PIRG released its third report, "Credit Bureaus: Public Enemy #1 At The FTC." Based upon a Freedom of Information Act (FOIA) request, U.S. PIRG found that between 1990-93, problems with credit bureaus were the leading cause of complaints to the FTC. The 1993 PIRG report found that 44% of complaints concerned mixed files, and that among those, 64% involved the mixing of data with total strangers. The study found that 94% of consumers complaining did so because of uncorrected errors in their reports and that 83% specifically named at least one of the three major CRAs – Equifax, TransUnion or TRW (now Experian).

FTC, State AGs Investigate

Officials at the FTC and the Offices of State Attorneys General (AGs) were keenly aware of these emerging patterns. In their view, the problems typically related to three inter-related areas: (1) inaccuracy and/or mixed files, (2) failure on the part of CRAs to reinvestigate disputed information in an adequate or timely manner, and (3) failure to correct inaccurate information or to prevent its reinsertion after it was corrected. Both the FTC and State AG officials concluded that complaints about CRAs and consumer reports were indicative of a larger problem, and launched investigations.

These investigations resulted in a series of settlements in which each of the three major repositories, although not admitting any wrongdoing, agreed to abide by more rigorous standards designed to improve accuracy, responsiveness and reinvestigations, and to better prevent the reinsertion of previously deleted data. The consent agreements set forth very detailed requirements and particularly focused on the problem of mixed files. They set specific 30-day reinvestigation deadlines.

The Consent Orders underscored the belief of the State Attorneys General and the FTC that the CRAs were exploiting the vagaries of the FCRA to the disadvantage of consumers, and that given widespread consumer complaints, it was necessary to articulate a higher and more specific standard of care.

The first two settlements were simultaneously reached December 10, 1991, between TRW and the FTC,[155] and 18 State AGs.[156]

Equifax came to a similar settlement with the State AGs in June 1992, and with the FTC in 1994.

In October 1992, Trans Union reached a similar settlement with eighteen States.

Next Stop: Congress

These agreements provided the foundation for the first set of legislative amendments to the FCRA. But the proposal still faced major hurdles. In 1992, pro-industry forces won a narrow vote on the House Floor to make the FCRA preempt all State law. Rather than let that happen, the bill's sponsors, including Representatives Henry Gonzalez

---

[155] FTC v. TRW Inc., USDC-N.D. Texas – C.A. No. 3-91CV2661-H; Dec. 10, 1991
[156] TRW v. Dan Morales, et al., USDC-N.D. Texas – C.A. No. 3-91-1340-H; Dec. 10, 1991

(D-TX) and Esteban Torres (D-CA), pulled the measure and let it die.

Never Give Up

In 1994, a compromise was reached on preemption of state law. But with just a few days left in the session, Senator Phil Gramm (R-TX), exercised his privilege to put a "hold" on the measure, effectively killing it.

Two years later, on September 30, 1996, Congress capped six years of public hearings and intense media coverage and enacted the Consumer Credit Reporting Reform Act of 1996.

The amendments included provisions to strengthen consumers' rights to prompt and effective reinvestigations, and to put an even stronger duty on CRAs to avoid mixed files, and to prevent reinsertion of previously deleted material. Many of the provisions in the 1996 Amendments paralleled the approaches taken by the State Attorneys General and the FTC in their consent agreements with CRAs.

The April 1994 House Banking Committee Report on the proposed amendments explained why, despite the consent agreements and subsequent industry guidelines, legislation was necessary: "Because the industry guidelines are simply voluntary, they are unenforceable and may be changed or revoked at any time. Many of the provisions in the consent agreements expire after a short period of time, are not enforceable by consumers, and do not apply in every state. Additionally, these agreements do not impose any reinvestigation obligations on furnishers of information or on credit bureaus other than the three largest. Because of these limitations, federal legislation is necessary to improve accuracy-related protections for consumers. Consequently, the bill contains new reinvestigation procedures which are intended to cut down on the number of errors in consumer reports and to reduce the delay in correcting those errors."

Inaccuracy Persists

Despite all of these efforts, these problems did not go away. In March 1998, U.S. PIRG conducted a study in which 88 consumers obtained 133 consumer reports, from either Equifax, Trans Union or Experian. The report found:

- 29% of the consumer reports contained serious errors -- false delinquencies or accounts that did not belong to the consumer -- that could result in the denial of credit;
- 41% contained personal demographic identifying information that was misspelled, long-outdated, belonged to a stranger, or was otherwise incorrect;
- 20% of the credit reports were missing major credit, loan, mortgage or other consumer accounts that demonstrated the creditworthiness of the consumer; altogether, 70% contained either serious errors or other mistakes of some kind.

The 1998 PIRG study found that non-responsiveness on the part of CRAs remained a problem:

- Of the consumers that did obtain their credit reports, at least 14% of them were forced to call back three or more times after receiving busy signals or had to write a letter in order to receive their report;
- Overall, 15% of consumers who attempted to participate in the survey either made at least three phone calls and never got through or requested their reports but never received them.

A 2000 survey by Consumers Union found that more than 50% of credit reports contained inaccuracies with the potential to result in a denial, or a higher cost of credit. The errors included mistaken identities, misapplied charges, uncorrected errors, misleading information, and variation between information reported by the various credit repositories. The study was based on a review of 63 reports by 25 consumers.[157]

Consumer Federation of America/National Credit Reporting Assoc. Study (2002)

Perhaps the most comprehensive study on consumer reports and credit scores was released in December 2002. It was conducted jointly by the Consumer Federation of America and the National Credit Reporting Association, which represents independent credit bureaus. The study covered a sample of 502,623 credit files combined from the three major repositories -- by far the largest independent statistical investigation of its type undertaken in the United States. Identifiers were stripped from all credit reports and the study was conducted without input from the consumers who were subjects of the reports. (We discussed the credit scoring aspects of this study in Chapter 2.)[158]

The study found that mixed files and multiple files continued to cause inaccuracies. For example, when researchers requested a "merged" report, consisting of a consumer report and credit score from each of the three major repositories, in 155 files out of 1,545-file sample (10%), "[I]t was very common for the additional report to contain a mixture of credit information, some of which belonged to the applicant and some of which clearly did not. In some cases, applicants had split files that appeared to be the result of applying for credit under variations of their name. Common reasons for returning additional repository reports included:

[157] "Credit Reports: How Do Potential Lenders See You?" *Consumer Reports*. July 2000. P. 52-3.
[158] CFA and NCRA, *Credit Score Accuracy and Implications for Consumers*, December 2002

- Confusion between generations with the same name (Jr., Sr., II, III, etc.).
- Mixed files with similar names, but different SSNs, and files with matching SSNs, but different names.
- Mixed files that listed accounts recorded under the applicant's name, but with the SSN of the co-applicant.
- Name variations that appeared to contain transposed first and middle names.
- Files that appeared to be tracking credit under an applicant's nickname.
- Spelling errors in the name.
- Transposing digits in the SSN.
- An account reporting the consumer as deceased.

The CFA-NCRA found that errors of "omission" and "commission" were rampant. Credit bureaus were particularly prone to not include positive credit history. Nearly 80% of all files examined were missing "a revolving account in good standing." One-third were missing a mortgage account that had never been late, and two-thirds were missing installment accounts that had been paid on time.

Since researchers did not communicate directly with the subjects of the credit reports, they could only analyze conflicting data between each of the three major repositories. Even then, the results were troubling. In 43.1% of the files sampled, there was conflicting data regarding 30-day late payments. In 29.4% cases, data conflicted on 60-day late payments, and in 23.5%, they conflicted on 90-day late payments. NCRA said it lacked data to estimate the potential impact on credit scores.

The Federal Reserve Board Study (2003)

In February 2003, the Federal Reserve Board (Fed) released a study concluding that changes were needed to improve the accuracy and completeness of the consumer data it contains.[159]

What was noteworthy about this study was that the Fed did not set out to examine credit report accuracy. Instead, it originally sought to determine whether examining credit bureau data on consumers would increase the Fed's understanding of the nation's economic health. The Fed study was based upon a random sample of nearly 250,000 (de-identified) consumer credit histories provided by an unnamed credit bureau.

Noting the long string of studies on credit report inaccuracy, the Fed said the issue was related to the potential usefulness of the data for measuring economic health.

"Despite the benefits that the credit reporting system offers, analysis reveals several areas of the current system that could be improved. A close examination of credit reporting company data reveals that the information is not complete, may contain duplications, and at times contains ambiguities about the credit histories of at least some consumers," the study found.

"The following are four particular areas of concern: (1) credit limits are sometimes not reported; (2) the current status of accounts that show positive balances but are not currently reported is ambiguous; (3) some creditors fail to report nonderogatory accounts or minor delinquencies; and (4) the reporting of data on collection agency and public record accounts is possibly inconsistent and inquiry data is incomplete."

In some instances, these deficiencies could harm a consumer's credit score; in others, they could help, the study continued. For instance, the failure to report credit limits could make it appear that consumers were "maxed out" on

---

[159] "An Overview of Consumer Data and Credit Reporting," was written by Robert Avery, Paul Calem, and Glenn Canner, of the Fed's Div. of Research and Statistics, and Raphael Bostic, of the Univ. of Southern California. www.federalreserve.gov/pubs/bulletin/2003/0203lead.pdf

their credit cards when they weren't. Duplications in mortgages, court judgments or collection accounts, could significantly drive down a credit score. On the other hand, the failure to report minor delinquencies could make consumers appear more creditworthy than they were. Like the CFA study, the Fed concluded that inaccurate data would reduce the reliability of credit scores.

Needed: Consumer Vigilance

The Fed listed consumer "vigilance" in the form of access to his or her own credit report as its first remedy. "Both growing consumer awareness of the importance of credit reports and easier consumer access to credit reports and credit scores serve to increase consumer vigilance," it said. It acknowledged that access by itself was not a panacea. "The credit granting system has moved toward risk-based pricing in which applicants are less likely to be denied credit (and thus given the reasons for denial) than to receive credit at prices that reflect the perceived risk."

"Consumers may not always be aware that they are paying higher prices for the credit. Similarly, an increasing share of consumer revolving credit is obtained through pre-approved solicitations as opposed to consumer initiated requests for credit," the Fed study continued.

"The credit reporting companies also could address some of the issues identified above," it said, recommending a system for coding collection accounts and public records, and for identifying out-of-date accounts.

"Most of the problems cited above result from the failure of creditors, collection agencies, or public entities to report or update items—areas that are beyond the direct control of the credit reporting companies. Thus, fully resolving these problems requires a more comprehensive and consistent reporting system, particularly with regard to major derogatories, collection agency accounts, and public records," it said.

General Accounting Office Study (2003)

In the heat of the 2003 legislative debate over the Fair Credit Reporting Act, Congress asked its research arm, General Accounting Office (GAO) to assess credit report accuracy. The GAO, a timid outfit to begin with, probably dreaded the assignment, as it knew that the opposing players in the legislative debate – the powerful financial services lobby and consumer-privacy advocates – would aggressively assail any conclusion that they did not like.

Not surprisingly, the GAO "punted." Rather than conduct its own study, the GAO surveyed previous studies (cited above) and other existing data. It reached the not-so-startling conclusion that the perfect study on accuracy had not yet been made.

"The lack of comprehensive information regarding the accuracy of consumer credit reports inhibits any meaningful discussion of what more could or should be done to improve credit report accuracy. Available studies suggest that accuracy could be a problem, but no study has been performed that is representative of the universe of credit reports," the GAO wrote. [160]

Shortcomings in the PIRG and CU studies included the lack of a statistically representative methodology and the absence of cooperation from the credit bureaus, GAO said. While the CFA study was based upon a review of actual credit reports, it lacked input from the consumers who the reports were about. The Federal Reserve study relied on only one credit bureau, GAO said.

None of the three major credit reporting agencies (Experian, Equifax and Trans Union), or its trade group, CDIA, kept statistics of credit report accuracy, GAO reported. A 1992 study by Arthur Anderson finding a miniscule level of inaccuracy was not seen by GAO as reliable.

---

[160] www.gao.gov/new.items/d031036t.pdf

The GAO came up with some useful findings. It noted that creditors who furnished inaccurate data to the CRAs were a major cause of errors. But it also noted that errors could occur at other points in the process.

CRA officials told GAO that five categories account for 90% of disputes. The most frequently received dispute was "not my account," CDIA said. (Remember, the 1993 U.S. PIRG study found that "mixed files" was the leading cause of inaccuracy.)

The other categories were: "account has been closed;" "account status, payment history, or payment rating;" "current balance;" and "account included in or excluded from a bankruptcy."

Industry Statistics

Although declining to provide a total number of disputes for 2002, CDIA provided the following percentages: 46% of disputes were verified as reported; 27% were modified/updated per furnisher's instructions; 10.5% had data deleted per furnisher's instructions; 16% had data deleted due to statutory time limit.

Critics of the credit bureaus questioned whether 46% of the disputes were actually "verified," given the bureaus' reliance on an automated message-exchange system that has been shown to cause creditors to "verify" information that in fact is inaccurate. Experts also said the CDIA statistics confirmed criticisms that the bureaus overly rely on the word of creditors and too often disregard the word of consumers.

The GAO also reported that consumer complaints to the FTC increased from 1,300 in 1997 to almost 12,000 in 2002. The most common complaints cited against CRAs in 2002 were: Provided inaccurate information (5,956); failed to reinvestigate disputed information (2,300); provided inadequate phone help (1,291); disclosed incomplete or improper credit file to customer (1,033); and improperly conducted reinvestigation of disputed item (771).

In the 2003 Amendments, Congress added several provisions to improve accuracy, including the right to one free credit report per year. Congress also ordered the FTC to conduct studies about credit report accuracy, and directed U.S. banking regulatory agencies, in conjunction with the FTC, to assess creditors' role in improving accuracy. But the FTC became mired in uncertainty over methodology, and consequently, had failed to complete a meaningful study on accuracy as of September 2007.

The CRAs sharply disagree that there are major accuracy problems. On its Web site, Experian points out that its credit files contain records on approximately 205 million credit-active consumers and 15 million U.S. businesses.

"Each month, there are more than 4.5 billion updates to credit report information throughout the U.S.," it stated. "The American credit databases are the most accurate and secure in the world. Experian has a long, distinguished record of responsible stewardship of the data in our care."[161]

Parallel History: Identity Theft & Credit Reports

In 1992, Trans Union started collecting a new statistic: the number of consumer "inquiries" to its fraud desk related to "true name fraud," otherwise known as identity theft.

It made sense that a major credit bureau like Trans Union would take an early interest, as identity theft usually leaves the innocent consumer with the debris of a polluted consumer report.

In that sense, identity theft is a sub-category of the more general category of mixed files, as the typical result of identity theft is that the imposter-generated fraudulent activity is mixed into the consumer report of the innocent victim. Moreover, a key moment occurs when the credit bureau actually helps the identity thief obtain credit by dis-

---

[161] http://www.experian.com/#

closing the innocent victim's report to the credit grantor holding the thief's application.

In 1992, the first year Trans Union began keeping track, it received 35,235 inquiries about identity theft. By 1997, the annual number of inquires had mushroomed to 522,922. Trans Union estimated that two-thirds of those inquiring were actual victims of identity theft.

Thus, in the years that credit report inaccuracy emerged as one of the key issues confronting American consumers, identity theft was born and quickly began escalating. By definition, this new problem would further denigrate credit report inaccuracy, as the victim's credit report would be polluted by the data generated by the fraudster.

GAO ID Theft Study (1998)

In 1998, the GAO released one of the first reports on identity theft. Using Trans Union's statistics, it concluded that the phenomenon was prevalent, growing, and damaging:

> On an individual level, the "human" costs of identity fraud should be acknowledged. Emotional costs are associated with identity-fraud incidents as well as the time and effort required to repair a compromised credit-history. One Secret Service field agent told us that victims of identity fraud feel they have been violated. Although not easily quantified, the financial and/or opportunity costs to victims can also be substantial. For example, the victims may be unable to obtain a job, purchase a car, or qualify for a mortgage.[163]

---

[163] (GAO/GGD-98-100BR, "Identity Fraud: Information On Prevalence, Cost and Internet Is Limited"

The next year, Congress enacted the Identity Theft Deterrence Act, specifically making it a federal crime to steal someone's identity. But the law did not place duties on credit grantors or credit bureaus to be more vigilant about stopping identity theft.

Identity theft did not stop; it got worse. And for good reason. First, for the thieves, it was a relatively low-risk crime, with a potentially big payoff. The most skillful identity thieves were able to run up bills of $100,000, loading up on jewelry, electronic equipment, even cars and homes. Criminalizing the activity had only minimal impact because many of the thieves probably thought they were breaking several laws to begin with.

Damages Similar To Mixed Files

The damages arising from identity theft, as they pertain to the interaction between consumers and the major credit bureaus, are similar to the damages arising from mixed files. In July 12, 2000, testimony before the Senate Judiciary Subcommittee on Technology, Terrorism and Government Information, Jodie Bernstein, then head of the FTC's Bureau of Consumer Protection, testified:

> The leading complaints by identity theft victims against the consumer reporting agencies are that they provide inadequate assistance over the phone, or that they will not reinvestigate or correct an inaccurate entry in the consumer's credit report. In one fairly typical case, a consumer reported that two years after initially notifying the consumer reporting agencies of the identity theft, following up with them numerous times by phone, and sending several copies of documents that they requested, the suspect's address and other inaccurate information continues to appear on her credit report. In another case, although the consumer has sent documents requested by the

consumer reporting agency three separate times, the consumer reporting agency involved still claims that it has not received the information.[164]

In her March 7, 2000 testimony before the Subcommittee, Bernstein elaborated:

> A consumer's credit history is frequently scarred, and he or she typically must spend numerous hours sometimes over the course of months or even years contesting bills and straightening out credit reporting errors. In the interim, the consumer victim may be denied loans, mortgages, a driver's license, and employment; a bad credit report may even prevent him or her from something as simple as opening up a new bank account at a time when other accounts are tainted and a new account is essential. Moreover, even after the initial fraudulent bills are resolved, new fraudulent charges may continue to appear, requiring ongoing vigilance and effort by the victimized consumer." …

> Identity theft victims continue to face numerous obstacles to resolving the credit problems that frequently result from identity theft. For example, many consumers must contact and re-contact creditors, credit bureaus, and debt collectors, often with frustrating results."[165]

ID Theft Becomes Number One Complaint To FTC

The parallel between identity theft and overall credit report inaccuracy was even reflected in FTC complaint stat-

---

[164] http://www.ftc.gov/os/2000/07/idtheft.htm
[165] http://www.ftc.gov/os/2000/03/identitytheft.htm

istics. As U.S. PIRG reported in its 1993 study, complaints about credit bureaus topped the list. Here's how the complaints broke down:

1)   Credit bureaus (30,901);
2)   Misc. Credit (22, 729);
3)   Investment Fraud (12,809);
4)   Equal Credit Opportunity (11,634);
5)   Automobiles (6,901);
6)   Truth-In-Lending (6,303);
7)   Household Supplies (5,835);
8)   Recreational Goods (5,747);
9)   Mail Order (4,687)
10)   Food/Beverage (2,738).

On January 23, 2002, the FTC announced that Identity Theft headed the FTC's Top 10 Consumer Fraud Complaints of 2001,[166] again, well ahead of other categories that involved out-of-pocket losses. The breakdown was:

1)   Identity Theft (42%);
2)   Internet Auctions (10%)
3)   Internet Services and Computer Complaints (7%)
4)   Shop-at-Home and Catalog Offers (6%)
5)   Advance Fee Loans and Credit Protection (5%)
6)   Prizes/Sweepstakes/Gifts (4%)
7)   Business Opports./Work at Home Plans (4%)
8)   Foreign Money Offers (4%)
9)   Magazines and Buyers Clubs (3%)
10)   Telephone Pay-Per-Call/Info Services (2%)

GAO 2002 ID Theft Study

In 2002, the General Accounting Office, although stating that hard statistics were not available, concluded that

---

[166] http://www.ftc.gov/opa/2002/01/idtheft.htm;

the problem continued to escalate, as did the costs to businesses. Importantly, the GAO noted the toll on victims.

"Identity theft can cause substantial harm to the lives of individual citizens -- potentially severe emotional or other non-monetary harm, as well as economic harm. Even though financial institutions may not hold victims liable for fraudulent debts, victims nonetheless often feel 'personally violated' and have reported spending significant amounts of time trying to resolve the problems caused by identity theft -- problems such as bounced checks, loan denials, credit card application rejections, and debt collection harassment."[167]

FTC Study (2003)

The studies kept coming. In September 2003, a major FTC survey, the first of its kind, left little doubt that identity theft had reached epidemic proportions and had escalated in the new century. Nearly 10 million people in the United States were victims in the previous year, costing them $5 billion, plus a total of 300 million hours to correct problems stemming from the theft, the FTC found. The five-year totals were 27.3 million individuals victimized by some form of identity theft, at $4,800 per victim, costing businesses $47.6 billion.[168]

Based on a random telephone survey of 4,057 adults, the survey found that 4.6% of the respondents said they were identity theft victims in the past year. That percentage translated into 9.9 million victims. The survey estimated 6.9 million victims two years ago and 3.4 million victims the year before that. The FTC said the most common form of ID theft – unauthorized charges on credit cards or telephone bills – was experienced by 3.1%. Another 1.5% reported

---

[167] General Accounting Office, *Identity Theft: Available Data Indicate Growth in Prevalence & Cost*
GAO-02-424T, www.gao.gov/new.items/d0242t.pdf
[168] Federal Trade Commission – Identity Theft Survey (Sept. 2003)
www.ftc.gov/os/2003/09/synovatereport.pdf

that new accounts were created in their name.[169] FTC Consumer Protection Chief Howard Beales called this latter form the most damaging type of identity theft because of the time it takes to correct and the toll it takes on consumers.[170]

The FTC survey was supported by separate studies by the Gartner Group, and by Privacy & American Business,[171] a New Jersey-based organization headed by Alan F. Westin, a consultant to several corporations and former Columbia Univ. professor.

Identity Theft Resource Center Study (2003)

Also in September 2003, the Identity Theft Resource Center (ITRC) published its survey of 173 victims, showing that the damage suffered by identity theft victims was escalating on all fronts. It found that fraudulent charges averaged more than $90,000 per name used, and that the average time spent by victims is about 600 hours, an increase of more than 247% over previous studies. It found that it was taking far longer than before to eliminate negative information from credit reports.[172]

Roughly half of the victims found it hard to understand their credit reports (particularly the "inquiries" section), the study said.

"Consistently all three bureaus did a very poor job of educating the public about fraud alerts and in helping people who called in for assistance. On average, only one in five people found it easy to speak with or reach a person after receiving a report. Once they did reach a fraud/customer service person, only 16% found the person "helpful and answered most, if not all, of my questions."

---

[169] *Id.*

[170] *Privacy Times,* September 12, 2003, pgs. 4-5

[171] www.pandab.org

[172] "Identity Theft: The Aftermath 2003," Identity Theft Resource Center (Sept. 2003); http://www.idtheftcenter.org/idaftermath.pdf

The study concluded that the most severe damages might be the emotional distress that victims endure. Paul Colins, a credit industry analyst and consultant who worked with the ITRC, commented, "The range of emotions is wide and rather painful to read. Three-fourths of victims were left with a feeling of financial insecurity, 88% experienced anger, and 75% expressed a feeling of helplessness. While these feelings do appear to subside a little over time, the survey clearly shows for many victims the feelings linger on. While most surveys have focused on the financial costs to victims, these psychological impacts are generally un-reported. They may, however, have far worse consequences for victims."

Dr. Charles Nelson, a licensed psychologist, and director of both the Crime and Trauma Recovery Program at the Family Treatment Institute, also reviewed the study:

Identity theft has been classified in many realms as a victimless crime," Nelson wrote. "This survey was designed to test the emotional impact of identity theft and to discover if sufferers of this crime exhibit similar responses as those of more commonly recognized victims including rape, repeated abuse, and violent assault victims. Many of the listed symptoms are classic examples of Post Traumatic Stress Disorder and secondary PTSD (from secondary wounding)."

In the years leading up to these studies, some states, particularly California, were very active in passing state laws to increase protections for victims of identity theft. Some of the state laws:

- Allowed victims to put a "security freeze" on their credit report, barring the credit bureaus from disclosing the report to anyone unless the consumer explicitly consented by lifting the freeze.[173]

---

[173] For more on state freeze laws, see: www.pirg.org/consumer/ or www.consumersunion.org/campaigns/learn_more/003484indiv.html; For example, Calif. Civil Code Sections 1785.11.2-1785.11.6; for California Credit Reporting Act, go to www.privacy.ca.gov/code/ccra.htm

- Required that credit bureaus remove fraud-generated accounts once the victim presented the credit bureau with a police report.[174]
- Allowed victims to request one free copy of their credit report every month for 12 months after becoming a victim.[175]
- Prohibited credit bureaus from disclosing a credit report unless three identifiers on the application matched the credit report.

The 2003 Amendments to the FCRA (FACT Act) created additional protections against identity theft. These included:

- Allowing consumers to block, and requiring CRAs to block, fraud-generated accounts from appearing on their credit reports.
- Requiring CRAs to notify furnishers that a blocked account is fraudulent.
- Allowing consumers with a "good faith suspicion" that they are fraud victims to place an "initial fraud alert" for (90 days).
- Permitting consumers who provide an official identity theft report (either the FTC report or local police) to place an extended fraud alert (up to 7 years).
- Requiring the CRA that received the alert to pass it on to the other CRAs.
- Permitting those on active military duty to place "active duty" alerts.
- When a report contains an alert, requiring CRAs to notify users of discrepancies in addresses.

---

[174] California Civil Code Sections 1785.16(k)
[175] California Civil Code Sections 1785.15.3

- Prohibit sale or collection of debts resulting from identity theft.
- Preventing fraud-related data from "re-polluting" a victim's credit report.
- Requiring the U.S. banking regulatory agencies to develop "Red Flag" guidelines, so financial institutions can spot patterns and practices related to identity theft.

In addition, the 2003 Amendments required rule-making and studies in a host of areas related to credit report accuracy, credit scoring and identity theft by the FTC and the U.S. banking regulatory agencies. These agencies dismally failed to meet these deadlines, and was scolded by Rep. Barney Frank, Chairman of the House Financial Services Committee, and other committee members, in a June 2007 hearing.[176]

These are all welcome and constructive additions to the FCRA. But upon their enactment, consumer advocates and privacy experts were quick to point out that they still did not go far enough. Worse, the federal law preempted state activity in too many areas.

More work lies ahead. Consequently, the history of the FCRA, or credit report inaccuracy, or identity theft, is far from over.

---

[176] www.house.gov/apps/list/hearing/financialsvcs_dem/ht061907.shtml

Chapter 11

Credit Repair & Credit Counselors

For every complex problem, there is a
solution that is simple, neat, and wrong.
—H. L. Mencken

If you want to find an industry with a horrible reputation, you need not look much further than credit repair. And for good reason. In this chapter, we will recount major enforcement actions against credit repair clinics. We will also touch on problems in the credit counseling and debt consolidation fields. But we will also hear from two small companies that say they ethically help consumers correct errors or otherwise improve their credit reports.

Over the years a steady drumbeat of warnings about credit repair scams have come from the Federal Trade Commission, state Attorneys General, AARP, and Call For Action. Despite these warnings, tens of thousands of consumers over the years, probably desperate to improve their credit reports, have turned to credit repair clinics. Consequently:

- Credit repair clinics collectively are making millions of dollar annually, typically charging consumers about $300-$500 dollars per year.
- Investigations of and enforcement actions and lawsuits continue against credit repair operators for ripping off consumers.

- Credit repair clinics continue advertising that they can help remove negative information from your credit report (regardless of its accuracy).

Steve Baker, Director of the Federal Trade Commission in Chicago and a leading enforcer of the credit repair law, said a prevailing myth about credit repair is that there are loopholes in the federal law that allow poor credit to be erased. It doesn't exist.

The Credit Repair Organizations Act

Let's start with the law. Under the Credit Repair Organizations Act (CROA),[177] and similar state laws, credit repair organizations must give you a copy of the "Consumer Credit File Rights Under State and Federal Law" before you sign a contract. A credit repair company cannot:

- Make false claims about their services
- Charge you until they have completed the promised services
- Perform any services until they have your signature on a written contract and have completed a three-day waiting period. During this time, you can cancel the contract without paying any fees.[178]

Your contract must specify:

- The payment terms for services, including their total cost.
- A detailed description of the services to be performed.

---

[177] 15 U.S.C. Sect. 1679(h)(b)
[178] These restrictions do not apply to a (1) non-profit organization; (2) creditor restructuring a consumer's debt or (3) depository instit.

- How long it will take to achieve the results.
- Any guarantees they offer, and
- The company's name and business address.

Bombardment & Technicalities

A typical technique used by credit repair outfits (CROs) is to flood consumer reporting agencies with letters disputing negative items in the credit report. CROs emphasize that when derogatory information is disputed, credit bureaus must remove it if they are unable to verify it within 30 days. They argue that with enough dispute letters, repeated over time, the credit bureaus will give up. However, the Big Three credit bureaus have ramped up their systems for countering this approach. Not only do their automated systems dispose of disputes with a few keystrokes, but also the bureaus often disregard repetitive disputes as "frivolous." Some CROs are known to try and mask their involvement by mailing in dispute letters from different locations around the country.

Some CROs proclaim that they exploit technicalities to remove negative data. For example, if the consumer owes $1,000.09 debt, and the credit bureau reports it as a $1,000.90 debt, some CROs argue that all references to the debt must be deleted when disputed. The FTC views such claims as false.

One case that illustrated the techniques and reach of credit repair was that of National Credit Repair. On August 11, 2003, the FTC announced that National Credit Repair, one of the country's largest credit repair operations, agreed to pay more than $1.15 million in consumer redress to settle charges that it violated the federal credit repair law. The FTC charged that the six Michigan-based defendants[179]

---

[179] The defendants were ICR Services, Inc.; a Livonia, Michigan-based company; and its three officers and directors, Bernadino J. Pavone, Jr., his mother Gloria Tactac, and Abood Samaan. The remaining defendants

falsely claimed that they could remove derogatory information from consumers' credit reports, even if that information was accurate and not obsolete. The defendants purported to do this through the use of a "one-of-a-kind" computer disk that they claimed could search and identify errors in the process used by the credit reporting agencies to enter negative items onto consumers' credit reports.

Since 1996, the defendants have sold their credit-repair service to more than 183,000 consumers, taking in more than $53 million on those sales (about $290 per consumer).[180] The company sold its services through a network of 50,000 sales representatives, who were paid commissions for each sale, the FTC said.

'Get A New Number'

Another approach that has drawn enforcement action is known as "File Segregation," in which the credit repair outfit shows the consumer how to obtain a new taxpayer identification number (TIN) or employer identification number (EIN) from the U.S. Internal Revenue Service. The consumer is then taught to create a new identity under the number on the theory that it will create a whole new file at the credit bureau and separate the individual from the negative credit history under his true Social Security number. The first problem with this approach is that it is a felony to put false data on a credit application. Second, the credit bureaus' algorithms are designed to accommodate discrepancies in identifiers, so that if the individual was still applying under the same or similar name or address, the information could end up in the same file anyway.

---

were National Credit Education and Review (NCER), based in Canton, Michigan, and its president Todd Renzi.
[180] FTC v ICR Services, Inc., et al.: U.S. Dist. Ct. – Northern Dist. Of Illinois (Eastern Div.) – No 03C-5532; complaint at http://www.ftc.gov/os/2003/08/icrcmp.pdf

In October 1999, sixteen defendants agreed to settle FTC charges that their "file segregation" schemes violated the CROA. The settlements were the result of an FTC's sweep entitled, "New ID, Bad IDea."[181] Thirteen of the sixteen defendants had to refund money to consumers. Three of the defendants showed they lacked enough money to pay refunds.

On May 9, 2001, Clifton W. Cross was sentenced to 49 months in federal prison and ordered to pay nearly $171,000 in restitution as part of a guilty plea resolving criminal charges stemming from a "file segregation" scam.[182] Cross and his company, "Build-It-Fast," promised consumers "perfect credit . . . instantly." It showed consumers how to get new Employment Identification Numbers and then substitute them for SSNs when applying for credit. Under a settlement with the FTC, Cross agreed to get out of the file segregation business.[183]

On February 17, 2004, a federal grand jury in Los Angeles returned a nine-count, criminal-contempt-of-court indictment against Richard Murkey Sr., 57, for returning to the credit repair business despite a previous court order that he stay out of it.[184]

---

[181] The settlements of the "Operation New ID - Bad IDea" sweep are with Mehmet Akca (FTC File No. X990018); Frank Muniz (FTC File No. X990020); LSQ International (FTC File No. X990024), Standard Business Services (FTC File No. X990021); Pro Se Publications (FTC File No. X990023); Ross Sanford Leiss (FTC File No. X990026); Michael Lyons (X990027); Edward Lane (FTC File No. X990032); All About Communications (FTC File No. X990030); Express Financial Planning (FTC File No. X990034); Financial Publishers of America (FTC File No X990033); New Start (FTC File No. X990028); Frederick P. Ray (FTC File No. X990066); Internet Publications (FTC File No. X990064); P.M.. Enterprises (FTC File No. X990047); Fresh Start (FTC File No. X990044).

[182] FTC v. Clifton W. Cross, et al.: U.S. Dist. Ct. – Western Dist. of Texas (Midland); No. M099-CA-018

[183] FTC News Release, June 21, 2001; ww.ftc.gov/opa/2001/06/cross.htm

[184] News Release (No. 04-020), Debra W. Yang, U.S. Attorney for Central Dist. of California, www.usdoj.gov/usao/cac/pr2004/020.html

The FTC brought a civil case against Murkey in 1998 for misleading consumers in connection with credit repair. In November 1999, a federal court in Los Angeles found that Murkey systematically violated the credit repair law and banned him from the business. The 2004 indictment charged that immediately following the court's order, Murkey continued to offer credit repair services through businesses such as "Credit Restoration Corporation of America, Inc." In 2001, the L.A. court held Murkey in civil contempt, but he again returned to credit repair, the indictment charged.

"There is only so much that civil enforcement can do against scams like credit repair," said Howard Beales, then Director of the FTC's Bureau of Consumer Protection. "We appreciate the Justice Department's willingness to pursue the criminal sanctions that con artists so richly deserve."

To Boldly Go . . .

An even more exciting scheme allegedly was operated by the husband-wife team that co-owned Second Chance Financial, a credit repair outfit based in Riverside, Calif.[185] According to an August 2004 federal grand jury indictment, Mickey Lynn Manning and her husband, Ross Smith "allegedly recruited employees from the major credit bureaus – Equifax, Experian and TransUnion – who would enter false and misleading information into their databases with the purpose of improving the credit scores" of Second Chance credit repair customers, stated Los Angeles U.S. Attorney Debra W. Yang in a press release.

Also indicted was Marcus Brandon Betts, of Ontario, Calif, a former "team leader" of Trans Union's Dispute Dept. in Fullerton, Calif., for falsifying credit report data on behalf of paying customers who wanted to improve their credit

---

[185] Remember, all those mentioned were only charged and had not been convicted of anything. People are presumed innocent until proven guilty. But the information is in the public domain and the story is quite compelling.

scores. The 16-count indictment named Dolores Guerrero, a Customer Service Representative on Experian's Dispute Team in the Dallas facility, as an unindicted co-conspirator. Guerrero pleaded guilty to fraud in May 2004 and is serving a prison term of more than three years, officials said, adding that she was paid $300-$500 a week in bribes.

No Equifax employees were named in the press release or the indictment, but a source said the husband-wife team had recruited operatives at Equifax's dispute facility in Jamaica. It was the first known case of credit bureau employees being accused of illegally working on behalf of outsiders.[186]

How They Did It

This investigation started in 2002 when, according to sources, Experian noticed a pattern of suspicious activity, specifically entries on credit histories that were made by one employee. That employee was terminated. A joint review by the credit bureaus prompted them to refer the matter to law enforcement authorities.

Second Chance Financial "helped" their credit repair customers in two ways. According to the indictment, in 2001, they would send to their accomplices at the credit bureaus fictitious "dispute letters" to justify deletion of negative data from their customers' credit histories. The credit bureau employees would then delete negative items from client credit reports and place the fictitious dispute letters in their credit bureau's files.

Second, they worked with at least three other conspirators who allegedly were employed at companies like "J&J Financial Services," of Fort Lee, N.J. (Jose L. Crespo); "Diamond Star Financial," of Teaneck, N.J. (Jamila Takiyah Davis); and "Superior Financial" of Valencia, Calif. These firms allegedly became subscribers of the major credit

---

[186] *Privacy Times*, Vol. 24 No. 16, Aug. 31, 2004

bureaus and then fraudulently reported positive loan histories on the credit repair clients. This, combined with the removal of negative data, had the effect of raising clients' credit scores. The indictment estimated $6 million in losses to more than 50 businesses. At the time, lawyers representing those who were indicted told reporters either that their clients would plead not guilty or that they had no comment.

Where To Draw The Line?

The Credit Repair Organization Act (CROA) is very broad in prohibiting *for-profit* companies from accepting advance payment for help in improving one's credit record, or providing advice or assistance to that effect.[187] But several consumers have alleged in separate federal lawsuits that credit monitoring services are doing just that in violation of CROA. One suit targeted ConsumerInfo.com, a Web site where consumers paid a $79.95 annual subscription for unlimited access to their Experian credit reports.[188] The suit said that the company acted like a credit repair outfit because it took money up front, provided consumers with a "Blue-print for Rebuilding Your Credit," and offered a service that helped generate dispute letters. Moreover, a Yahoo search using the term "'credit repair' consumerinfo" turned up the phrase, "How Can I Repair My Credit Rating" and a link to the www.consumerinfo.com. The company strongly denied it engaged in credit repair and defended itself in the lawsuit, which was pending when this book went to print.

Similar suits were pending against Trilegiant Corp.'s "PrivacyGuard."

---

[187] While some legal experts wonder whether such a broad prohibition on commercial speech could withstand Constitutional scrutiny, no successful challenge has yet been brought.

[188] Ronald W. Helms v. ConsumerInfo.com, Inc.: U.S. Dist. Ct. N. Dist of Alabama (Middle Div.) – No. CV-03-RRA-1439-M

The Modern Landscape

As of January 2005, it appeared that a handful of companies dominated the credit repair industry.

One market leader was Lexington Law Firm, based in Salt Lake City, Utah. According to its Web site, Lexington began operating in 1991 and has served over 100,000 consumers. It claimed to have "challenged and deleted" 350,174 negative items on credit reports in 2003.[189] (Lexington cannot "delete" items; presumably, it meant that its disputes prompted the CRAs to delete the negative items.)

Lexington required a $99 payment covering what it called a "case setup." New clients were required to sign a retainer agreement.

"In accordance with federal regulation, Lexington charges retroactively for the service it performs," billing $39-$79 for the dispute work performed in the previous month, depending on the tier of service. (Remember, the Credit Repair Act prohibits for-profit companies from collecting fees in advance for disputing credit report errors.)

Lexington's Web site said its system works in cycles. Clients begin by sending in their three credit reports. The firm enters the information in a database, and presents the client with a list of disputable items. The client chooses which items to dispute, and Lexington then sends dispute letters to the CRAs. (Lexington considers these dispute letters to be trade secrets and will not share them with anybody, including the client.)

"When you receive a response from a bureau, make a copy of the updated report for your records then send the original to Lexington to move your case forward. Thus the cycle begins anew, this time hopefully with fewer negative items on your credit report," the Lexington Web site stated, describing the fourth step in the cycle.

---

[189] www.lexingtonlaw.com

The annual cost is $508 ($79.00 initial + 11 months $39.00/ea). After 12 months, clients are entitled to a refund if Lexington does not effectuate deletion of at least 11 negative items. It calculates that each deleted item has a $50 value. So, if only two items are deleted, the client is entitled to a $408 refund, according to the Web site.

The Lexington Web site sports both the Better Business Bureau seal (BBB) and separate seal for BBB's Online Reliability Program. Clicking on the first seal takes you to a BBB Web page stating:

> Based on BBB files, this company has a satisfactory record with the Bureau. Any complaints processed by the Bureau in its three-year reporting period have been resolved. The number and type of complaints are not unusual for a company in this industry.
>
> To have a "Satisfactory Record" with the Bureau, a company must be in business for at least 12 months, properly and promptly address matters referred to it by the Bureau, and be free from an unusual volume or pattern of complaints and law enforcement action involving its marketplace conduct. In addition, the Bureau must have a clear understanding of the company's business and no concerns about its industry.

Other credit repair companies that take approaches similar to Lexington at similar prices, and which feature a BBB seal, include "CreditAttorney,"[190] "Ovation Law," and "Legacy Legal Services."[191] A Google search, and the accompanying ads, turned up a host of credit repair clinics.

Not every consumer has been satisfied with Lexington Law's services. In 2000, the Tennessee Office of Attorney General investigated the firm for possible viola-

---

[190] www.creditattorney.com, Dana Facemyer, Provo, Utah
[191] www.legacylegalservices.com, Brian Rollins, Tempe, Arizona

tions of the telemarketing sales law. The result was a consent agreement in which Lexington, while not admitting any wrongdoing, agreed not to "request payment ...to remove derogatory information from, or improve, a person's credit history, credit record, or credit rating before the expiration of the time frame in which [Lexington] has represented all of the goods or services will be provided to that person."[192]

A Different Approach

Stephen Gardner knows a lot about the credit reporting system, and about credit repair outfits. As the Texas Assistant Attorney General in the late 1980s and early 1990s, he led investigations that resulted in landmark settlement agreements with the "Big Three" consumer reporting agencies (CRAs). Under those agreements, the CRAs vowed to take steps to prevent mixed files, reinsertion of previously deleted data, and to conduct adequate investigations upon receiving consumer disputes (see Chapter 10). Those agreements served as the foundation for the 1996 FCRA amendments.

Gardner, now the litigation director for the Center for Science in the Public Interest, said the only organization he knew that ethically helps consumers was First Stone Credit Counseling (FSCC),[193] and its affiliate company, the People's Credit Bureau (PCB).[194] Based in Dallas, the two companies are run by Bruce J. Danielson, a former pilot and military veteran. Danielson said First Stone is the only Consumer *Advocate* Credit Counseling organization in the

---

[192] State of Tennessee v. Lexington Law Firm: U.S. Dist. Ct. – Middle Dist. Of Tennessee; Civil No. 3-96-0344; Agreed Final Order, 9/29/00.
[193] http://www.firststone.com/
[194] http://www.peoplescreditbureau.com/; The Peoples Credit Bureau sells annual memberships ($150 for singles, $200 for couples), offering "fast-track" credit restoration, a newsletter, and other consumer education material.

country because it helps the consumers organize their matters *and* clean up their credit reports.

On behalf of an estimated 300 clients each year, Danielson engages in what he called "accountability combat," in which the "average client's credit report is cleaned up in four-to-seven months, and no one takes longer than two years." Danielson pointed out that the FCRA not only requires that credit reports be accurate, but that they are "relevant, confidential, and properly utilized" as well.

Danielson said he leverages the consumer's willingness to repay a loan so that the creditor reports information to the credit bureau in a manner most beneficial to the consumer. As an example, he cited the negative hit a credit report takes when a consumer pays an old charge-off or collection because it can "re-freshen" the "date-of-last-activity" (DLA), making the negative account "more recent," and consequently, cause greater damage to the credit score.

"FSCC believes people need to pay their bills and timely. Therefore, we 'fairly settle' many situations. However, we also get the proper paperwork in hand before payment is delivered, which protects our consumer clients from further abuse and victimization," the company stated in a fact sheet.

Danielson, who for years has hosted weekly radio shows focused on consumer finance, said that many of the people in the credit counseling industry are "collection agencies in disguise."

He said the most famous organizations, the non-profit National Foundation For Consumer Credit (NFCC) and Consumer Credit Counseling Services (CCCS), are actually a set of "non-profit franchises" that earn billions of dollars each year, primarily serving creditors' interests.

"The CCCS Web sites state that their average client takes five years to complete their program, and worse yet, there is no credit file clean-up. The bottom line is that you may end up having seven to fifteen more years of 'credit hell,'" he said. Danielson also warned of private companies that offer credit counseling, referring to them as "NFCC clones."

NFCC has a different view. On its Web site, it described how its member organizations help millions of debt-laden consumers at a low or reasonable price. It claimed to help some consumers by giving them a Debt Management Plan (DMP).

"Fair Isaac and Company (FICO), has publicly stated that since 1999 FICO has completely ignored any credit report mention of a Debt Management Plan arrangement with any counseling agencies. This is great news for consumers and credit counselors both. Therefore, credit counseling and DMP services *do not* negatively affect credit scores. As to consumers' ability to obtain credit, it is the discretion of individual creditors as to how they interpret a consumer's credit report history and their decision to extend credit," NFCC stated on its Web site.[195]

In 2003, the National Consumer Law Center (NCLC) and Consumer Federation of America (CFA) published a report, "Credit Counseling in Crisis," detailing the severe threat to consumers from a new generation of credit counseling agencies. The study found that, unlike the previous generation of mostly creditor-funded counseling services, these new agencies often harm debtors with improper advice, deceptive practices, excessive fees, and abuse of their non-profit status. An estimated nine million Americans have some contact with a consumer credit counseling agency each year, it found.[196]

Susan Keating, who in 2004 became the chief executive at NFCC, acknowledged to Michelle Singletary of the *Washington Post* that the credit-counseling industry was "in transition."

"I believe there are agencies out there that are not doing the right thing morally and ethically on the part of con-

---

[195] http://www.nfcc.org/AboutUs/nfccfactsbckgnd.pdf
[196] http://www.nclc.org/initiatives/credit_counseling/content/press_cc.pdf

sumers and are taking advantage of individuals when they are vulnerable," she said.[197]

Keating said she planned to work with Congress to push for federal legislation to weed out bad credit-counseling agencies. "NFCC remains committed to ensuring that consumers have access to high-quality, affordable financial-management advice and debt-relief services," she said.[198]

Keating said she wanted to get rid of the quick-fix debt operations that do little if any worthwhile credit counseling. She favored an industry that would not push "cookie-cutter" debt-repayment plans, but rather put more emphasis on financial education and counseling.[199]

A central problem with the approach of many credit counselors is that they often focus on negotiating lower monthly payments with credit card companies. But the card companies respond by reporting to the credit bureaus delinquencies each month because they are not receiving the required monthly payments. This approach continues to damage the consumer's credit score and represents a recipe for keeping a financially-strapped consumer in "credit jail."

Beyond Credit Report Errors

Daryl Yurek and J. Madison Ayer don't like the term "credit repair." Instead, they prefer to describe their young and growing company, Veracity Credit Consultants,[200] as representative of a new, pro-consumer approach in which helping customers remove errors from their credit reports is only one part of a suite of "optimization" services.

---

[197] Singletary, Michelle, "Growing Consumer Debt Requires Reliable Credit Counseling,"
    March 4, 2004; Page E03
[198] *Id.*
[199] *Id.*
[200] www.veracitycredit.com

"Traditional credit repair clinics focus strictly on the credit history, but that's only 35% of your credit score," Ayer said. "In addition to tackling the derogatory disputes, our service is heavily consultative, allowing us to educate and advise our clientele on the most effective way to ensure optimization of the remaining 65% of the credit score."

"Areas that are unclear to most consumers but can yield very meaningful improvements in credit scores include the use of revolving credit, ensuring the proper reporting of revolving credit limits, removal of any recent unauthorized inquiries, optimizing the mix of credit accounts for length and balance, etc. At this time we are not aware of any other fully consultative services."

The Denver-based firm doesn't advertise. Most of its customers come via referrals from mortgage lenders and brokers across the country.

Veracity conducts an initial consultation with prospective customers, but only ends up working with 75% of applicants, Ayer said.

"If someone is currently overextended and unable to make their monthly payments, then our program is not going to help them, as they'll just be piling up more delinquencies. We advise them to put the fee they would pay us towards existing bills until they are indeed stable. We want them as clients at some point, but only when we're really going to be able to help them," Ayer said.

Customers are charged $69 to set up a file and provide a detailed analysis and consultation. After that, they are billed $45 at the end of each 30-day period that service is provided. Customers can cancel at any time. About 80% of the customers renewed monthly, Ayer said.

'Rate Optimization'

Because most of its business comes from mortgage professionals, Veracity traditionally has focused on the "big-ticket" items: Mortgages and refinancing. But Ayer said that consumers need help with their credit card rates as well.

"As the credit industry moves more into risk-based pricing using credit scores, rates become more dynamic," he explained. "Each month, credit card companies check the credit scores of their cardholders for any drop in score from the previous month, and raise rates accordingly. However, interest rates do not automatically go down when the credit score goes up – this has to be specifically requested."

Veracity began testing services along these lines, he continued. One customer had several serious, inaccurate delinquencies, including a collection account, a credit card more than 150 days past due, three separate 30-day delinquencies on a bank line of credit, and a 30-day late on a Texaco gas card. Ayer said Veracity helped the customer get these errors removed. But the bad credit history had caused his credit card issuers to hike his rates to: 27.99% (MBNA); 20.99% (Chase); 20.49% (Advanta) and 12.74% (Citi).

"After correspondence with either the 'Customer Service,' 'Credit,' or 'Retention' departments at each of these four card companies, the rates were changed to the following: MBNA: 11.99% fixed; Advanta: 13.68%; Chase: 8.99% and CITI: 8.74% + 0% Balance Transfer for life of balance," he said.

The shrinkage of credit opportunities resulting from the subprime lending crisis has exposed weaknesses in risk-based pricing and heightened the importance of removing errors, Ayer said. "This is where accuracy will really begin to matter, because for consumers, their credit rating won't be the difference between a few points on the loan interest – it will be the difference of getting a house, or not getting a house," he explained.

Are we entering a new era in which companies can make a profit by ethically helping consumers not only fix credit report errors, but improve their overall credit standing? Yurek said he already saw this happening, and considered it a rational market response.

One can only hope he's right. Only time will tell.

Chapter 12

Debt Collection

> *Beautiful credit! The foundation of modern society...I wasn't worth a cent two years ago, and now I owe two millions of dollars.*
> – Mark Twain
> "The Gilded Age"

Unpaid debts, especially ones that have gone to collection, are bad news for your credit report.

Debt collection companies and creditors view the credit reporting system as a tool for debt collection. Often, debtors will pay or settle an account to avoid negative information appearing on their credit reports. For this reason, credit reporting is a "powerful tool designed, in part, to wrench compliance with payment terms."[201]

Of course, it's appropriate for companies to inform consumers that unless they take care of a valid debt by a certain deadline, accurate derogatory data will be reported to credit reporting agencies (CRAs). But it is highly improper to threaten to report—and to report—inaccurate data as a tactic to pressure a consumer to pay an amount that is in dispute.

Unfortunately, this happens all too often. Collectors of all stripes that "parking" an unpaid debt on a consumer's report is an easy and effective to collect a debt. That is because no creditor is going to extend credit to a consumer until he or she "resolves" outstanding unpaid collections or

---

[201] Rivera v. Bank One, 145 F.R.D. 64, 623 (D.P.R. 1993)

charge-offs. "Resolving" it means either removing it from your credit report, or paying it. Since deleting errors can be such a time-consuming or otherwise daunting task, there have been instances where consumers have paid debts that they did not owe – simply to be approved for a pending credit transaction.

One common problem is accounts that have gone to collection often result in duplicate or even triplicate negative accounts. Say your Chase card account was charged off and sent to collection. It is not uncommon for the debt to be reported separately by Chase and by the debt collector. If that collector fails to collect and the debt is sold to a third collector, still another negative entry to your credit report could result. Of course, there should only be one entry.

'Re-Aging'

A second common problem is known as "re-aging." This involves the debt collector reporting an account with a more recent date, like the date it began trying to collect on it, as opposed to the actual date the debt became delinquent, which is what is supposed to be reported.

The Federal Trade Commission already has brought two cases against debt collectors over re-aging, as well as other alleged violations of the Fair Credit Reporting Act and Fair Debt Collections Practices Act.

In the most recent case, the FTC brought suit against DC Credit Services, Inc., and its owner David Cohen. "In numerous instances, in the course and conduct of their business, defendants have reported information about debts to consumer reporting agencies using a date of delinquency other than the month and year of the delinquency that immediately preceded date,"[202] stated the FTC complaint, filed in a Los Angeles federal court on June 27, 2002.

Four days later, on July 1, 2002, DC Credit Services and Cohen settled the charges, agreeing to pay a $300,000 civil penalty and to notify CRAs to delete all adverse information the collection agency previously reported to them over the past seven years. The consent decree permanently banned Cohen from engaging in debt collection activity.[203]

Performance Capital Management

Two years earlier, the FTC filed suit against Performance Capital Management (PCM), another California debt collector. According to the complaint, PCM systematically reported accounts with delinquency dates that were more recent than the actual date of delinquency, resulting in negative information remaining on consumers' credit reports long beyond the seven-year period mandated by the FCRA. The Commission's complaint also alleged that PCM violated Section 623 by ignoring or failing to investigate consumer disputes referred by credit bureaus and by failing to notify credit bureaus when consumers disputed collection accounts with PCM.[204]

The FTC charged that PCM's practice of merely comparing the name, address, and information in PCM's computer database with the information provided on each consumer dispute verification form was inadequate.

"Where the two match, PCM reports that it has verified as accurate the information in its files. The actual records of the original creditor are not reviewed, nor is the

---

[202] U.S.A. v. DC Credit Services, Inc., et al.: U.S. Dist. Ct. – Central Dist. of California; Case No. 02-5115; The FTC alleged that this violated 15. U.S.C. § 1681s-2(a)(5) of FCRA; www.ftc.gov/os/2002/07/dcscmp.pdf
[203] "California-based Debt Collector Agrees To Pay, $300,000," FTC press release, July 1, 2002; www.ftc.gov/opa/2002/07/dccredserv.htm
[204] U.S.A. v. Performance Capital Management, et al.: U.S. Dist. Ct. – Central Dist. of California; www.ftc.gov/os/2000/08/performcomp.htm

matter referred to the original creditor for the original creditor to verify the accuracy of the information," stated the complaint.

"Because PCM collects accounts that are often old, information in its computer files may not be accurate for a variety of reasons, including incorrect updating of addresses, errors in recording names and information, and problems with the original creditor's records. Accordingly, verifying information in the computerized PCM file does not constitute an 'investigation' for purposes of Section 623(b) of the FCRA when a consumer disputes the accuracy of the information," the complaint stated.

Under an August 24, 2000 settlement, PCM was enjoined from "serious violations" of the FCRA. Because PCM was in bankruptcy, the FTC waived a $2 million fine.[205]

Re-Aging Grows Old

There are indications that some debt collectors have continued to use re-aging tactics to improve their chances of collecting old debts. In Chicago, Georgia Redd was the lead plaintiff in a potential class action lawsuit against Arrow Financial Services, LLC. Ms. Redd defaulted on a car loan in 1990; the car was repossessed and the debt charged off.

However, in October 2002, she received a letter from Arrow Financial Services, advising that the client was "willing to settle for 45% of full balance," and that if Ms. Redd paid $4,449.33, "the appropriate credit bureaus will be notified that this account has been settled."[206]

---

[205] "California Debt Collection Agency Settles FTC Charges," FTC Press Release, August 24, 2000; www.ftc.gov/opa/2000/08/performance.htm

[206] Amended Complaint, <u>Georgia Redd v. Arrow Financial Services, LLC</u>: USDC-N.D. Illinois (Eastern Div.); CA No. 03 C 1341; filed February 24, 2003; Ms. Redd is represented by Edelman, Combs & Latturner of Chicago.

Citing the FCRA's seven-year limit for derogatory information, the complaint stated, "No report concerning the (12-year-old) debt could legally appear on plaintiff's credit reports. The statement that if plaintiff paid money on account of the debt credit bureaus would be notified is misleading in that it tells the unsophisticated consumer that a credit bureau could report the payment, when that is not the case." (The case was pending when this book went to print.)

In October 2003, Ruth Zitka filed a separate suit against Asset Acceptance, LLC, over its alleged failure to remove duplicate accounts. Zitka's Trans Union report already listed her First USA credit card account, which was charged off as a bad debt in July 2000. However, the report also showed a collection account with an October, 2002 date for a First USA Bank as an "open account." When Zitka disputed the duplication with Trans Union, Asset Acceptance allegedly verified the debt as accurate.

"When Asset Acceptance reported it to Trans Union, it dated the debt October, 2002 or 27 months later. It also reported the debt as an 'open account,' which was not true (none of the debts purchased by Asset Acceptance remained 'open'), and which tells the credit bureau that the delinquency being reported is recent," the complaint charged.[207]

Recipe For Disaster

Imagine combining debt collectors' aggressive tactics with the credit bureaus' propensity to mix files so that collectors go after the wrong person. Then add in the credit bureaus' failure to correct the errors that are causing the problem in the first place.

That's what happened to Eric W. Carroll, a 29-year-old Newton, Massachusetts resident, whose financial life was

---

[207] Proposed Second Amended Complaint, <u>Ruth Zitka and Dyvonne Brown v. Asset Acceptance, LLC,</u>: USDC-N.D. Illinois (Eastern Div.); CA No. 03 C 1601; filed October 27, 2003; Plaintiffs are represented by Edelman, Combs & Latturner of Chicago.

hopelessly interwoven with that of a Florida man of the same name who, according to credit reports, appeared to have stiffed more than two dozen creditors, from banks to utilities, and had a history of bouncing checks. As a result, the Massachusetts Eric Carroll, living with his fiancé Nancy and their new baby, couldn't get a mortgage, couldn't rent an apartment in his own name, and could not buy an engagement ring without his father's help.

Carroll was one of scores who contacted the *Boston Globe* after its summer 2006 series on debt collection abuses.

"Many felt victimized by the power and ruthless tactics of debt collectors. But Carroll and others complained of another maddening aspect of the system: The glacial and ineffectual response of the three giant keepers of consumer credit records – Experian, Equifax, and TransUnion – to any errors in their files, even those that appear to result from fraud," the Globe reported. "Until the errors are corrected, debt collectors will try again and again to squeeze out a payment. Some back off when they find they're after the wrong consumer, but often, another firm buys the account and goes after the likes of Carroll again."[208]

One leading opponent of unethical debt collection practices is Bud Hibbs, a radio personality and author of "The American Credit System: Guilty Until Proven Innocent." His Web site listed 250 "Debt Collection Agencies, Scavenger Debt Buyers, & Collector Attorney - Law Offices" to avoid. (www.budhibbs.com)

"An often unfair credit system discriminates against those who do not understand how it works and can adversely affect the consumer on a daily basis," Hibbs said.

---

[208] Beth Healy, "Credit Agencies Lag on Errors, Fraud Consumers Struggle to Untangle Reports," *Boston Globe*, December 28, 2006; www.boston.com/news/local/massachusetts/articles/2006/12/28/credit_agencies_lag_on_errors_fraud/. The series prompted Rep. Frank to hold an oversight hearing in June 2007. "If you can't correct the report, that's a problem. You've got to be able to correct it," Frank told the *Globe*.

Chapter 13

Auto Insurance

Every move you make, Every vow you break,
Every smile you fake, Every claim you stake,
I'll be watching you

– The Police (Rock Group)
"Every Breath You Take"

When it comes to credit reports and how they are used, insurance may be the least known and most mysterious area. This is an oddity in a sense because from the beginning, the Fair Credit Reporting Act has declared that "insurance" is a permissible purpose for using credit reports. In this chapter, we will explore the insurance industry's use of traditional credit reports and scores, and then examine the rise and spread of a newer kind of report that details consumers' driving records and property claims history.

In the late 1990s, it became increasingly common for auto insurers to use credit scores in the course of deciding whether to cover drivers and what premium they should be charged. The practice grew increasingly controversial as public knowledge of the practice spread. Many people could not see the connection. Why should you have to pay a higher rate for your car insurance because you had unpaid bills or some other financial problem. Some consumers who had never had an accident or a moving violation were faced with sharply raised premiums when their renewal notices arrived.

The controversy quickly spread to state legislatures. As of January 2004, three states—Maryland, Utah, and

Washington—banned the practice outright. Twelve states have laws setting restrictions, often allowing insurers to use credit scores, but requiring that the score not be the sole determinant or reason for raising rates or denying coverage.[209]

Twenty-six states regulate insurers' use of credit scoring by requiring greater notice and reporting.[210]

Despite the movement to restrict use of credit scores, they are, in fact, used widely, particularly by auto insurers.

Stress & Risk-Taking

In fact, auto insurers are passionate in their belief the credit scores they use are one of the best predictors of future losses. Allstate Counsel Steven R. Sheffey said, "Credit-based insurance scoring is the most significant advancement in cost-based pricing in at least the past 30 years."[211] In the insurance world, you do not have to explain why certain kinds of data predict risk, only that they do, he said.

Sheffey said that authoritative research[212] showed there are two basic explanations as to why insurers are able

---

[209] Arkansas, Georgia, Hawaii, Idaho, Illinois, Louisiana, Minnesota, Missouri, Montana, Oklahoma, Washington, and Wisconsin. See the Web site of the National Association of Mutual Insurance Commissioners, http://www.namic.org/state/credithistory.asp, for an overview and, http://www.namic.org/state/creditlaws.asp, for a brief description of each State's law

[210] Arizona, California, Colorado, Delaware, Florida, Georgia, Idaho, Kansas, Maine, Maryland, Massachusetts, Missouri, Montana, Nebraska, New Hampshire, New Jersey, New York, Ohio, Oregon, Rhode Island, South Carolina, Texas, Utah, Virginia, Washington, and West Virginia. Some states have more than one kind of insurance-credit scoring law, hence the overlap. (See Footnote 209.)

[211] Letter from Steven R. Sheffey to Evan Hendricks (undated), received in February 2004.

[212] Sheffey said there were over 30 articles or studies supporting the stress and risk taker theories. One of them was "The Use of Credit History for Personal Lines of Insurance; Report to the National Association of Insurance Commissioners," American Academy of

to find information in your credit report that is predictive of future losses.

"The first explanation relates to stress. People under stress are more likely to have auto accidents. They may be more easily distracted or not react as well to certain situations (the difference between an accident and a near-miss is often just a fraction of a second). Financial problems are a known cause of stress. Therefore, some people with poor scores are more likely to experience stress and thus more likely to incur losses," Sheffey wrote.[213]

"The second explanation relates to risk-taking behavior," he continued. "Different people have different aversions to risk. Some people like to skydive. Some people are afraid of the amusement park roller coaster. Some people will run a yellow light if it was yellow when they first saw it. Some people will stay under 55 on the highway. People who are more likely to take risks are more likely to get into serious financial difficulties (bankruptcies, liens, foreclosures, etc.) than those who are more risk averse. As the studies show, people who are more likely to take risks are also more likely to get into auto accidents. Therefore, some people with poor scores are more likely to engage in risky behavior and thus more likely to incur losses. Similar reasoning probably applies to homeowners insurance as well."

"Neither, either, or both of these theories may be true for a particular individual. In some instances, financial difficulties might not be caused by risk-taking behavior, but will still produce stress. In other instances, however, it is the risk-taking behavior rather than stress that leads to a greater likelihood of loss," he wrote.

Sheffey said another theory is that "credit history reflects personal responsibility" and that one who prudently manages one's finances is prudent and responsible in the

---

Actuaries Risk Classification Subcommittee of the Property/Casualty Products, Pricing, and Market Committee., November 15, 2002
[213] Sheffey letter, op. cit.

realms of homes and cars as well.[214] A derivation would be that financially stable people would be more likely to pay for a minimal loss themselves "because they have the financial wherewithal, rather than file a claim."[215] Similarly, some insurers believe that financially stable individuals are likely to exhibit stability in many other aspects of their lives.[216]

Sheffey said Allstate was not aware of any research that supported these theories, but was emphatic that the risk-taking and stress theories were well supported by research.

Key Factors For Insurers

According to the American Insurance Association, here are some of the kinds of data from credit reports that are of most interest to insurance scoring models:

- Payment History
- Bankruptcies
- Collections
- Length Of Credit History
- Amount Of Outstanding Debt
- New Applications For Credit
- Types Of Credit In Use

The debate over the link between credit reports and insurability promises to continue, as few consumer advocates have been persuaded by Sheffey's arguments.

---

[214] Insurance Information Institute, *The Use of Credit Information as an Underwriting Tool in Personal Lines Insurance,* Brookings Institution Presentation, February 27, 2003.

[215] From an April 11, 2003 presentation by NAIC President and Arkansas Insurance Commissioner Mike Pickens, reported by AM Best on April 14, 2003.

[216] Insurance Information Institute, *The Use of Credit Information as an Underwriting Tool in Personal Lines Insurance,* Brookings Institution Presentation, February 27, 2003.

A Contrary View

Birny Birnbaum executive director of the Council for Economic Justice in Austin, Texas has led the fight against insurance credit scoring. He continually has challenged industry assertions that it is fair, that there is a correlation between credit history and insurance, or that the studies supporting it were credible.

"The 'evidence' supporting the correlation claim comes almost exclusively from insurers, insurer trade associations, and credit scoring vendors who refuse to divulge the methodology of their studies, details of the study results, and/or the underlying data for independent verification," Birnbaum wrote in a January 2003 report for the Ohio Civil Rights Commission.[217] "For those studies about which some information is known, the industry claims become more suspicious. For example, Fair, Isaac and Company continues to bring out the Tillinghast 'study' as support for the correlation—even though the National Association of Insurance Commissioners Credit Reports subgroup dismissed the 'study' as 'counterproductive and misleading.'"

Birnbaum said there is plenty of evidence to raise questions about the industry's correlation theory. For instance, while economic conditions vary greatly by geographic region, credit scoring models are developed on a national basis. One survey showed that in the fourth quarter of 2000, mortgage delinquencies in the South were almost 60% higher than in the West. "Consumers with high credit scores in a region with weak economic conditions were more likely to encounter problems than consumers with lower scores in a region with stronger economic conditions," Birnbaum wrote.[218]

---

[217] Birnbaum, Birny, "Insurers' Use of Credit Scoring for Homeowners Insurance In Ohio: A Report For the Ohio Civil Rights Commission," January 2003
[218] *Id.*

Then, there is bankruptcy data. "If consumers who have filed for bankruptcy in the past five years are far more likely to have claims than consumers who have not filed for bankruptcies, then we would expect an increase in loss ratios if the number of bankruptcies increases dramatically. Personal bankruptcies did increase dramatically during the 1990's, yet private passenger auto insurance loss ratios *declined.* The following data show a *negative* correlation— just the opposite of the positive correlation claimed by the insurance industry," he wrote.[219]

Birnbaum argued that credit scoring allows insurers to price based on the profitability of the consumer, as opposed to the expected risk of loss. In sum, it provides a shortcut for underwriting and rating consumers by income.

He said that other profitability factors include:

- Credit scoring makes possible the expansion beyond the traditional tiers of "preferred, standard, and non-standard." With more tiers, consumers can be identified for higher rates because of their place on the credit scoring scale.

- In most states, insurers' changes to underwriting guidelines receive no scrutiny. Consequently, an insurer could simply raise the cutoff score for rating tier eligibility by, say, ten points, and effectively create a 10% rate increase without making a rate filing or any other regulatory oversight.

- Credit scoring enables larger insurers to build a base of customers more likely to purchase other financial products, including life insurance, retirement products, and traditional banking products.

- Since the FCRA allows insurers to use credit reports to market to consumers without their permission (prescreening), insurers can essential-

---

[219] *Id.*

ly "redline," that is, target consumers based upon their economic profiles.[220]

Insurers' use of credit reports and credit scores proved controversial for other reasons. Some companies were accused of failing to provide consumers with "adverse action notices" informing them that they were being charged more for insurance because of information in their credit report. Other insurers have been accused of pulling the credit reports of spouses and even non-family housemates who were not included in the policy. But before discussing these issues, let's briefly examine the way in which auto insurers typically use credit reports.[221]

Silence Of The Agents

Birnbaum said an important voice was not being heard: insurance agents.

"There are hundreds of agents who want to come forward and tell why they are opposed to credit scoring, why credit scoring has worsened insurance availability, and how credit scoring has a disproportionate impact on poor and minority consumers. But they won't be here today because of their fear of reprisal by the insurance companies they represent. To hear from these agents, they must be given protection against these reprisals. To give you a sense of who these agents are, the following agent organizations have come out against credit scoring—National Association of State Farm Agents, National Association of Professional All-state Agents, and the United Farmers Agents Association.[222]

---

[220] *Id.*

[221] Birnbaum, "Insurance Credit Scoring: An Unfairly Discriminatory Practice," before the Michigan Insurance Committee, July 2003

[222] *Id.*

The Texas Study

In a Jan. 31, 2005, Texas Insurance Commissioner Jose Montemayor said that his study found that credit scores were a reliable predictor future losses, "finding there was a strong relationship between credit scores and claims experience on an aggregate basis."[223]

"Prior to the study, my initial suspicions were that while there may be a correlation to risk, credit scoring's value in pricing and underwriting risk was superficial, supported by the strength of other risk variables," he wrote.

If that proved to be the case, Montemayor said he would have effectively banned insurers' use of credit scores.

"The study, however, did not support those initial suspicions," he wrote. "Credit scoring, if continued, is not unfairly discriminatory as defined in current law because credit scoring is not based on race, nor is it a precise indicator of one's race. Recall that not all minorities are in the worst credit score categories. Further, its use is justified actuarially and it adds value to the insurance transaction. Without a change in statute that disallows credit scoring as a matter of public policy, any action to ban may be tied up in court for several years, further frustrating public expectation."

On the other hand, the study found a "consistent pattern of differences in credit scores among the different racial/ethnic groups. The average credit scores for Whites and Asians are better than those for Blacks and Hispanics. In addition, Blacks and Hispanics tend to be over-represented in the worse credit score categories and under-represented in the better credit score categories."

It also found "a consistent pattern of differences in credit scores depending on an individual's age, with younger people having worse credit scores than older people. The best average credit scores are for individuals older than 70."

---

[223] Jan. 31, 2005 letter by Jose Montemayor to Gov. Rick Perry, et al. www.tdi.state.tx.us/general/pdf/credit05sup.pdf; also see Dec. 31, 2004 study www.tdi.state.tx.us/general/pdf/creditall04.pdf

It Started With Marketing

The move to start using credit reports probably was in part due to effective marketing by the "Big Three" credit reporting agencies (CRAs). The pitch was that credit scores were a better predictor of future losses than were the insurers' customary methods at the time. To test this theory, some insurers provided CRAs with a list of customers, some of whom had losses. The CRAs would then append each customer's credit score and return the list. This allowed the insurers, using their own statistical tools, to correlate credit scores to losses. Most insurers became convinced that consumers with lower credit scores were more likely to have future losses.

It used to be that car insurers only used "underwriting" criteria when deciding whether to grant insurance or how much to charge for it. "Underwriting" criteria includes age, driving record, geographic location, and type of car. But given their belief that credit scores were reliable predictors, insurers had to find a way to integrate credit scores into their "decisioning" models.

To accomplish this, insurers had to create a whole new formula, or matrix. An example was the new approach taken in the late 1990s by The Progressive Corporation, which sells auto insurance in most states.[224] Progressive traditionally had divided consumers into five "markets" or "tiers" based upon their predicted risk or future losses:

- Ultra-Preferred (The Best)
- Preferred (Good)
- Standard (Regular)
- Mid-Market (Not Good)
- Non-Standard (Very Bad or Sub-Prime)

---

[224] Information about Progressive's policies and practices was included in court filings in U.S. District Court for the Northern District of Florida (Gainesville Division), in Cathryn Smith, et al. v. The Progressive Corp., et al. (Case No. 1:00-CV-210-MMP). The lead attorney was Terry Smiljanich of James, Hoyer, Newcomer and Smiljanich, of Tampa, Fla.

Again, in the old, pre-1997 system, it was purely underwriting criteria that placed you in one of these categories. Presumably, if you had a perfect driving record, and you were the right age, drove the right kind of car, and met the other *driving-related* underwriting criteria, you would get the Ultra-Preferred rate.

The Progressive Matrix

Under the new system, Progressive created its own insurance-credit scoring system that divided consumers into the same five categories. That is to say, Progressive did not obtain from the CRAs a traditional FICO score. Rather, Progressive developed its own proprietary scoring model. Progressive's scoring model would then examine the information in the consumer's credit report that it believed was most predictive of future loss, and rate the driver. The credit score was then blended or cross-matched with the consumer's underwriting status. If you had an Ultra-Preferred credit score and an Ultra-Preferred underwriting rating, you would get the Ultra-Preferred rate. However, it did not matter if you had a perfect driving record. If you did not have a top-notch credit score according to Progressive's proprietary model, you were not eligible for Progressive's Ultra-Preferred rate. Progressive put such emphasis on information in your credit report that a bad credit score "dragged you down faster" than a bad underwriting rating.

To better understand the impact of credit scores and how they were cross-matched against the underwriting rating in order to rate consumers, take a look at the chart on page 239. The "A-E" row at the top, running left to right, represents the consumer's credit score, or "financial responsibility," with "A" being the best and "E" being the worst.

The "A-G" row, running down the left side of the page, represents the consumer's underwriting rating or "value." As mentioned the five categories are:

- Ultra-Preferred ("UL," The Best)
- Preferred ("PR," Good)
- Standard ("ST," Regular)
- Mid-Market ("MM," Not Good)
- Non-Standard ("NS," Very Bad or Sub-Prime)

The top row, running left-to-right, describes a consumer with the highest underwriting rating ("A"), but whose status drops with her credit score ("UL-to-MM"). Only with the best credit score can this consumer obtain the Ultra-Preferred rate. If her credit score is good or average, she gets the Preferred Rate, but if her credit score is below average, she gets the Standard rate. If her credit score is sub-prime, she gets the Mid-Market rate, second from the lowest.

The Progressive Matrix

	Credit Score (Financial Responsibility)				
	A	**B**	**C**	**D**	**E**
Underwriting					
Value Column					
A	UL	PR	PR	ST	MM
B	UL	PR	ST	ST	MM
C	PR	ST	ST	MM	MM
D	PR	ST	ST	MM	NS
E	PR	ST	MM	MM	NS
F	ST	MM	MM	NS	NS
G	ST	MM	NS	NS	NS

Now compare that to the bottom left corner, describing a problem driver with the worst possible underwriting value ("G"), who still gets a regular— "Standard" rate—because his credit score is top-notch. Similarly, someone with the worst underwriting value, but with a good ("B") credit score, pays the Mid-Market rate— the same rate as the person we described above with the best driving-underwriting record and a subprime credit score. This Matrix underscored Progressive's apparent belief that the credit score was as good or better a predictor of future losses than its traditional underwriting criteria.

This Matrix enabled Progressive and independent insurance agents to give preliminary quotes to drivers. If the consumers indicated they were interested in purchasing insurance at the given quote, Progressive (or the insurance agent in some instances) would seek to verify their driving and claims history by ordering a separate report from Choice-Point. A spin-off of Equifax, ChoicePoint gathers publicly available data from federal, state and local courts, state motor vehicle departments, other state licensing agencies, and sometimes, voting records. Just as the CRAs receive data from their customers—the credit grantors—so does ChoicePoint receive regular reports from insurance companies on people who file insurance claims. This information is stored in its database, "Claims Loss Underwriting Exchange" or CLUE. A driving history (MVR) or CLUE report can affect the final quote given the consumer. (ChoicePoint and CLUE Reports are discussed in more detail below and in subsequent chapters.)

Progressive officials testified they only applied this model to new customers, not to renewing customers. This apparently meant that if you were initially covered by Progressive when you had a good credit rating, it would not hurt your renewal rate if your credit score went down. But if the opposite were true—you signed up when you had a bad credit rating but had since improved it—you were stuck at the less favorable rate, unless you knew to ask to be re-rated.

Although there is limited data about how each insurer uses credit reports, there is reason to believe many use them in a fashion similar to Progressive. They develop their own proprietary model for scoring credit report data and then cross-match it against traditional underwriting criteria.

Adverse Action Notices

Progressive's practices came to light because it was sued for not giving adequate adverse action notices. Rather than inform each consumer that their car insurance quote was higher because of data in their credit report, Progressive gave all customers a form letter stating that the company some-times used credit reports, and that these reports "may" have affected the premium. The lawsuit charged that a generalized form letter, telling all consumers that their premiums "may" have been affected, was not specific enough. (The case settled, with Progressive agreeing to send proper notices.)

The discovery in the case revealed that the FTC staff in 2000 advised Progressive that its generalized form letter was not specific enough to meet the FCRA's adverse action requirements.

Even before that, the Independent Insurance Agents of America (IIAA) in 1997, said in a policy statement that its members were "not presently convinced that there exists a clear and relevant correlation between an individual's credit history and a consumer's actual or potential loss experience." The IIAA recommended that credit information only be used if "insurance companies prove to the satisfaction of state insurance regulators that there exists a direct and relevant correlation between an individual's credit history and actual loss experience." The IIAA also called on insurance commissioners to ensure that insurers' use of credit data does not result in race or sex discrimination.

If insurers were to use credit scores, it was vital that adverse action notices be given when information causes a denial of coverage or increase in the rates, it concluded.

ChoicePoint: Key Auto Insurance Player

In recent years, ChoicePoint has emerged as the premier player in both auto insurance and homeowners insurance. In fact, one insurance official referred to Choice-Point "as the only game in town" when it came to driving records. Starting as a spin-off of Equifax, ChoicePoint has grown dramatically in recent years. During 2002, the company produced $753.0 million in core revenue, a 19% increase from $631.7 million in 2001.[225] In 2004, the company earned $148 million on revenue of $919 million.

It has expanded in many directions. It services the insurance industry through its electronic data exchange network in which insurers provide claims data and ChoicePoint sells it back to insurers. This system in many ways mirrors the traditional credit reporting system presided over by Equifax, Experian, and Trans Union.

Another key to ChoicePoint's success has been its ability to harvest public records maintained mainly by state and local governments—motor vehicle records, court records, licensing records, and voting records. In this area, ChoicePoint has moved aggressively to purchase smaller, local companies that specialized in public records—much the same way the Big Three CRAs bought up smaller credit bureaus and consolidated their hold over the market from the 1980s to the present.

First, we'll look at ChoicePoint's driving-related information services. Then, we'll examine its property-related services. Remember, much of the consumer information maintained by ChoicePoint qualifies as a consumer report regulated by the Fair Credit Reporting Act. At the end of this chapter, we will provide contact information for obtaining your various CLUE reports, which you can now get once a year at no charge.

---

[225] www.corporate-ir.net/ireye/ir_site.zhtml?ticker=CPS&script=2100

Driving: 'CLUE' & "MVR' Reports

ChoicePoint serves as a clearinghouse for both insurance claims information through its CLUE Personal Auto database, and through its Motor Vehicle Records (MVR) service. CLUE stands for Comprehensive Loss Underwriting Exchange.

"CLUE Personal Auto is a claim history information exchange that enables insurance companies to access prior claim information in the underwriting and rating process," ChoicePoint stated on its Web site. "CLUE Personal Auto reports contain up to five years of personal automobile claims matching the search criteria submitted by the inquiring insurance company. Data provided in CLUE reports includes policy information such as name, date of birth, and policy number; claim information such as date of loss, type of loss, and amounts paid; and vehicle information. More than 95 percent of insurers writing automobile coverage provide claims data to the CLUE Personal Auto database."[226]

ChoicePoint Codes & Categories

In addition to the identifying information, the CLUE Personal Auto report typically features the following codes to denote who was at fault (if known):

- **(AF)** – At Fault
- **(NF)** – No Fault
- **(UN)** – Undetermined
- **(PF)** – Partial Fault
- **( )** – Unknown or Unreported

---

[226] www.choicepoint.com/business/pc_ins/us_5.html

Another set of codes reflects the loss that was incurred:

BI – Bodily injury	**PD** – Physical/Property damage
CD – Collision deductible	**PI** – Personal injury protection
CO – Collision	**RR** – Rental reimbursement
CP – Comprehensive	**TL** – Towing and labor
ME – Medical Expense	**UM** – Uninsured motorist
MP – Medical Payment	**UN** – Underinsured motorist
OT – Other	

A typical Personal Auto report lists the disposition of the claim (closed, open, or in "subrogation"), the amount paid and date of first payment, type of vehicle, vehicle identification number (VIN), and disposition of the vehicle (e.g., repaired, stolen, totaled, damaged, no compensation).

'Possible Related Claims'

The Personal Auto report also may include information on "Possible Related Claims" (PRC) defined as a "match" between the consumer who the insurer is inquiring about, and other individuals at the same address. "PRC means there is a match found on the address and at least one other identical data element, such as driver's license, SSN, policy number or last name," ChoicePoint explained in its sample report.[227] "ChoicePoint encourages the insurance company to resolutely determine if these claims relate to the subject on whom the search criteria is underlined."

In other words, ChoicePoint "encourages" insurers to avoid misjudging consumers on the basis of mixed files or other inaccuracies. But in traditional credit reporting, as well as among law enforcement agencies using criminal history data exchanges, such nuances can be lost among users. Too often, once the user sees the data on the computer screen, a

---

[227] http://www.choicepoint.com/sample_rpts/CLUEAutoUnderwriter.pdf

match is assumed, and the consumer is judged accordingly.

Similarly, the report can include "Possible Additional Drivers." ChoicePoint said it "encourages the insurance company to verify this information prior to making business decisions." At the top of the "Possible Additional Drivers" section, it reads, "Additional driver might not reside in household or be associated with insured. This information should be independently verified prior to use. This report is not a recommendation."[228]

Insurers wanting to investigate drivers also can order the following "supplemental reports:"

- **ADD** – Additional Drivers in Household
- **SAFESCAN** – Potential Fraudulent Information Warnings. Informs the insurer if the applicants address has been subject to "misuse," or is a post office, campground, hotel/motel, check cashing facility, storage facility, telephone answering service, or unverifiable.
- **VIN-D-CODE** – Vehicle descriptions based upon vehicle information number
- **ISO/GUS Automobile** – Risk address territory rating
- **ISO/GUS Crime** – Risk address crime indices, showing how many crimes and what kinds, in the neighborhood of the insurance applicant
- **Inquiries** – Six month history of insurance applications
- **Current Carrier** – Past or present lapses in insurance coverage

Through the MVR service, "ChoicePoint provides driving records, including standard violation codes, from all 50 states and three Canadian provinces in an easy-to-read standardized format," the ChoicePoint Web site explains.

---

[228] *Ibid*

"Online access to driving records is available for 40 states and two provinces, and ChoicePoint continues to add to the list of states with online access," the company said on its Web site. It said the advantages of the MVR included a "single interface to all state Departments of Motor Vehicles," and "Standard input and output record format."[229] A sample of a driving report, and an explanation of how to read it, was available at the ChoicePoint Web site.[230]

When compared with the traditional credit reporting agencies, ChoicePoint's CLUE reports were relatively new and had stayed under the radar screen. Thus, it had not been subjected to the same level of public scrutiny. To date, there has been no independent assessment of the accuracy of data in ChoicePoint's varying and large and growing databases.

Harbinger, Or Fluke?

There was abundant reason to believe that Choice-Point would experience the same inaccuracy issues as its brethren in the credit reporting industry.

For example, in one case, an insurer raised a consumer's auto insurance premium based upon a ChoicePoint report of a traffic citation, even before the court rendered a decision on the citation. The consumer disputed the inaccuracy, pointing out that the citation had not even been adjudicated. But ChoicePoint said it was merely passing on information, serving as an electronic go-between the insurance companies and the Department of Motor Vehicles (DMV). ChoicePoint said it could not correct the information because it was not responsible for it. Only the DMV could correct it, ChoicePoint argued.

Like so many other issues involving personal information, the question of which entity is responsible for ensuring accuracy under the FCRA will have to be decided by the courts.

---

[229] http:// www.choicepoint.com/business/pc_ins/us_5.html
[230] http://www.choicepoint.com/sample_rpts/mvrhowtoread.pdf

How To Obtain Your CLUE Reports

Under the 2003 amendments to the FCRA, known as the "Fair and Accurate Credit Transactions Act (FACT Act)," consumers are entitled one free copy of their consumer file during each 12-month period.

ChoicePoint said it has three "products" that are free under the FACT Act: the C.L.U.E. (auto and homeowners insurance); "WorkPlace Solutions" (employment background screening) and "Tenant History" (apartment rentals). You can order these online, via toll free phone number, or through the mail. Here's the contact information:

www.choicetrust.com
C.L.U.E. Auto or Homeowners Reports
ChoicePoint Consumer Disclosure Center
P.O. Box 105295
Atlanta, GA 30348
1-(866) 312-8076

WorkPlace Solutions
ChoicePoint Consumer Disclosure Center
P.O. Box 105292
Atlanta, GA 30348
1-(866) 312-8075

Tenant History
Resident Data Consumer Disclosure Center
P.O. Box 850126
Richardson, TX 75085-0126
1-(877) 448-5732

ChoicePoint said there would be no C.L.U.E report on you if you had not filed an auto or home insurance during the last five years.

However, it also said it would not have an employment history or tenant history report "if you have not applied for employment with a customer that we serve," or "have not submitted a residential lease application with a customer that we serve."[231]

How could it not have a "report" on you, but then sell one to an employer or landlord when they asked for it? Under ChoicePoint's interpretation, you apparently could not check the accuracy of a report *before* it was sold to a landlord or employer. But the FCRA requires that *every* CRA shall, upon request, disclose to the consumer "*all information in the consumer's file.*" This fundamental question of access might have to be decided by the courts.

ChoicePoint 'Full File' Disclosure

Because of a class-action settlement, you can request your ChoicePoint "Full File Disclosure," which includes such public records items on file as real estate transactions and ownership data, lien, judgment, and bankruptcy records, professional license information, and historical addresses. You need to fill out the form found at the link in footnote 231, which you can also find it at www.ChoiceTrust.com, and clicking on "Access Your Personal Information."[232]

ChoicePoint Consumer Center
Attn. Full File Disclosure
PO Box 105108
Atlanta, Ga. 30348-5108

---

[231] www.choicepoint.com/factact.html, visited March 13, 2005
[232] www.choicetrust.com/servlet/com.kx.cs.servlets.CsServlet?channel=welcome&subchannel=disclosure; The 2007 settlement came in Campos v. ChoicePoint Services, Inc., 1-03-CV- 3577 (N.D. Ga. 2007). James Pietz, of Pittsburgh, PA, & Leo Bueno, Coral Gables, FL, were lead attorneys.

Unregulated Data?

In addition, ChoicePoint claimed that other consumer data it sold was not subject to the FCRA and therefore need not be disclosed to consumers. This is because the company and its subsidiaries tap a wide range of taxpayer-subsidized sources, including local property records; driver records; boating, pilot and professional licenses; and court records showing bankruptcies, liens, judgments and divorce. The company had accumulated 19 billion records with personal data, according to media reports. It was not entirely clear how ChoicePoint organized and "housed" all of the information. But presumably much of it was out of reach to the average consumer. That meant you could not see your data or correct errors -- even though other companies and government agencies could buy the same data and use them for making decisions about you.

The Electronic Privacy Information Center challenged ChoicePoint's claims of not being regulated by any federal law, particularly for its "AutoTrackXP," which "locates and verifies assets" or helps investigate fraud, and for its "Customer Identification Programs," which mainly help banks verify the identities of new customers.

At a March 15, 2005 hearing before the Senate Banking Committee, Sen. Charles Schumer (D-NY) told a ChoicePoint executive that given the company's poor performance in preventing identity theft, it did not belong in the business of selling personal information.

Citing the Mary Boris case (see next chapter), Sen. Jim Bunning (R-KY) castigated ChoicePoint for its inability to protect sensitive information like Social Security numbers. "And this is information you probably should not be selling in the first place," said Bunning, an advocate of greater protection for SSNs.[233]

---

[233] "Identity Theft: Recent Developments Involving the Security of Sensitive Consumer Information," Senate Banking Committee hearing, March 10 & 15, 2005

ChoicePoint responded by appointing a Chief Privacy Officer and improving its internal policies, as well as its communications with privacy experts and the public. It even endorsed the concept of legislation to give consumers stronger rights, akin to the FCRA, in relation to non-credit database companies like ChoicePoint, LexisNexis/Seisint, Westlaw and Acxiom. While none of the several legislative proposals to that effect were adopted by Congress as of September 2007, many felt it was only a matter of time.

http://banking.senate.gov/index.cfm?Fuseaction=Hearings.Detail&HearingID=144 and
http://banking.senate.gov/index.cfm?Fuseaction=Hearings.Detail&HearingID=142

Chapter 14

Homeowners Insurance

> *You have the right to remain silent.*
> *Anything you say, can and will be used*
> *against you . . .*
>
> -- Criminal Suspect's Rights Under
> <u>Miranda v. Arizona</u> (45 US 123)

One ChoicePoint product that has aroused controversy is "CLUE Personal Property." [234] This system was designed to keep track of claims filed by homeowners going back five years. More than 90 percent of homeowner insurance companies furnish data to CLUE Personal Property, ChoicePoint said on its Web site. [235]

According to the rather drab description on the company Web site, "The CLUE reports include policy information such as name, date of birth, and policy number, and claim information such as date of loss, type of loss, and amounts paid."

This product became controversial for a couple of reasons. First, anecdotal information indicated there was a significant error rate that directly caused wrongful denials of

---

[234] C.L.U.E. stands for Comprehensive Loss Underwriting Exchange
[235] http://www.ChoicePoint.com/industry/insurance/pc_ins_up_2.html, visited January 23, 2004

homeowner policies or hikes in premiums. Second, some people have found their premiums were raised for simply asking questions about their coverage. Others saw their rates go up after they reported minor damage, but refrained from filing a claim.

Put simply, because of ChoicePoint's CLUE, you should be very careful about communicating with your insurer about your homeowners policy, because anything you say can and might be used against you. Even what you might ask could hurt you.

Complaints On The Rise

For these reasons, complaints over property insurers were on the rise. The California Department of Insurance (CDI) said in 2001 it only received 318 formal complaints. By the third quarter of 2003, it had received 1,200 written complaints. In 2003, it continued receiving over 100 complaints per month.[236]

Some of the complaints came from Californians who simply inquired about their insurance policies, such as:

- Ken Pfeffer, 71-year-old Carlsbad homeowner who said he was "blacklisted" after his wife Patricia made a telephone inquiry about their policy coverage with State Farm. They had homeowner's insurance for 30 years and had never filed a claim.
- Rachelle Goldberg, a San Diego resident whose homeowner's policy was "non-renewed" by Travelers Insurance after making a telephone inquiry regarding her coverage. Her insurer listed this inquiry as a claim on the national CLUE Report.
- An unnamed San Francisco woman was denied coverage by Nationwide Insurance due to CLUE

---

[236] http://www.insurance.ca.gov/PRS/PRS2003/fs057-03.htm

data that reported a "water claim" she filed while insured by State Farm. The consumer never filed a water claim, but rather called her agent to see if a clogged pipe would be covered by her policy. The information was entered by State Farm into the CLUE database as a claim. There was no claim and no loss in this case. The consumer was unaware that these data existed. It was not until CDI intervened on her behalf that State Farm corrected the record.[237]

Other complaints concerned inaccurate or misleading data, such as:

- Joe and Clementine Whelan, of Spring Valley, whose homeowners' policy was cancelled by Meritplan Insurance Company due to a leaky pipe under their sink. The leak actually occurred before they purchased the home, but the claim showed up on a CLUE report.
- One unnamed Southern California man was rejected by 45 insurance companies before somebody told him the problem stemmed from a CLUE report.[238]
- A first-time homebuyer was denied coverage due to a "water damage claim" at his previous address. In reality, this consumer did not own the home where the damage had occurred. It was his brother's home and he merely stayed with him for a period of time. But because he listed it as his previous address, it popped up on the CLUE database and the previous activity wrongfully affected his ability to obtain insurance.

[237] *Id.*
[238] Walter, Bob, "Home Insurance Now At A Premium," *Sacramento Bee*, March 16, 2003, Page: A1

Drawing Commissioner Attention

The complaints prompted California Insurance Commissioner John Garamendi to adopt emergency regulations to strengthen his residents' rights in regard to their CLUE data, and to curb the insurers' policy of "you use it, you lose it." Several California lawmakers introduced bills to regulate CLUE, but none were enacted into law.[239]

"ChoicePoint, the company that owns and manages the CLUE database, is quick to compare CLUE to a credit report. Consumers are at a serious information disadvantage because they do not know the database exists, may not be told by insurers that their denial of coverage is due to a CLUE report, and do not know how to obtain a copy of their report to review it and dispute errors," Garamendi Web site stated.[240]

He expressed concern that CLUE reports were replacing basic underwriting principles. Instead of studying the probability of future losses, companies were making too many decisions based on CLUE loss history reports, he told the *Sacramento Bee*. For example, consider a water claim that results when a tree falls on a roof during a storm. "If the tree is removed and the roof is replaced and the damage is repaired," he said, "then the future risk is lower, not higher."[241]

Garamendi's assistant, Nanci Kramer, added, "What we can't tolerate is seeing somebody who files one claim after 15 years and finds himself in insurance no man's land. We don't want people to be afraid to use the insurance they are paying for."[242]

Despite these anecdotes, insurers defend CLUE reports as generally reliable and as simply one of many tools

---

[239] See SB 64, by Senator Jackie Speier; SB 691 by Senator Martha Escutia, AB 81 by Assemblyman Wyland
[240] http://www.insurance.ca.gov/PRS/PRS2003/fs057-03.htm
[241] Walter, Bob, *Sacramento Bee*, op cit.
[242] *Id.*

they use to assess risk. After all, they said, past history is a critical element for evaluating both properties and customers.

Industry: One Loss Leads To Another

"Our analysis shows that if you had a loss in the last three years, you are 25-30 percent more likely to have a loss in the next 12 months," said Kevin Kelso of Farmers. "If you had two losses, it's 75 percent more likely. This seems to be pretty intuitive in auto insurance, and it's always been true in homeowners as well."[243]

Robert Hartwig of the Insurance Information Institute said the CLUE reports are invaluable for aspiring homebuyers as well as legitimate tools for setting rates.

"Insurance inherently draws a distinction between different groups," he said. "The fact is that some people file very few claims and others file quite a few. If you restrict the tools, you create a less equitable system in which everybody pays the same ... you effectively have low-risk customers subsidizing the rest."

As for the issue of consumer inquiries, Ernest Burley Jr., a Maryland-based insurance agent for State Farm, told the *Washington Post's* Michelle Singletary that policyholders should make it clear when they call their insurer that they are only seeking advice and do not want a claim filed.[244]

In July 2003, ChoicePoint sent a letter to insurers reminding them what information should be reported, according to ChoicePoint V.P. Jeffrey A. Skelton.

"Claim information should be reported to CLUE when there has been a request from an insured or claimant for payment as a result of a loss," the letter stated. "Claims information should not be reported when a customer merely asks questions about their coverage or deductible."[245]

---

[243] *Id.*

[244] Singletary, Michelle, "Loose Lips, Higher Premiums?" *Washington Post,* October 5, 2003; pg. F1

[245] *Id.*

Important Call

But insurance companies argue that calls about a possible claim can tip them off to future problems, especially in regards to such prevalent and expensive claims as mold or water damage.

"The issue is not really a question of defining what is a claim and what is not, but what information has a bearing on future risk," P.J. Crowley, vice president of the Insurance Information Institute, wrote in a response to questions submitted by the *Post's* Singletary.

"Consumers tend to look at dollar amounts and conclude that something that happened didn't cost the insurance company any money, so no harm, no foul. Insurance companies pay a lot more attention to the frequency of problems occurring in the home, as opposed to the severity, as being a key predictor of future risk and future claims."

For example, suppose your home was broken into and a television set was stolen. You might call your insurance company to report the burglary but then decide not to file a claim because the television set is worth less than your deductible.[246]

"In the consumer's mind, there is no claim," Crowley wrote. "However, to the insurance company, there is information that is associated with higher risk, since the house was broken into."

Crowley said claims or calls that indicate damage or losses in the home are used by insurers to evaluate the likelihood that another claim will be filed on that property over the next 12 months and what the homeowner should be charged in premiums as a result.

Some insurance companies ignore information that didn't involve a payment, what insurers refer to as a "zero paid claim" or "claim closed without payment." Travelers, for example, did not consider zero-paid claims when consid-

---

[246] *Id.*

ering renewals or new customers, said Travelers Spokeswoman Marlene Ibsen.

Other insurers pay attention to everything in the
CLUE report. How a company treats the information will
vary by company, market, and state regulation, Crowley
said. Crowley recommended that when shopping for
insurance, ask the agent about the insurer's policy on
handling claims closed without payment.

The debate assuredly will rage on and occupy state
insurance commissioners and policy makers for years to
come.

Subject To FCRA

However, it should not be forgotten that ChoicePoint,
CLUE and like services are all subject to the FCRA. One
consumer who remembered was Mary Boris, a Kentucky
woman who sued after inaccurate data caused CNA
Insurance not to renew her automobile and homeowners
policies. Boris' CLUE report showed she had made four fire
claims and an "extended loss" claim over a short period of
time. In fact, Boris had made four water-related claims.

After some back-and-forth, ChoicePoint finally corrected the errors, but they all reappeared a few months later.
This frustrated Boris' effort to get affordable insurance.
Although she filed suit in May 2001, the mistakes remained
on her report until March 2002.

In court, ChoicePoint argued that it satisfied the
FCRA's requirement of reasonable procedures for accuracy
(§1681e(b)) because it "accurately transcribed information
from a reputable third party." It also asserted it was
absolved from liability because CNA was circulating the
same false information to other consumer reporting agencies.

But the jury was not persuaded. It slapped
ChoicePoint with $250,000 in punitive damages and
$197,000 in compensatory damages. Chief U.S. District
Judge John G. Heyburn II said that punitives were justified

because of the need to "punish" a "corporate conglomerate like ChoicePoint."

Considering ChoicePoint was notified several times about the mistakes and still didn't correct them, Judge Heyburn said, "A jury could certainly conclude that a reasonably prudent company would have prevented a similar outcome."

"ChoicePoint never took responsibility for assuring that its data was accurate," he continued. "Third, Choice-Point never really explained the computer glitches which apparently caused this problem. To this day, the court is still unclear what procedures, if any, ChoicePoint uses to insure the accuracy of its mass circulated reports."

"To be sure, this is not a case, as ChoicePoint seeks to paint it, where there was an isolated instance of human error which ChoicePoint promptly cured, or where, upon discovery, ChoicePoint quickly took ameliorative action. Nor is it an instance where ChoicePoint can defend itself by simply claiming it relied on information it assumed was accurate, or where it assumed its actions were lawful," he wrote.

"With that in mind, the following facts likely account for the large verdict: 1) ChoicePoint knew the FCRA's requirements; (2) it was on notice that there was a problem with Plaintiff's report, but failed to correct those problems; (3) ChoicePoint failed to take seriously the computer problems even after they became known; (4) not one of ChoicePoint's employees ever accepted responsibility for the accuracy of the claims data and, in fact, everyone blamed others; (4) ChoicePoint showed a complete lack of sympathy for Plaintiff's problems; and (5) throughout trial, ChoicePoint made several ill-advised efforts at trial to blame or criticize Plaintiff for her own problems. Second, the punitive damages are not out of proportion to the compensatory damages nor do they appear disproportional to the resources of the company. The Sixth Circuit has said, since the FCRA is intended to protect consumers, it is to be liberally construed in support of that purpose," Judge Heyburn wrote.[247]

In a March 15, 2005 Senate Banking Committee hearing, Sen. Jim Bunning (R-KY) cited Judge Heyburn's opinion and asked ChoicePoint Vice President Don McGuffey what procedures his company had in place to ensure accuracy.

Seemingly unprepared for the question, McGuffey said the company had a dispute-handling process in place to comply with the FCRA, but would have to get back to him about the specifics.[248]

How To Obtain Your CLUE Reports

Under the 2003 amendments to the FCRA, known as the "Fair and Accurate Credit Transactions Act (FACT Act)," consumers are entitled one free copy of their consumer file during each 12-month period.

ChoicePoint said it has three "products" that are free under the FACT Act: the C.L.U.E. (auto and homeowners insurance); "WorkPlace Solutions" (employment background screening) and "Tenant History" (apartment rentals).

You can order these online, via toll free phone number, or through the mail. Proceed to the next page for contact information:

---

[247] (Mary Boris v. ChoicePoint Services, Inc., et al.: USDC-W.D. Kentucky (Louisville) – No. 3:01CV-342-H; March 14)

[248] http://banking.senate.gov/index.cfm?Fuseaction=Hearings.Detail&HearingID=144; (go to "Click here to view hearing.")

www.choicetrust.com
C.L.U.E. Auto or Homeowners Reports
ChoicePoint Consumer Disclosure Center
P.O. Box 105295
Atlanta, GA 30348
1-(866) 312-8076

WorkPlace Solutions
ChoicePoint Consumer Disclosure Center
P.O. Box 105292
Atlanta, GA 30348
1-(866) 312-8075

Tenant History
Resident Data Consumer Disclosure Center
P.O. Box 850126
Richardson, TX 75085-0126
1-(877) 448-5732

ChoicePoint 'Full File' Disclosure

Due to a class-action settlement, you can request your ChoicePoint "Full File Disclosure," which includes such public records items on file as real estate transactions and ownership data, lien, judgment, and bankruptcy records, professional license information, and historical addresses. Find the required form by going to www.ChoiceTrust.com, and clicking on "Access Your Personal Information." (Or, go to the link in footnote 249.)[249]

ChoicePoint Consumer Center
Attn. Full File Disclosure
PO Box 105108
Atlanta, Ga. 30348-5108

---

[249] www.choicetrust.com/servlet/com.kx.cs.servlets.CsServlet?channel=welcome&subchannel=disclosure; The 2007 settlement came in Campos v. ChoicePoint Services, Inc., 1-03-CV- 3577 (N.D. Ga. 2007). James Pietz, of Pittsburgh, PA, & Leo Bueno, Coral Gables, FL, were lead attorneys.

Chapter 15

Mortgage Insurance

> You say potato and I say 'po-tah-to,'
> You say tomato and I say 'to-mah-to;'
> Potato, po-tah-to, tomato, to-mah-to
>
> – George & Ira Gershwin
> "Oh, Let's Call The Whole Thing Off!

In 1998, in a little-noticed action, the Federal Trade Commission staff warned the mortgage insurance industry that it needed to give homebuyers adverse action notices whenever their credit reports caused a mortgage insurer to deny coverage.

The FTC considered the issue after a lawyer representing the Mortgage Insurance Companies of America asked the FTC whether mortgage insurers were exempt from giving adverse action notices under the loophole in the Fair Credit Reporting Act.

"No," was the basic answer of Clarke Brinckerhoff, an FTC staff attorney who specializes in credit reporting. Brinckerhoff summed up the industry's position, and then shot it down.

"You support your belief that a Mortgage Insurer should not be required to provide this notice with (1) a legal argument that the section does not apply where a mortgage insurer declines to insure a consumer residential loan based on the credit report on the applicant, and (2) a policy argument that consumers will be confused or distressed by the notices. We disagree," Brinckerhoff wrote.

"In our view, the plain language of Section 615(a) requires mortgage insurers (MI) to provide notice. First, an MI takes 'adverse action'—in both the common sense and legal definition of that term—when it declines to extend insurance coverage that is a prerequisite for approval of the consumer's residential mortgage loan application... An MI's refusal to insure a consumer loan is certainly a 'denial in connection with the underwriting of insurance,'" he wrote.

"First, the reason the MI is allowed to obtain a report on the loan applicant is because FCRA Sect. 604(a)(3)(C) provides a permissible purpose 'in connection with the underwriting of insurance on the *consumer*.' Second, the party evaluated by the MI is the *consumer*. Third, the premium when coverage is granted is paid by the *consumer*."

"Finally, we are unpersuaded by your policy argument that consumers will be confused by receiving the notices . . . We believe that the benefit provided by the notice . . . outweighs any problems that might arise when consumers get the notice."

Brinckerhoff's analysis was logical and straightforward. However, while it said notice was required when coverage was *denied*, it was silent on whether notice was required when rates were *raised* because of information in a credit report. That issue would return another day.

Established Industry, New Controversy

Mortgage insurance grew in popularity during the home-buying boom of the late 1990s. It was used mostly by first-time homebuyers and others who could not make a full 20-percent down payment and therefore need to have their mortgage insured against default. Each year, an estimated one million homebuyers pay for mortgage insurance.

In January 2003, Anthony and Alethea Preston were sitting at the settlement table in Clermont, Florida, about to close on their mortgage. But they were shocked to learn that the deal could not go through unless they agreed to pay a monthly mortgage premium of $762.29. No explanation was given. Their investigation later revealed that the mortgage company, Flagstar Bank, had passed their credit report or credit score to Mortgage Guarantee Insurance Corporation (MGIC). MGIC allegedly came up with the $762.29 figure after reviewing the Prestons' credit report or score.

The Prestons ultimately sued MGIC under the FCRA for not providing an adverse action notice. The Mortgage Insurance Companies of America (MICA), the industry trade association, filed an *Amicus* brief supporting MGIC's argument that mortgage insurers did not have to comply with the FCRA's adverse action requirement for insurance.

The mortgage insurance industry disagreed that the FCRA required its member companies to give adverse action notices when a consumer's credit report resulted in higher rates. In the kind of highly technical argument that high-paid lawyers are known for, the industry contended that mortgage insurance wasn't really an "insurance transaction." Instead, they argued, it was part of the mortgage-granting process and it was really a "credit transaction." Thus, mortgage insurance fell within the so-called "counter-offer" loophole for creditors. Under that loophole, creditors who raise rates because of credit reports don't have to give adverse action notices when they counter-offer at a higher rate, and the counter-offer is accepted by the consumer. No such loophole existed for insurers. (What's more, even the creditor's loophole was somewhat closed by the 2003 Amendments to the FCRA: any significant increase in an interest rate based upon a credit report would require a "risk-based" pricing notice, regardless of whether or not the consumer accepted the counter-offer.)

On December 19, 2003, U.S. District Judge William Terrell Hodges ruled that under the plain meaning of the FCRA, the Prestons' arrangement with MGIC was an "insurance" transaction requiring an adverse action notice. The ruling cleared the way for a trial.[250]

Moreover, Judge John Steele, also of the Middle District of Florida, rejected arguments by PMI, another major mortgage insurer, that it did not have to give adverse action notices.[251]

[250] <u>Tony Preston & Althea Preston, et al. v. MGIC</u>: U.S. Dist. Ct. – Middle Dist. Of Florida (Ocala Div.) No. 5:03-cv-111-Oc-10GRJ; December 19, 2003. The Prestons were represented by Terry Smiljanich, of James, Hoyer, Newcomer and Smiljanich, of Tampa, Florida. However, Judge Hodges declined to certify a class action.
[251] <u>Clayton Glatt, et al. v. PMI Group, Inc., et al</u>: U.S. Dist. Ct. – Middle Dist. of Florida (Ft. Myers Div.) – No. 2:03-cv-326-FtM-29SPC; January 2, 2004.

Chapter 16

The Color Of Credit Scores

> *We must rapidly begin the shift from a "thing-oriented" society to a "person-oriented" society. When machines and computers, profit motives and property rights are considered more important than people, the giant triplets of racism, materialism, and militarism are incapable of being conquered.*

> – Rev. Martin Luther King
> "Beyond Vietnam: A Time
> To Break Silence" (April 1967)

Is there a connection between credit scoring and racial discrimination? Despite a slough of studies, the question remains unsettled, and the debate rages on. A 2004 study by Missouri Insurance Commissioner Scott Lakin indicated that credit scoring system was disproportionately harsher on minorities. [252] Separate studies in 2007 by the Federal Trade Commission and Federal Reserve Board both found that minorities tended to have lower scores, but still concluded that credit scoring itself was not discriminatory.

In a 1996 report, Freddie Mac, the giant mortgage underwriter, acknowledged in a report that African-American borrowers were about three times as likely than white borrowers to have high-risk credit scores—defined as FICO scores below 620. Hispanic borrowers were twice as likely as white borrowers to have high-risk scores. [253]

---

[252] Kabler, Brent Ph.D., "Insurance-Based Credit Scores: Impact on Minority and Low Income Populations in Missouri," Missouri Dept. of Insurance Statistics Section, January 2004

[253] "Automated Underwriting: Making Mortgage Lending Simpler and Fairer for America's Families," Report By Freddie Mac, September 1996 (Herein cited as "Freddie Mac Report")

In a footnote, Freddie Mac was quick not to blame it all on Fair Isaac. "This pattern, while not well understood, seems to reflect less about credit markets and more about the general economic condition of many minority families. African-American and Hispanic house-holds tend to have higher unemployment rates, less job security, and significantly lower levels of wealth. For example, in times of financial difficulty, minority households may be less able to get help from parents or other family members and more likely to fall behind in their payment obligations."[254]

Using Freddie Mac's data from its 1999 National Consumer Credit Survey, Birny Birnbaum, executive director of the Council for Economic Justice in Austin, Texas, compared overall scores to those of minorities. "When combining African-Americans, Hispanics, and Whites into one group, he estimated that:

- 30% had "bad" credit records
- 13% had "indeterminate" credit records
- 57% had "good" credit records[255]

For African-Americans he estimated that:
- 48% had "bad" credit records
- 16% had "indeterminate" credit records
- 36% had "good" credit records[256]

For Hispanics he estimated that:
- 34% had "bad" credit records
- 15% had "indeterminate" credit records
- 51% had "good" credit records

---

[254] *Id.*
[255] Birnbaum, Birny, "Insurers' Use of Credit Scoring for Homeowners Insurance In Ohio: A Report For the Ohio Civil Rights Commission," January 2003
[256] *Id.*

For whites, in contrast, he estimated that:

- 27% had "bad" credit records
- 12% had "indeterminate" records
- 61% had "good" credit records

Like SAT Scores

When this author was in college, a group of African-American students invited black and white students to take a multiple-choice test patterned after the Student Achievement Tests (SATs) that have become a rite of passage for high school students preparing to enter college. But the test they gave was heavily weighted with questions about African-American history and culture. After struggling through so many unfamiliar topics, many of the white students would ask, "How am I supposed to know the answer to these questions?" The African-American organizers of the event made their point: they who create and give the test, likely will influence who succeeds.

Credit scores have been favorably compared to SAT tests because both systems rate achievement according to where the individual's score falls within the percentile, as compared to the entire group.

Credit Scores and SAT tests share another commonality: they reflect the assumptions of a narrow group of Caucasian-Americans who created them and have grown to be a widely accepted standard that touches the lives of millions of Americans. As one observer quipped, "Credit scores are just one more reminder that it's still a White Man's world."

Freddie's 'Seal of Approval'

FICO's defenders, on the other hand, insist the scoring system is both colorblind and the most effective predictor of credit risk. In its 1996 study, for instance, Freddie Mac found that regardless of whether the borrower was white, black or Hispanic, loans to borrowers with scores above 660 performed better than loans for borrowers with scores between 620 and 660, which in turn performed better than loans with FICO scores below 620.[257]

Freddie Mac also cited an August 1996 "Discussion Paper" by Fair Isaac that sought to determine whether minorities were adequately represented in credit bureau data. Fair Isaac found that residents of "high-minority areas" accounted for 7.8 percent of adults, and for 6.7 percent of consumers with credit reports maintained by the three major CRAs. Fair Isaac conceded that the figures indicated a "slight under-representation of high-minority-area residents" in credit bureau files. But the company said the "data clearly cover a significant number of minority households."[258]

Looking at Fair Isaac's data, Freddie Mac said it was satisfied: "The fact that credit-bureau scores are powerful predictors for minority borrowers confirms that they are sufficiently represented."[259]

Freddie Mac and Fair Isaac separately examined whether heavy use of finance companies, as opposed to major banks or other mainstream creditors, push their credit scores into a high-risk category. Fair Isaac "detected little variation in the number of finance company accounts used by consumers regardless of racial composition ... (and) Freddie Mac reached a similar conclusion."[260]

Freddie Mac noted that more lenders were turning to alternative means for documenting credit history of low-income people, including rent and utility payments and other recurring obligations.

---

[257] Freddie Mac Report (see Footnote 2)
[258] Fair Isaac and Company, Inc., "Low to Moderate Income and High Minority Area Case Studies," Discussion Paper, August 1996, as cited in the Freddie Mac Study.
[259] Freddie Mac Study
[260] *Id.*

It concluded that the system would welcome with open arms those consumers that were willing to conform their behavior to its standards. "Fortunately, consumers are able to go from no credit history to an acceptable one relatively quickly, in perhaps one or two years. To do this, they need to open and use several credit accounts and make timely payments without running up large balances."[261]

Insurance Scoring and Discrimination?

Throughout 2003 and into 2004, the debate intensified over the alleged discriminatory effects of insurance scoring.

As one insurance industry official recently said, "We live in a racist society. Scoring is not at fault; it simply reflects what's there, whether we like it or not."

But before more closely examining the Missouri research, it is useful to examine, albeit briefly, the evolution of one insurer's practices and how that insurer historically discriminated against minorities.

The 'Negro' Factor

For nearly 100 years, the Metropolitan Life Insurance Company had a policy of selling sub-standard insurance policies to "Negroes" and other non-whites.[262] Some of these policies were known as "burial" policies, as they were touted as a means for poor people to have enough money to pay for a decent burial. MetLife agents would go door-to-door to

---

[261] *Id.*

[262] The following information about MetLife is from the opinion and order of U.S. District Judge Harold Baer, Jr., in <u>Karl Thompson, et al. v. Metropolitan Life Insurance Co.</u>: USDC – Southern District of New York -- 00 civ. 5071; June 21, 2001. Christa Collins was co-counsel on the case; she currently is partner at James, Hoyer, Smiljanich & Newcomer, in Tampa, Florida. The Insurance Library in New York City is also a useful resource.

collect weekly premiums. In some cases, the premiums exceeded the policy's payoff.

In its manual entitled, "Instructions To Agents," dated June 1940, MetLife advised agents,

> In designating race, state the race definitely; for example: White; colored; Indian; Mexican; Hawaii; Porto Rican (sic); West Indian; etc. Colored includes not only the Negro, but the Mulatto and all other persons having colored blood. Only persons of pure Caucasian blood are designated as white; all other races should be designated by their proper term or distinction.[263]

As blatant discrimination became less acceptable, MetLife found other ways to continue its practice of selling sub-standard policies to African-Americans and other non-whites. One approach was to classify policyholders by job classification. Since blacks typically were the only ones who worked as "porters," or "black boots," this approach temporarily succeeded at separating whites and non-whites.

A 1964 memo showed that MetLife could distinguish between blacks and whites by classifying them by neighborhood, sometimes called "geo-coding," other times, "redlining."

"This memo and attached map identified 108 neighborhoods in Manhattan that had 'the least favorable population and housing characteristics,' including the Lower East Side; south of 14th Street; in east and central Harlem; and in the lower parts of Washington Heights,'" wrote Judge Harold Baer, Jr., in his 2001 order.[264]

Judge Baer quoted from the 1964 memo to underscore MetLife's preoccupation with race. "About two-fifths of the residents in these areas are nonwhites and an additional one-fifth are Puerto Rican. This compares with

---

[263] *Id.*

[264] *Id.*

one-fourth nonwhite and one-eighth Puerto Rican for Manhattan as a whole," said the memo.[265]

As time passed, MetLife needed to delve more into personal details of applicants to continue its discriminatory practices. This trend was reflected in the "Mercantile" reports, which were the product of questionnaires only required of non-whites. Some of the questions included:

> Number of rooms in the home?
> Number of persons living in the home, including lodgers?
> Does home contain toilet facilities? Running water?
> Is the home in good repair? Clean?
> Does the applicant or premium-payer associate with criminals or gamblers such as those in the policy number game?
> Does the applicant or premium-payer get into fights?
> Have the applicant's or premium payer's drinking habits been criticized?[266]

MetLife believed that blacks had higher mortality rates than whites, even though some experts said the company's actuarial tables were flawed. A 1950 memo showed that MetLife was concerned that some state anti-discrimination laws might be unfair to whites: "Since the laws of several states do not allow us to take race into account in appraising an applicant for insurance, we have had to adopt other means of avoiding unfair discrimination against white policyholders in the cost of their insurance."[267]

Allstate In California

In the previous chapter on automobile insurance, we noted how California Insurance Commissioner John Garam-

---

[265] The memo was authored by "Paul H. Jacobsen Ph.D.".
[266] Thompson, et al. v. Metropolitan Life, op cit.
[267] *Id.*

endi consistently voiced concerns about the use of credit scoring.

In 2002, he brought a formal action against Allstate for its use of credit scoring in homeowners insurance. Garamendi charged that Allstate's proprietary score "in underwriting or tier placements results in excessive, inadequate, unfairly discriminatory, or unreasonable rates." His department made the move after an Allstate motion for a rate increase confirmed that the company was using credit scores in rating homeowner policies.[268]

In possibly the first order of its kind, Administrative Law Judge Lisa Williams ordered Allstate to reveal its scoring algorithms to prove they were not discriminatory or unreasonable. Soon thereafter, Allstate settled, agreeing to stop using credit scores in setting homeowners insurance. It also agreed it would not try to re-introduce credit scoring unless it first revealed its credit scoring methodologies with the department.

Allstate said the debate on the use of credit scoring, which it referred to as "insurance financial stability" in underwriting, "would best be served in a public policy forum such as the legislature, or a formal rulemaking by the department, rather than in the context of a rate hearing."[269]

In a subsequent filing, Garamendi charged that Allstate's use of credit scoring, or "insurance financial stability (IFS)," in auto insurance, violated California insurance law.

Noting that IFS was used to "predict the likelihood of future losses" based upon credit reports, the complaint said that Allstate's credit scoring program used a "scorecard approach where a consumer credit report's value for a particular attribute or combination of attributes receives a

---

[268] Order Adopting Proposed Decision, <u>In The Matter of a Rate Application by Allstate Insurance Company</u>, Calif. Dept. of Insurance, No. PA02026201; Admin. Law Judge Lisa Williams, April 25, 2003
[269] *Id.*

score. The total score for the credit report is then an aggregation of all the individual attribute scores."[270]

"The use of an aggregate score, such as that generated by [Allstate's] IFS program, which combines various credit characteristics that may or may not have a direct substantial relationship to loss exposure, developed without disclosure of the components . . . does not allow the [Calif. Dept. of Insurance] to determine compliance with the applicable statutes and regulations," the complaint alleged.

The complaint also charged that Allstate "failed lo maintain reasonable records and has failed to make available information regarding the IFS program to the Commissioner so that a determination can be made whether its use of the IFS program complies with the California Insurance Code."

The Allstate Class Action

A credit score-discrimination lawsuit charged that, "Over the years Allstate has employed various artifices to conceal its discriminatory conduct. Initially, Allstate established geographical districts to identify and target non-Caucasian neighborhoods for the purpose of charging the non-Caucasian residents of these districts higher premiums because of their race."[271]

In the early 1990's, however, Allstate began "making extensive use of credit reports to assess 'financial stability'" so it could continue its racially discriminating practices under a more objective veneer, the lawsuit charged.[272]

---

[270] Fifth Amended Notice of Noncompliance Pursuant to CIC 51858, In the Matter of the Rates, Rating Plans, or Rating Systems of Allstate Insurance Company et al., Calif. Dept. of Insurance, File No.NC01017552

[271] Jose C. DeHoyos v. Allstate Corp., et al.: U.S. District Court for the Western Dist. Of Texas; class action complaint filed Nov. 2, 2001.

[272] Id.

Next came credit scoring. "In recent years Allstate has intensified its use of credit scoring through development of the Insurance Financial Stability score and the Strategic Risk Management system. Allstate designed each of these artifices for the purpose of using them as a pretext to discourage sales to non-Caucasians and to charge non-Caucasians higher premiums."

Jose DeHoyos and Eva Perez-DeHoyos, Mexican-Americans living in Texas, had maintained good driving records since 1984, the year they took out auto and homeowners insurance policies with Allstate. They also had good credit histories. But in July 2001, Allstate said their premiums for both their homeowners and automobile policies were being substantially increased. When the DeHoyos asked why, they were informed that Allstate's new use of Insurance Financial Stability Scores caused the increase in their premiums.

Four other plaintiffs, African-Americans and other non-Caucasians from Texas or Florida, recounted similar experiences. The complaint indicated that a major motivating factor for Allstate was to use credit scoring to identify "High Lifetime Value" customers (i.e. the kind that have more money and the greatest potential to buy additional policies).

In court, Allstate argued that 1930s-era law[273] barring federal involvement in insurance issues prevented plaintiffs from suing under federal civil rights laws. But a federal court in the Western District of Texas disagreed, allowing the suit to go forward.

On September 3, 2003, in a 2-1 opinion, a three-member panel of the U.S. Court of Appeals for the Fifth Circuit also rejected Allstate's argument, stating, "Every circuit that has considered the question has determined that federal anti-discrimination laws may be applied in an insurance context, even where the state insurance agencies have

---

[273] McCarran-Ferguson Act, 15 U.S.C. § 1012(b)

mechanisms in place to regulate discriminatory practices."[274] The case was pending at the time this book went to press.

The Missouri Study

Missouri law prohibits sole reliance on credit scoring to determine whether to issue a policy. However, there are no limits on price increases that can be imposed due to credit scores so long as such increases can be actuarially justified. Accordingly, auto insurers use credit scores widely. To understand how minority populations were affected, the Missouri Insurance Department collected scoring data on 330,000 applicants from the top-20 auto insurers.

The study found a major gap between "all-minority" and "no-minority" neighborhoods. The average credit score in the "all-minority" neighborhood fell within the 18.4 percentile, meaning the average score was in the lowest one-fifth of Missouri residents. Meanwhile, average credit scores in the "no-minority" neighborhoods were in the 57.3 percentile (close to the top two-fifths)—a gap of 38.9 points.[275]

Even after eliminating a broad array of socioeconomic variables, such as income, educational attainment, marital status and unemployment rates, the relationship between below-average credit scores and minority concentration in a zip code remained.

"Indeed, minority concentration proved to be the single most reliable predictor of credit scores," it said.[276]

Moreover, the study examined the percentage of minority and white policyholders in the lowest three-fifths of credit score ranges and found that minorities were overrepresented in this worst credit score group by 26.2 percentage points.

---

[274] Jose C. DeHoyos v. Allstate Corp., et al.: 345 F.3d 290 (5th Cir.) Dissent by Judge Edith Jones. The Fifth Circuit rejected Allstate's *en banc* appeal, raising the possibility of an appeal to the U.S. Supreme Ct.
[275] Kabler, op cit.
[276] *Id.*

In response, Missouri Governor Bob Holden said he favored legislation to ban the use of credit scoring in auto or homeowners insurance. "The concern is that credit scoring is unfairly penalizing low income citizens with inflated insurance prices, with much of the burden falling on African-Americans and Hispanics. This places unnecessary obstacles in the way of many people and many communities that are struggling to move forward."

Holden expressed concerns that credit scoring techniques were secretive, not well understood by the public, and possibly not an accurate indicator of a person's financial responsibility.

Scott Lakin, director of the Missouri Insurance Department, said that Missouri would head a national study of credit scoring that will test whether similar patterns exist in other states. More than ten states agreed to join the project.

Defenders Of The System

The Maryland Insurance Administration subsequently criticized the study, as "inconclusive," partly because insurers don't collect data about race. Joe Thesing, Missouri manager for the National Association of Mutual Insurance Companies (NAMIC), said the Missouri study was based on "faulty methodology." "Most professional researchers think ZIP codes are far too large for accurate analysis," he said. The study also failed to focus on actual purchasers of insurance and claims experience, he said, adding, "All previous evidence indicates that insurance scoring actually allows companies to insure more people at a lower cost."[277]

The FTC and Federal Reserve Board found that Blacks and Hispanics, on average, had lower scores than whites and Asians, but still concluded that scoring models were not biased against any demographic group.[278]

---

[277] NAMIC Press Release, Jan. 30, 2004
www.namic.org/newsreleases04/040130nr1.asp
[278] www.ftc.gov/opa/2007/07/facta.shtm

Chapter 17

Special Challenges

When it comes to identity theft or credit report accuracy, some groups face special challenges. In this chapter, we'll briefly examine emerging issues for minorities and other people with little or no documented credit history, Spanish-speakers, students, divorcees, filers for bankruptcy, and the elderly.

Minorities

Among some of America's largest minority populations, including African-Americans and Hispanic, there traditionally has been a "low-trust" level in the banking system. According to one survey, as recently as 2003, 87% of African-Americans believed that lending institutions discriminated against borrowers, and 42% had no relationship with a bank.

Similarly, 40% of Hispanics had no relation with a bank, according to this financial survey. In terms of credit reports, this translates into what's known as "thin files." If a consumer doesn't have credit or there is insufficient activity in his or her credit report, a credit score cannot be generated.

The survey estimated that 30% of the Hispanic U.S. population and 20% of the Asian population lacked a credit score. Overall, 26% of the U.S. population lacked a credit score. A study by the University of North Carolina's Center For Community Capitalism found that 22% of Hispanics had no credit score.[279]

"Thin Files" mean that millions of people, who quite possibly are financially responsible, face difficulties in buying a home or getting a car loan because their payment history is not documented by the credit bureaus.

The irony is that the financial services industry sees the traditionally underserved minority populations as one of the better opportunities for growth. Minorities accounted for nearly 40% of home ownership growth from 1994 to 2000 and will contribute 64% of household growth over the next 10 years, with 67% being first-time homebuyers, and 33% being renters. One out of ten Americans was born in another country. It is projected that the number of all immigrant homeowners will increase to 6.8 million people by 2010.

A Response To 'Thin Files'

Many people who do not have credit scores actually have credit histories, but they are not documented by Equifax, Experian, and Trans Union, the "Big 3" consumer reporting agencies (CRAs). Those payment histories can include payments for rent, utilities, and phone service.

Seeking to serve the underserved, Michael Nathans in 2004 launched "PRBC," a new kind of credit bureau. The service allows consumers to register at its Web site[280] so that their on-time rental, cable, utility, day care and other payments are recorded, enabling the renter to build a credit history.

---

[279] Stegman, Michael A., et al., "Automated Underwriting: Getting to 'Yes' for More Low-Income Applicants," presented at the 2001 Conference For Housing Opportunity

[280] www.prbc.com; (originally named "Pay Rent, Build Credit, Inc.")

PRBC steadily has progressed towards its goal of creating a "supplement" to standard credit reports that allow creditors to "fill in the blanks," and permit the data to be factored into credit scoring models.[281]

To that end, PRBC has partnered with various organizations, including the National Credit Reporting Association, the National Association of Mortgage Brokers and Mortgage Guarantee Insurance Corp., on different projects.

The company is subject to the Fair Credit Reporting Act.

Spanish

The Hispanic population in the United States is extremely diverse.[282] The majority are fluent in English. But for a significant percentage of Latinos in the U.S., Spanish is their first language. For example, in 2000, of the 7.8 million Latino students enrolled in U.S. public schools, 3.6 million were Spanish-speaking students enrolled in "English Language Learners" (ELL) programs. Thus, the National Council of La Raza estimates that 46% of Latino students are ELLs.[283] The parents of these children presumably consider Spanish their first language.

As most American telephone users realize, a wide array of U.S. firms, including banks, credit card companies,

---

[281] Harney, Kenneth, "Renters Soon Get A Chance To Boost Credit Records," *Washington Post*, January 10, 2004

[282] The terms "Hispanic" and "Latino" are used interchangeably to refer collectively to Mexicans, Puerto Ricans, Central and South Americans, Cubans, Dominicans and others of Spanish and Latin American descent. Hispanics can be of any race.

[283] Yzaguirre, Raul, "State of Hispanic America 2004," National Council of La Raza

phone companies, and utilities, voluntarily provide Spanish-language options.

However, the three major credit-reporting agencies (CRAs) – Equifax, Experian, and Trans Union – have not offered Spanish-language options.[284]

This created challenges for significant portions of the U.S. population who were fluent in Spanish but not English. The credit reporting system is complicated enough for Americans whose first language is English. Moreover, the "Centralized Source" for obtaining free credit reports (www.annualcreditreport.com), does not include assistance features in Spanish or other languages, as it was not required by FTC rules.

Several organizations offer guides and assistance in Spanish. Consumer Action, a California-based group, has published booklets on credit and credit reports, fraud, and a host of other issues in Spanish,[285] Chinese, Vietnamese, Korean, Russian, and Japanese.[286]

Other organizations offering Spanish-language information on credit reports and identity theft include the California State Office of Privacy Protection,[287] and as mentioned previously, the Privacy Rights Clearinghouse[288] and the Identity Theft Resource Center.[289]

---

[284] Linda Foley, of the Identity Theft Resource Center, has pressed the CRAs to provide Spanish language assistance, but to no avail.

[285] http://www.consumer-action.org/English/library/privacy_rights/index.php

[286] www.consumer-action.org/OtherLang/library/index.php

[287] www.privacyprotection.ca.gov - (866) 785-9663

[288] www.privacyrights.org

[289] www.idtheftcenter.org

Individual Taxpayer Identification Numbers

Since 1996, the Internal Revenue Service has issued 6.9 million Individual Taxpayer Identification Numbers (ITINs), mainly to recent immigrants who were not eligible for Social Security numbers. According to National Council of La Raza (NCLR), not all CRAs treat consumers with ITINs equally, which can lead to significant discrepancies in information reported and in FICO scores.[290]

Identity Theft & Hispanics

While mainly anecdotal, there was growing evidence that identity theft is hitting Hispanics particularly hard. Some observers were not surprised. A larger percentage of the Latino population in the United States share common names—Garcia, Gomez, Perez, Ramirez, Rodriguez, Sanchez, and Torres, to name a few.

Los Angeles Police Detective Lyle Barnes regularly investigates identity theft cases involving Hispanic names. "I've seen it where somebody connected with one of the credit bureaus will look up a name and then get information on, say, 10 people with the name Juan Perez. Then they'll sell it to somebody who will use the stolen IDs in stores," he told the Associated Press.[291]

In 2002, Barnes said he started to see an uptick in the trend of Hispanic-on-Hispanic ID thefts for the purpose of stealing credit cards and opening bogus lines of credit. He attributed the increase to thieves who branched out from other crime to the white-collar arena. "The criminal has probably already been a criminal ... and now this is an easier way for him to make money," he said.

---

[290] NCLR has asked the FTC to examine this issue as part of the accuracy study mandated by the 2003 FACTA (FCRA) amendments.

[291] Bryan, Dave, "Investigators Say ID Theft Rising Among Common Hispanic Names," Associated Press, Dec. 7, 2003 in the *Bradenton Herald* (Florida) http://www.bradenton.com/mld/bradenton/7437684.htm

The Federal Trade Commission, which tracks identity theft nationally, does not compile ID theft data based on the ethnicity of the criminal, according to Naomi Lefkovitz, an FTC attorney.

Linda and Jay Foley, co-executive directors of Identity Theft Resource Center in San Diego, were convinced that the number of Hispanic victims was growing. Jay Foley said that in 2003 there were at least two active cases in Southern California in which thieves stole computers from an office and took them across the border to Mexico. Once in Mexico, the thieves took all the Hispanic names out of the computer and sold the personal information to Mexican nationals, who in turn used the data to create IDs for crossing the border into the United States.

Linda Foley said another problem was that Equifax, Experian, and Trans Union did not include Spanish-language instructions or assistance on their Web sites or telephone recordings. She repeatedly has urged the Big Three to add special-language assistance for Hispanics and other sizeable second-language groups in the U.S., but to no avail.

Sgt. Tim Crews, chief of the Orlando, Fla., police department's economic crimes unit, told the AP that stolen common Latino last names had always been part of the larger pool of ID theft. The crime was easier to carry out for the criminal who already had a legitimate driver's license with the same last name as the victim, Crews said. When the thief went to buy a car using someone else's identity, for example, an unsuspecting salesperson might be more willing to overlook discrepancies.[292]

Crews said the victims were not always wealthy Hispanics with a long history of good credit. He had seen cases in which a Latino couple of modest means labored for years and saved their money only to realize that their IDs had been stolen and their credit ruined when they applied for their first mortgage.

---

[292] *Id.*

"They finally are making a decent wage and are on their feet and, lo and behold, somebody in Texas has stolen their ID," Crews said.

Officials said the theft of personal information that ended up in the hands of undocumented workers had been a facet of identity theft in the United States for years. The demand for Social Security numbers continued to be at a premium among illegal immigrants who used the numbers to get employment.

The AP reported the case of Adriana Sanchez who actually had to pass a credit history check to get hired as a Los Angeles police officer. When Sanchez applied for a car loan, her credit report showed several open accounts that had been turned over to collections agencies. Someone living in the Atlanta area with almost the same name had stolen her identity and run up $70,000 in debt.

Sanchez's research uncovered the addresses of the Georgia accounts. She contacted Gwinnett County investigators, who tracked down and arrested 33-year-old Adriana Sanchez-Palacios of Sugar Hill, and charged her in September 2003 with identity theft and fraud.[293]

"Everything was compromised, from my date of birth and my mother's maiden name," she said in a telephone interview. "You feel like you're being violated. ... She even had my mom's address."

Lupe Rodriguez, a detective with the Chula Vista, California police department said cleaning up the mess left by identity theft is especially difficult for people for whom English is a second language. "It's a paper nightmare," he said. "Victims have to make a lot of calls, and it consumes a lot of time."[294]

One dramatic example was "Carlos," who according to computer records, had racked up $68,000 in debt, owed $4,700 in child support and had three warrants out for his

---

[293] *Id.*
[294] http://www.privacyrights.org/spanish/pi17a.htm

arrest for failing to appear at DUI hearings. But Carlos was six-years-old.

Jay Foley, of the ID Theft Resource Center said Carlos' father was divorced and was expelled from the U.S. "He's been living and working as his son for four-and-a-half years," he said. Foley withheld the last name because the case was ongoing.

The Identity Theft Resource Center and the Privacy Rights Clearinghouse both offer guidance in Spanish for identity theft and other issues.

www.idtheftcenter.org/aiuda.shtml

www.privacyrights.org/spanish/PaginasInformativas.htm

Students

The challenges faced by college students and recent graduates stem from two sources: student loans and credit cards.

Because of the exorbitant cost of college, many students graduate owing anywhere between $5,000 and $70,000 in student loans. It is important that students realize that any late payments will stay on their credit report for seven years. Late payments will lower credit scores and disadvantage graduates when they want to buy a car or home.

It is doubly important that students check their credit history because student loans can complicate a credit report. This is because student loans are often sold by the originator, and often are resold after that. The problem is that the credit report often records the "sold" student loan as a new "student loan," making it look like the student has doubled her debt load. For some graduates, the sale and re-sale of their student loans can make it look like they have four outstanding loans instead of one. That in itself can damage a credit score.

Accordingly, the damage can escalate if there are late payments, as the loose reporting practices of lenders could make it look like you are tardy on multiple accounts when you truly are only late on one.

Sallie Mae's Quiet Move

In 2003, a separate controversy arose involving Sallie Mae, formally known as the Student Loan Marketing (SLM) Corporation, which oversees the student loan program.[295]

In 2002, Sallie Mae quietly decided to report loan information on more than 7 million of its borrowers only to Equifax and to Innovis Data Solutions, a small credit bureau, and to halt all reporting to Experian and Trans Union. Sallie Mae said the move was intended to protect privacy, as only Equifax agreed not to sell lists to credit card companies for pre-approved offers. Critics accused Sallie Mae of trying to hide its borrowers from competitors who might offer better loan deals.

But Sallie Mae never told anyone. It came to light in the Autumn of 2003 when Chris Neuswanger, a Colorado mortgage broker, noticed that a young home-buying client had been pushed into a high-rate loan solely because two of his three credit bureau reports omitted his large, on-time student loan payments with Sallie Mae, depressing his credit score by 40 points. Eric Borgeson, a 31-year old architect, said Sallie Mae's less-than-full reporting practice cost him $200 a month more than it should have, plus higher closing costs and a $5,000 prepayment penalty. "I got shafted by Sallie Mae," said Borgeson, who reportedly was considering legal action. Kenneth Harney of the *Washington Post* broke the story.[296]

Caroline Wright, a 34-year-old student from Virginia, said a mortgage broker told Wright she would have trouble getting a good interest rate on a home loan if her on-time

---

[295] www.salliemae.com
[296] Harney, Kenneth, "Sallie Mae's History Lesson," *Washington Post,* November 15, 2003, pg. F1

payments to Sallie Mae were missing from her Experian and Trans Union reports files.

"They weren't protecting me," Wright said. "They were doing exactly the opposite."[297]

The controversy came in the latter stages of Congress's consideration of amendments to the Fair Credit Reporting Act. After the story broke, Senator Richard Durbin (D-IL) prepared legislation to require Sallie Mae to resume reporting to all three credit bureaus. Soon thereafter, Sallie Mae sent a letter, promising to continue reporting to Experian and Trans Union. Undeterred, Durbin said he would offer his amendment as part of the Higher Education Act, instead of the FCRA.

Students & Credit Cards

Another challenge facing graduates is a high level of credit card debt, often at high interest rates.

Professor Robert Manning of Rochester Institute of Technology, and author of Credit Card Nation,[298] told Congress, "What is striking in the acknowledgement of the credit card industry is that college students are a desirable market because of their ignorance of personal finance and their lack of consumer debt."[299]

"The marketing of credit cards has shifted rapidly over the last five years from college upperclassmen to college freshmen and high school seniors. More significantly is the recognition that student consumption has a large debt component that is increasingly financed by family loans, federally subsidized student loans, summer earnings, and

---

[297] Singletary, Michelle, "Giving Students Due Credit for History," *Washington Post,* Nov. 6, 2003, pg. E3

[298] Credit Card Nation: America's Dangerous Addiction to Consumer Credit (Basic Books, 2001).

[299] Statement of Professor Robert Manning before the House Financial Services Subcommittee on Consumer Credit, June 12, 2003. http://financialservices.house.gov/media/pdf/061203rm.pdf

part-time employment during the academic year, and even with other credit cards."

"Three out of five students with credit cards in our survey had already maxed them out during their freshmen year and, three out of five freshmen with multiple credit cards were already using bank cards to pay for other revolving credit accounts. Furthermore, this survey reveals that nearly three-fourths of students use their student loans to pay for their credit cards. Not incidentally, recent studies indicate that this indiscriminate marketing to college students has led to high incidences of fraud and identity theft among this young adult population," Manning testified.

Not surprisingly, Manning recommends that students check their credit reports.

Clearly, today's graduates face greater challenges in managing their finances so as not to jeopardize their finances. The National Consumers League has a page on its Web site dedicated to student debt issues.[300]

Divorce

Divorce can have a dramatic impact on the divorcee's credit score and credit report. A major problem is that divorcees often don't realize the extent to which their credit relationships can continue to entangle each other's lives well after divorce. Or, they are so overwhelmed with the emotional and logistical difficulties of separation that there is little time left for separating and straightening out credit relationships.

But that is precisely what you need to do: ensure that your name is no longer on accounts for which you are not responsible for paying. During the divorce, the husband and wife usually work out a division of debts that receives final approval from the judge. Divorcees often think that any debt

---

[300] www.nclnet.org/moneyandcredit/index.htm

assigned to their ex-spouse by the court frees them from that debt for ever after.

The problem is that your creditors usually don't know about your divorce. In terms of the credit report, problems arise when the ex-spouse who is responsible for paying an account, fails to, and the other spouse, according to the creditor's records, is still a co-signer or joint user or otherwise associated with the account. The failure to pay goes on the credit report of the innocent spouse, creating a fresh derogatory that slams that spouse's credit score.

Thus, it is vital that divorcees identify all of their accounts and separate them completely. This includes mortgages, credit cards, bank loans, debit cards, store charge cards, lines of credit, and overdraft checking. Some authors suggest that spouses begin separating accounts as soon as they consider separating. [301]

Of course, it's also crucial that divorcees obtain their credit reports to check the accuracy of information.

Bankruptcy

Bankruptcy is the most derogatory item that can appear on your credit report. Under the Fair Credit Reporting Act, a bankruptcy can stay on your report for 10 years.

But that does not mean you can no longer get credit. As Gerri Detweiler, a renowned expert on credit explains in her 1997 book, The Ultimate Credit Handbook, (Plume) people can rebuild their credit after bankruptcy or other traumas. It requires patience and a plan. It starts with checking the credit report to see where you stand. If you still have open accounts, try to negotiate with creditors to improve the way they report on you to the credit bureaus, Detweiler advises. Try to catch up on any accounts for which there might be late payments. Next, try to re-establish

---

[301] Ventura, John The Credit Repair Kit (Dearborn 1998 3rd Edition); or see Sember, Brette McWhorter, Repair Your Own Credit and Deal With Debt (Sphinx 2003 2nd Edition)

positive lines of credit. A bank card, paid on time over time, is one of the stronger credit references you can add. In the beginning, she says, you might need to get a "secured" credit card, which requires you to deposit money so use of the card is secured against those deposits.[302] But be careful: both Detweiler and the FTC warn there are a lot of scam artists offering secured credit cards. CardTrak.com provides a list of institutions offering secured cards.[303]

Perhaps the best scholarship on bankruptcy is found in the books of Harvard Law Professor Elizabeth Warren.[304] Warren has pointed out that of the 1.66 million bankruptcies filed in fiscal year 2003, nearly 40% were by husband-wife couples, meaning that the number of people who actually filed for bankruptcy in that year was 2.14 million.[305]

Warren said that women were both the fastest growing and largest demographic group in bankruptcy.

There were 1,661,996 bankruptcies filed in fiscal year 2003, up 7.4% from the 1,547,669 filings in fiscal year 2002. Since 1994, when filings totaled 837,797, bankruptcies in federal courts have increased 98%. From 1991-95, annual bankruptcy filings hovered around 870,000. The biggest noticeable jump occurred in 1995-1996, when they went from 874,642 to 1,125,006.[306] Interestingly, that is when credit card companies sharply escalated their use of direct marketing solicitations offering pre-approved credit card

---

[302] Detweiler continues to advise consumers and publish, see www.ultimatecredit.com, and www.DebtConsolidationRX.com, or for her new E-Book, www.stopdebtcollectorscold.com

[303] www.cardtrak.com/cards/categories/secured.html; Also see http://www.ftc.gov/bcp/conline/pubs/credit/secured.htm

[304] Warren, Elizabeth, Bankruptcy (West 2002), and, Warren and Amelia Warren Tyagi, The Two-Income Trap, (Basic Books 2003)

[305] http://www.bankruptcyaction.com/USbankstats.htm

[306] http://www.abiworld.org/stats/1980annual.html

offers. It is estimated that the industry now sends out five billion unsolicited credit card applications annually.

Many consumers who complete a bankruptcy find that bad debts that were supposed to be discharged as part of the bankruptcy are later erroneously included on their credit reports. Bankruptcy attorneys, like Robert Weed, of Alexandria, Virginia, said he regularly must file motions in federal bankruptcy court in order to get creditors to stop reporting discharged debts and to get the credit reporting agencies to remove them.

Included In Bankruptcy

A special problem arises for individuals who are co-signers, or are otherwise legally obligated for credit cards or loans, when the other co-signer files for bankruptcy. For many years, the CRAs would report such accounts as "Included In Bankruptcy"—even if the non-bankrupt co-signer met his or her obligation and paid the bill on time. This had an adverse impact on the creditworthiness of non-bankrupt consumers. Not only did it seem to have a negative impact on their credit scores, but also major institutions like Freddie Mac, Fannie Mae, and insurance companies do an automated scan of credit reports for serious derogatory items like bankruptcy, "foreclosure," or "judgment." This meant that a co-signer could be denied credit for an account that he or she in fact paid responsibly.

A class action lawsuit was filed over the issue in federal court in South Carolina. Under a settlement approved by U.S. District Judge Cameron Currie, all three CRAs agreed to stop reporting the term "bankruptcy" to the credit reports of consumers who had not filed for bankruptcy.[307]

---

[307] <u>Franklin E. Clark, et al. v. Experian Information Solutions, Inc.</u>: C/A No. 8:00-1217-22; www.fcraclassaction.com; Equifax had proposed allowing it to continue reporting "included in the bankruptcy of another," but the proposal was abandoned after additional attorneys entered the

Seniors

Because it recognized years ago that a host of credit reporting issues affected its members, the American Association of Retired Persons (AARP) has closely followed the FCRA and produced research and surveys on various aspects of it, and on identity theft.

In his June 2003 testimony before the Senate Banking Committee, Michael W. Naylor, AARP's Director of Advocacy said, "Our research does indicate a greater vulnerability of older Americans, based on the higher proportion of those age 50 years and older who report being victimized by identity theft, compared to the proportion of all age groups making such reports."[308]

Among the myriad of problems identified by Naylor was inaccuracy caused by debt collectors. "Inaccuracies can also occur when a creditor sells a delinquent account to a debt collector. Once the original creditor sells the account to a debt collector, the debt collector becomes the furnisher of information on this account to the CRAs. The main source of inaccuracy in this case results from incorrect reporting of the date of initial delinquency on the account."[309]

In a footnote to his prepared statement, Naylor added, "One concern is that debt collectors may report the date they purchased or received the account as the date of initial delinquency, even though the actual date of initial delinquency was likely much earlier. Because the FCRA stipulates that most negative information remains on a consumer credit report for seven years from the date of

---

case to object. The objectors were led by Michael Caddell, of Caddell and Chapman, Houston Texas.

[308] Statement of Michael Naylor, "The Growing Problem of Identity Theft and Its Relationship to the Fair Credit Reporting Act," Senate Banking Committee, June 19, 2003

[309] *Id.*

initial delinquency, establishing this date is important to consumers attempting to restore their credit."

Chapter 18

Opting Out From Pre-Screening

> *The makers of our Constitution undertook to secure . . .the right to be let alone—the most comprehensive of rights and the right most valued by civilized men.*
>
> – Justice Louis Brandeis (dissenting)
> <u>Olmstead v. U.S.</u> 277 U.S. 438 (1928)

If you are tired of the barrage of "pre-approved" credit card offers, you can stop it. If you do "opt out," it should also prevent telemarketers from learning that you just applied for a mortgage or refinancing, and thus allow you to avoid their shady bait-and-switch offers. Separately, you have the right to stop large financial conglomerates from sharing data about you among their affiliates for marketing purposes.

The right to opt-out from "pre-screened" offers, created by the 1996 Amendments, might be the least known right under the Fair Credit Reporting Act – and no wonder. Scan one of the pre-approved credit card offers that you've received in the mail and see if you can find the legally-required notice that (1) the credit card company got your name from either Equifax, Experian, or Trans Union, and (2) you have the right to call a toll-free number in order to stop the credit bureaus from selling your name. This effectively opts you out from future offers that are generated from your credit report data. (*For the toll-free number, turn the page.*)

The Toll Free Number For Opting Out Is:

(888)-5-OPTOUT / (888) 567-8688

By calling the number and *carefully* following the prompts, you can opt out from pre-screening from all three credit bureaus. When you call, be prepared to press "2." By doing so, you get a choice of opting out for two years (Press "one"), or opting out permanently (Press "two") or opting back in if you previously opted out (Press "three").

The recording advises that the personal identifying information you provide will only be used to process the opt-out request. It then asks for your (1) home telephone number; (2) full name; (3) Zip code; (4) street address; and (5) Social Security number. It's that easy. It's also the most effective opt-out right that Americans have under law.

The recorded greeting is confusing to some because it first asks, "If you are calling as a result of the recent e-mail that appeared over the Internet regarding a July 1st law affecting personal financial data, press '1' now." It is referring to the famous bogus e-mail that circulated on the Internet, warning everyone that "on July 1," the credit bureaus were going to start selling your sensitive financial information to everyone. By pressing one, the recording explains that the July 1st date related to opt-out rights with banks under a different law, the 1999 Gramm-Leach-Bliley Act. It also explains that the credit bureaus were not allowed to sell credit report data under the FCRA.[310]

'Pre-Screening & The FCRA'

Under the FCRA, the Big Three CRAs and a fourth bureau, called Innovis, can use their credit report data to

---

[310] For more on this misleading e-mail, go to the National Consumers League Web site, www.nclnet.org/moneyandcredit/financialprivacy.htm, or to www.ftc.gov

produce lists of people that are sold to credit card companies and other lenders. But under the law, these lists can only be used by creditors to offer the recipient a "firm offer of credit." Even though they are called "pre-approved" offers, if the consumer accepts the offer, the law permits a credit card company to pull that consumer's report again. If the company finds something it doesn't like on the newly-pulled report, it can still reject the consumer for the pre-approved offer. This process can result in unseemly "bait-and-switch" offers. (More on this later.)

Remember, responding to a pre-approved offer creates the kind of inquiry to your credit report that shows you applied for credit, and thus, can negatively impact your credit score. Whether it does negatively impact it, or how much, depends on several other factors. But if you suddenly decided to accept two or more pre-approved offers, it probably would make your score drop.

The credit industry started experimenting with pre-approved solicitations in the very late 1980s as CRA records became increasingly computerized. The practice began taking off in the mid-1990s. It was estimated that between 2000-2003, the average American adult received 32 credit card offers through the mail, regardless of their credit history. In those years, industry was estimated to send out more than four billion pre-approved solicitations per year. The consumer response rate to all those solicitations is said to be well below one percent.

Technology allows the credit bureaus to produce lists of all shapes and sizes. They generally produce a list after a credit bureau provides criteria for a target audience. American Express presumably wants to promote its top-tier "Platinum" card to people with high credit scores. Conversely, sub-prime lenders target people with lower scores.

But it's usually more specific. A lender might want a list of women who have two or more credit cards, between the ages of 30 and 40, living in the Boston, New York, and Washington metropolitan areas. Or, they might want a list of elderly women with a minimal number of active accounts who live in the suburbs. Or, how about providing a list of 20-40 year olds who live in rural zip codes in the eight western most states? Some say it's only a list. But the list you are on can say a lot about you.

The 1996 Amendments to the FCRA formally authorized pre-screening and required that pre-approved credit offers inform consumers that their credit report was the basis for the offer, and that they have a right to opt out. To quote part of the law, creditors must "provide with each written solicitation . . . a clear and conspicuous statement that the CRA was the source of the information and that the consumer can opt out."

Clear and Conspicuous?

There was nothing "clear and conspicuous" about the notices on pre-approved credit card offers. In fact, it's more accurate to say that these were the kinds of "notices" that were designed not to be noticed. Let's examine one more closely. The following example of a notice from Bank of America was located near the bottom of the back page, below the section on "Authorizations, Terms, and Conditions," written in typically tiny type:

Notice Regarding Pre-Screened Offer

Information contained in your credit report was used in connection with this offer. You received this offer because you satisfied the criteria for creditworthiness used to select you for this offer. The credit may not be extended if, after you respond, we find that you do not meet the criteria used to select you for this offer or any applicable criteria bearing on creditworthiness. If credit is extended, the exact account type and credit line will be based on a review of your income and current credit report. You have the right to prohibit use of information in your file with any credit-reporting agency in connection with any transaction that you do not initiate. To assert this right with respect to your file, you may write to: Trans Union, Name Removal Option, P.O. Box 97328, Jackson, MS 39288-7328; Equifax Options, P.O. Box 740123, Atlanta, GA 30374-0123; or Experian, Consumer OPT-OUT, 901 West Bond, Lincoln, NE 68521; or you may notify all three agencies by calling 1-888-567-8688.

Now, Let's Translate

"Information contained in your credit report was used in connection with this offer. You received this offer because you satisfied the criteria for creditworthiness used to select you for this offer."

Translation: Our software programs scan your credit report so we can decide whether to sell you a credit card. You made the cut this time because you have three credit cards with fairly high balances and a credit score between 540-690. We figure you'll jump at our 0% introductory interest rate and no-fee balance transfer and end up switching to our card in the long run.

"If credit is extended, the exact account type and credit line will be based on a review of your income and current credit report."

Translation: Even though the term "pre-approved" is plastered all over the front page in big, bold type, you're not really pre-approved. If you actually respond to our offer, we will pull your credit report again so we can do one last, *individualized* (though automated) check before deciding if we really want you as a customer.

"If credit is extended, the exact account type and credit line will be based on a review of your income and current credit report."

Translation: Here's the "bait-and-switch," or "counter-offer." If after pulling your credit report a second time, we decide you're a bit too risky, we will still send you a credit card. But, it won't be the 0% card that we promoted to you. It will be a 12% APR.

"You have the right to prohibit use of information in your file with any credit reporting agency in connection with any transaction that you do not initiate . . . . (blah, blah, blah) . . ."

Translation: You can block all offers based on your credit report by opting out. (Notice how the last thing they tell you about is the toll-free number.)

'Bait-and-Switch'

The "bait-and-switch" is a real possibility. Some credit card companies will lure you into responding with the "pre-approved" 0% introductory offer, only to send you a card that charges a 12% or higher interest rate. Moreover, when they send you the higher rate card they don't tell you that you were rejected for the better card, or that your credit report caused your rejection. Under the old FCRA, they did not have to give you an "adverse action" notice because they made you a counter-offer and you accepted. Unless you read the fine print, you could start using your new card and incur interest charges that you won't discover until your first monthly statement arrives.

Mail Theft & Identity Theft

Another reason to opt out from pre-screening is identity theft. In the early days of pre-approved credit offers, identity thieves would change the address so that a new card in the victim's name would be sent to the destination of choice. During the 2003 legislative debate, credit card companies insisted they had changed their procedures so that if the applicant changed the address on a pre-approved offer, it would be flagged and the card would not be sent. Several industry officials said the rate of identity theft was much lower with pre-screened offers than with other kinds.

But the identity thieves adjusted as well. In fact, theft of mail by organized gangs or loosely affiliated criminals has gotten worse. Even if they are unable to convert the pre-approved offer or "convenience check" into quick cash or credit, they are often able to sell the personal data to a "fence" that traffics in identifiers in order to service identity thieves.

In June 2003, *Privacy Times* broke a major investigative news story about how various criminal gangs across the nation, intent on committing identity theft and credit fraud, were targeting mail boxes for consumers' personal information and financial instruments. Their favorite targets included "convenience checks," pre-approved credit card offers and bank statements. The gangs involved with these have demonstrated different levels of sophistication. Some consisted of drug addicts, especially "meth-amphet-amine" users known as "Tweakers;" others were associated with specific foreign nationals. Some of the more active gangs hit 200-300 mailboxes in one day. When possible, they used convenience checks or pre-approved credit card offers to get credit quickly. If not, they sold the personal data to other gangs specializing in identity theft, credit fraud and counterfeiting.[311]

"Some thieves will steal a pre-approved application, send it in, and either change the address or come back to take the credit card out of the mail box. Others will get checks, call the bank and try to change the customer's address," said Phil Bartlett, the U.S. Postal Inspection's manager for external crimes and identity theft.[312]

Between October 2002 and May 2003, postal inspectors had made 2,264 identity theft-related arrests stemming from mail theft investigations. In one month in

---

[311] *Privacy Times*, June 16, 2003, Vol. 23 No. 12
[312] *Id.*

2003, in one mid-sized western city, there were 20 arrests and 14 prosecutions. In that city, one law enforcement team had four of its six investigators dedicated to identity theft.

Bolstering Opt-Out Rights

The FCRA Amendments of 2003 attempted to strengthen consumers' rights in a couple of ways. First, they required the FTC to set new rules directing creditors to present opt-out notices "in such format and in such type size and manner as to be simple and easy to understand." Second, the Act closed the counter-offer loop-hole that made it easier for credit card companies to pull the bait-and-switch. The FTC and the Federal Reserve Board must publish "risk-based pricing" rules explaining how and when creditors must give consumers notice when something in their credit report caused the consumer to receive a "materially less favorable" offer. The Amendments permitted creditors to give oral, written, or electronic notice, but do not allow consumers to sue for violations. Enforcement will be up to the FTC and U.S. banking agencies.

Third, the Amendments, for the first time, permitted consumers to opt out from the sharing of their data *for marketing purposes* by affiliates of financial conglomerates. The new provisions were controversial among consumer advocates and privacy experts because they did not go further and regulate other types of affiliate sharing, such as the ones that result in detailed profiling of customers. A California State law sponsored by Senator Jackie Speier went further, but major banks convinced a federal court to declare that portions of the Speier law were preempted by the FCRA.[313]

Still, for those who want to cut down on junk mail, the 2003 Amendments should provide additional relief. A large financial conglomerate like Citigroup has over 1,500

---

[313] The case was pending before the U.S. Court of Appeals for the Ninth Circuit in March 2005.

affiliates. In testimony before the Senate, Martin Wong, Citibank Global Consumer General Counsel confirmed that his company aggressively used affiliate data:

> "Citigroup is able to use the credit information and transaction histories that we collect from affiliates to create internal credit scores and models that help determine a customer's eligibility for credit. This information supplements credit reports and FICO scores to paint the most accurate picture possible of a customer. For example, CitiMortgage underwriters have access to information from affiliates that includes a customer's deposit, loan, and brokerage account balances, as well as the customer's payment history and available lines of credit. This allows our credit analysts to verify the customer's creditworthiness quickly and efficiently, minimizing the burden on the customer associated with providing this documentation."[314]

And, if you are a current or former customer of Citibank, and you receive a pre-approved credit card offer from the banking giant, notice how the FCRA notice is not included. This indicates that Citibank's "internal" information is detailed enough for it to make you a credit card offer without pre-screening against the credit reporting databases.

Quick On The 'Triggers'

Reputable mortgage brokers and consumer advocates alike became outraged to discover in 2007 that the three

---

[314] Statement of Mr. Martin Wong, U.S. Senate Committee on Banking, Housing, and Urban Affairs, "Affiliate Sharing Practices and Their Relationship to the Fair Credit Reporting Act," June, 26 2003; http://banking.senate.gov/index.cfm?Fuseaction=Hearings.Testimony&HearingID=46&WitnessID=189

major credit reporting agencies were selling a service to brokers and lenders which revealed, sometimes within 24 hours, when a consumer had applied for a mortgage or refinance.

The Big Three defended the practice, first marketed as "Triggers" by Experian, as merely a more efficient and targeted form of pre-screening. Triggers services were possible because the inquiries section of a credit report showed whether a consumer had applied for a mortgage or refinance. The credit bureaus could almost instantly convert the data into profitable telemarketing lists.

This is how Equifax described its service:

> Increase your likelihood of a sale. Consumers with a recent credit inquiry, new trade line, or loan maturation event have a higher statistical probability to open new credit than traditional credit pre-screened populations. Increase your response rate. Focus marketing dollars on consumers with a demonstrated need for credit by identifying "in market" consumers with TargetPoint Acquistion. Some customers have seen a 4-6 time improvement in response rates compared to traditional pre-screening. Delivery of fresh prospects, weekly. TargetPoint Acquisition delivers "fresh" names on a weekly basis, suppressing previously delivered names for 30, 60, or 90 days. TargetPoint Acquisition enables on-going weekly marketing campaigns, ensuring a constant flow of new customer prospects.

One problem was that people receiving "Triggers" telemarketing pitches did not realize that the salesmen already knew they had applied for a mortgage.

A second problem was that the practice was of questionable legality. When credit report data are used to market a credit product, the FCRA requires the solicitation to include a "firm offer of credit." How could a telemarketer make a truly "firm offer of credit" based upon a credit report inquiry and a phone call?

Third problem: a growing list of anecdotes indicated that unscrupulous lenders and brokers were using Triggers-styled leads to make deceptive "bait-and-switch" proposals.

Douglas Braden, of Delta Mortgage in Fort Collins, Colo., said one of his long-time customers was persuaded to agree to a high-risk, adjustable rate mortgage by an Ohio lender operating off a Triggers list. However, the loan he closed on turned out to be far more costly than the one described to him by the lender. The customer also said the lender failed to make a promised mortgage payment, thereby damaging his credit score. He complained to the Ohio Consumer Affairs Department. But for the time-being, his financial life had been thrown into chaos because he couldn't afford the loan he was "switched" to, Braden said.

Rhonda Harper, a mortgage broker in Washington State, said both she and her clients received calls, some of them from what sounded like telemarketing operations in India. Other U.S.-based telemarketers delivered hard-sells, berating her for not being interested or for not offering other leads, Harper said. When she told one Florida-based marketer that she was on the Do-Not-Call List (DNC), he kept hounding her for an alternative number that was not on the DNC. Harper said the mortgage-leads list appeared to be an effective way to get around DNC restrictions.

Harry H. Dinham, president of the National Association of Mortgage Brokers, charged that such loose sharing of loan applicants' financial information would open the door to identity theft. He also said that Triggers services did not meet the FCRA's legal standard for "firm offers of credit." His group advocated legislation to either ban the practice altogether, or to require that consumers must first opt-in, and that all offers be in writing. Representative Barney Frank (D-MA), chairman of the House Financial Services Committee, indicated he would move legislation to regulate Triggers.

Of course, the financial services industry is only one source of junk mail. The rest of it comes from retailers, catalog companies, publishers, and non-profits, just to name a few. With a few notable exceptions, federal law is silent on this front. One federal law requires state motor vehicle departments (DMVs) to obtain drivers' permission first before selling their data to marketers. This was a major change for the direct marketing industry, as it was largely built upon free or low-cost drivers' data until Congress passed the Drivers Privacy Protection Act in the mid-1990s.

The Direct Marketing Association runs a voluntary opt-out program known as the "Mail Preference Service (MPS)." Registering with the MPS is supposed to reduce unsolicited commercial mail, though it cannot eliminate it. Contact: Mail Preference Service, P.O. Box 643, Carmel, NY 10512; www.dmaconsumers.org/consumerassistance.html or www.dmaconsumers.org/privacy.html

You have a better ability to **stop junk phone** calls: sign up for the FTC's "Do Not Call" Registry. (888) 382-1222, or, www.donotcall.gov.

Chapter 19

Impermissible Access

Benjamin Marchese III must have thought he had found a sure-fire way of making money—fast and easy.

As the son of the owner of Marchese Chevrolet/GEO in the Philadelphia suburbs, Marchese was in charge of credit applications and review. He quickly saw the value of credit reports and the valuable data they contained. Beginning in 2001 and continuing for more than a year, Marchese allegedly pulled the credit reports of 150 individuals and used the information to pocket $4 million. Marchese was arrested in 2003 and charged with fraud. He was awaiting trial when this book went to press.[315]

Bruce Castor, District Attorney for Montgomery County (Penn.) informed banks and lending institutions that victims of Marchese's scheme, like Rhonda and Michael

---

[315] Michael M. Ciccarone, et al. v. B.J. Marchese, Inc., et al.: U.S. Dist. Ct. – Eastern Dist. of Penn.; C.A. No. 03-1660; class action complaint filed March 19, 2003. Plaintiffs are represented by Cary L. Flitter, Timothy T. Myers and Mark A. Kearney.

Meksoh were not at fault, but they continued to be harassed by creditors and collectors seeking payments.[316]

Rhonda Meksoh of Pottstown, said the fraud caused extreme damage to her credit. "We're going to have to tell our son, 'Mom and Dad can't help you apply for a car loan'. And (the interest rates on) our credits cards are getting raised because of someone else.' "[317]

The Purpose Test

The Fair Credit Reporting Act (FCRA) specifies that credit reports can only be used for "permissible purposes," meaning for credit, insurance, or employment.

It is not allowed to use credit reports to snoop into the finances of an ex-spouse or prospective lover, or a critic of your organization, or an opponent in litigation. It is also not permissible to access credit reports for the purpose of committing identity theft.

But these things happen—all of them and more.

If someone wants to invade your privacy, the credit report is the first document of choice. It's a convenient roadmap to your financial standing and relationships. The FCRA imposes civil and criminal penalties for impermissibly accessing credit reports.

To detect impermissible access to your credit report, you need to examine the "inquiries section," which lists the companies who have obtained your credit report and their stated reason for doing so.

In addition to the FCRA, companies are bound by the contracts they sign with Equifax, Experian, and Trans Union to only use credit reports for permissible purposes.

Clearly for many entities, it has proved a tremendous convenience and privilege to enjoy instant access to the con-

---

[316] Melissa Milewski, "Bill Would Protect Identity Theft Victims," *Buck County Courier Times*, Oct. 21, 2003; http://www.phillyburbs.com/pb-dyn/news/111-10212003-181732.html

[317] *Id.*

sumer reports of some 205 million Americans. However, with that privilege goes major responsibilities.

Accordingly, it is incumbent upon companies to ensure that their employees only use credit reports for permissible purposes. Several courts have ruled that if an employee illegally accesses someone's credit report, the company he works for can be held liable.

Companies Are Liable

The potential for abuse of consumer reports, as well as the importance of users of consumer reports being vigilant about their duty to obey the FCRA's permissible purposes restriction, was illustrated by a 1987 court case. An attorney (Ms. Ryan) used her connection with a credit union to access the credit report of her ex-husband. The U.S. Court of Appeals for the Fourth Circuit ruled that obtaining consumer reports under such false pretenses subjected both the attorney and the credit union to civil and criminal liability.[318] The credit union was on the hook because of a legal doctrine known as *"respondeat superior,"* which imposes vicarious liability on organizations for the actions of their agents who have "apparent authority."

"Ryan was an agent of the Credit Union and had apparent authority to obtain the credit report, even if Ryan lacked actual authority to do so," the Fourth Circuit panel wrote. "Accordingly, the Credit Union is liable to Yohay (the ex-husband) for Ryan's wrongful actions as its agent pursuant to the doctrine of *respondeat superior*. A principal is liable for the acts of an agent who had apparent authority to act regardless of whether the principal benefited by the acts of the agent or ratified the acts of the agent, if either the plaintiff or a third-party relied upon the principal's representations which created apparent authority."

---

[318] Yohay v. City of Alexandria Employees Credit Union, Inc. (827 F.2d 967).

The court reasoned that the employer was in the best position to protect consumers with internal safeguards. "Seemingly anyone who used the Credit Union's computer to access [the CRA's] files appeared – from [the CRA's] perspective – to have authority to gain such access. In that regard it is to be noted that the Credit Union had not posted any guidelines to users of the computer informing them of the circumstances under which such credit information could be obtained," the Fourth Circuit wrote.

Sixth Circuit

In a 1998 case, the U.S. Court of Appeals for the Sixth Circuit came to the same conclusion, finding that whenever a creditor has expressly allowed an employee to access consumer reports on its behalf, that person will invariably have apparent authority in the eyes of the CRA to request and receive a consumer report. Thus, the credit grantor can be liable for that employee's actions.

"Protecting consumers from the improper use of credit reports is an underlying policy of the FCRA. An apparent authority theory is in keeping with FCRA's underlying deterrent purpose because employers are in a better position to protect consumers by use of internal safeguards," the Sixth Circuit wrote, citing the Fourth Circuit's opinion in Yohay.[319]

"Because application of the apparent authority doctrine advances the FCRA's goals and produces no inconsistencies with other FCRA provisions, we conclude that such a theory of liability is an appropriately operative theory of liability under the statute," it continued.

"Failure to impose vicarious liability on a corporation like Federated would allow it to escape liability for 'willful' and 'negligent' violations of the statute. Because a company like Federated can act only through its agents, it is difficult

---

[319] Jones v. Federal Fin. Reserve Corp. (144 3d 961)

to imagine a situation in which a company would ever be found to have willfully violated the statute directly by obtaining a credit report for an impermissible purpose. The FCRA's deterrence goal would be subverted if a corporation could escape liability for a violation that could only occur because the corporation cloaked its agent with the apparent authority to request credit reports," the Sixth Circuit wrote.

Another court commented that sloppy practices, like posting computer access codes where anyone could see them, "would almost invite violations" of the FCRA.[320]

Car Dealers

Unfortunately, it seems many companies that regularly use credit reports never got around to installing safeguards and conducting the employee training necessary to discourage misuse of credit reports.

Car dealers have emerged as one problematic sector—and for understandable reasons. When someone walks into a showroom, a salesman naturally would like to know if that person is a serious candidate for a car purchase, or just a "window shopper" on whom it would be better not to waste time. Pulling a credit report can help the salesman "size up" a consumer and see what they can afford and for what kind of financing they would qualify. It's easy to do while the consumer's out for a test drive and the auto dealer is holding his drivers license.

But it's illegal. On more than one occasion, auto dealers have been told that it's illegal.

Window Shoppers?

In fact, the Texas Automobile Dealers Association (TADA) in 1997 wrote a letter asking the Federal Trade

---

[320] <u>Kodrick v Ferguson</u> 54 F. Supp.2d 788 (N.D. Ill. 1999)

Commission if it was permissible for salesmen to pull credit reports on window shoppers.

The FTC responded with an emphatic "no," stating that dealers only have a permissible purpose when the prospective customer applies for financing or otherwise consents to use of his credit report to see if he qualifies.

David Medine, then associate director of the FTC's Division of Credit Practices, wrote that a dealer is not justified in pulling a credit report when a consumers asks about prices, takes part in comparison-shopping, or goes for a test drive. Dealers also can't pull credit reports when the consumer pays cash.

If the dealer would like to see a consumer's credit report before answering general questions about the availability of financing, this must be explained to the consumer and written permission must be obtained.

Only in those circumstances where it is clear both to the consumer and to the dealer that the consumer is actually initiating the purchase or lease of a specific vehicle and, in addition, the dealer has a legitimate business need for consumer report information, may the dealer obtain a report without written permission.[321]

A "legitimate need" would be to arrange financing or to confirm the creditworthiness of a consumer who wanted to pay by check, Medine wrote.

At least one trade association has warned its members not to abuse their access to credit reports, particularly in light of the FTC opinion letter and the 1996 Amendments to FCRA. The Independent Automobile Dealers Association (IADA) posted a column—written by Keith E. Whann—on its Web site entitled, "Permissible Purposes To Run A Credit Report:"

---

[321] Staff Opinion Letter, David Medine to Karen Coffey, Chief Counsel, Texas Automobile Dealers Assoc., Feb. 11, 1998 (www.ftc.gov/os/statutes/fcra/coffey.htm)

While it is naturally important to have some sense of the consumer's ability to qualify for financing prior to spending a great deal of time with that customer throughout the sales process, the dealership must understand what constitutes a legitimate business need and, more importantly, the consumer's initiation of the transaction.

A consumer merely asking questions about prices and financing is not necessarily indicating intent to purchase a vehicle from that particular dealership. Accordingly, the dealership does not then have a legitimate business need for a credit report in this situation. If the consumer is simply comparison-shopping, as they would be in a situation such as this, the dealer would have to obtain written permission from the consumer prior to obtaining a credit report. Similarly, a request by a consumer to test drive a vehicle does not indicate an intent to initiate the purchase of a vehicle.[322]

Not An Isolated Incident

Over the years, there have been a string of cases involving auto dealers' unauthorized access to credit reports. On December 8, 1993, *The New York Times* reported that the Secret Service had arrested 15 salesmen in the Autoland car dealership in Springfield, N.J. for fraudulent purchases that stemmed from salesmen's access to credit bureau databases. The arrests were part of a crackdown on a fraud ring.

Daniel Greenstone, an Assistant U.S. Attorney who prosecuted the case, said, "Merchants and credit reporting agencies have to be more vigilant in insuring that those who access credit reports are authorized to do so. This case shows it's too easy."

---

[322] Whann, Keith, "The Fair Credit Reporting Act Made Simple" http://www.independentdealer.com/finance/finance18.asp

In the same article, Janis Lamar, a TRW spokeswoman, said the credit reporting agency, beginning January 1, 1994, would stop giving auto dealers the account number for individuals' credit card and charge accounts.

In the Autoland cases, the frauds generally involved ordering credit cards or loans in other peoples' names and then collecting large cash advances. Usually, the most credit-worthy people, with few charge accounts or bad debts, were picked out, and applications were made by the fraud ring.

Autoland changed its procedures. Previously it allowed its 170 salespeople to search the credit histories from any of the company's 21 terminals. After the fraud case, Autoland designated two employees as authorized to access credit bureau databases, according to the *New York Times*.

In October 2001, a federal jury in Miami returned a 34-count indictment against a car salesman for pulling credit reports without authorization and allegedly selling consumers' data to identity thieves. According to the Oct. 26, 2001 *Consumer Financial Services Law Report (CFSLR)*, the indictment charged that from April to September 2001, the salesman gained access to the Equifax and Experian credit files on 130 consumers. Potential losses were estimated at $1 million, according to the *CFSLR*.

At Wayzata Nissan in Minnesota, salesman Chris Ochtera apparently felt he was not performing up to expectations, so he began accessing the reports of past customers with good credit histories to help less-qualified individuals qualify for financing. Before getting caught, he pulled the credit reports of 34 unsuspecting consumers, many of whose credit histories were damaged and whose current and previous addresses were changed. Ochtera was sentenced for identity theft and mail fraud and sentenced to federal prison.[323]

---

[323] Andrea M. Johnson, et al. v. Wayzata Nissan LLC, et al.: U.S. Dist. Ct. – Minnesota; C.A. No. 03-4553; plaintiffs were represented by Tom J. Lyons and Associates of Little Canada, MN. The case settled.

Chapter 20

Damage & Damages

> *"That doesn't mean that it's not actual. It just means that it's hard to quantify, but you've had the emotional harm. Why isn't that an ... actual harm?"*
>
> – Justice Antonin Scalia
> Oral Argument, <u>Doe v. Chao</u>,
> (December 2003)

TransUnion had put Judy Thomas through the wringer. Unbeknownst to her, it had first mixed the negative credit history of Judith Upton into her credit report in 1996. Thomas disputed the errors. Some, but not all of them, were deleted. More inaccuracies returned to her TransUnion (TU) credit report again in 1998, right when Thomas, a Klamath Falls, Oregon realtor, was applying for a mortgage. The episode painfully delayed approval of her mortgage and the purchase of her home, as it took TU months to clear up her credit report. Thomas remembered being in tears, sitting beside her mortgage broker, as the broker tried explaining and re-explaining to a TU phone representative that the bad data did not belong on Thomas' report.

TU grudgingly cleared up Thomas' credit report a second time, and she was able to buy her house. But the experience gnawed at her for many months. After finally finding a pair of experienced lawyers to take her case in 2000, Thomas filed suit under the Fair Credit Reporting Act.[324]

---

[324] Thomas was represented by Robert Sola and Michael Baxter, of Portland, Oregon.

In a quiet moment just days before the start of her July 2002 trial, Judy Thomas was asked, "Why did this bother you so much?"

"It wasn't me," she responded.

After a four-day trial which delved deeply into TU's standard operating procedures, a federal jury in Portland awarded Thomas $300,000 in compensatory damages and $5 million in punitive damages. The smaller amount was to compensate Thomas for the harm she endured; the latter amount was to punish TU so the company would not do to others what it did to Thomas.[325]

'But What Are The Damages?'

Normally, when people think of damages in the legal context, they think of lost jobs or broken legs. In fact, when confronted with complaints about credit report errors or other invasions of privacy, the common refrain from the financial services industry and their lawyers is, "Yeah, but what are the damages?"

Thomas' case was a watershed because it demonstrated the high value that Americans place on two simple components of privacy in the information age: one's "good name," and reasonable control over one's own personal data. If measured in hours, or in out-of-pocket expenses, Thomas' damages were relatively small – especially considering that the FCRA's statute-of-limitations was only two years.[326] But the jury apparently placed profound importance on the humiliation and emotional distress that Thomas endured be-

---

[325] Thomas v. Trans Union LLC: U.S. Dist. Ct. – Oregon – No. 00-1150; In a Jan. 29, 2003. Opinion & Order, U.S. Magistrate Judge John Jelderks reduced the punitive damages from $5 million to $1 million, reasoning that the case only warranted a 4-1 ratio of punitive to compensatory damages. He awarded Sola and Baxter roughly $110,000 in fees and costs.

[326] Under the 2003 FCRA Amendments, the statute of limitations has been modified and in some cases extended to five years.

cause of the unjust besmirching of her good name and the associated hassles.

That's what Congress intended. The FCRA states that the "banking system is dependent upon fair and accurate credit reporting," and that "inaccurate credit reports directly impair the efficiency of the banking system, and unfair credit reporting methods undermine the public confidence which is essential to the continued functioning of the banking system." The FCRA also states, "There is a need to insure that CRAs exercise their *grave responsibilities* with fairness, impartiality, and a respect for the consumer's right to privacy."

To achieve this, the FCRA provides for actual damages for negligent violations. "Actual damages" include out-of-pocket expenses, financial harm and emotional or mental distress. To recover for the latter, a consumer generally needs to provide evidence that he or she actually experienced distress. Such evidence can come in the form of credible testimony or medical or other records.

The FCRA also provides for punitive damages for "willful" violations, which are intended to deter companies from making such violations by punishing them if they do. In 2007, the U.S. Supreme Court ruled that "willful" means the company acted in "reckless disregard" of a consumer's FCRA rights.[327] Finally, the FCRA provides for attorney's fees when the consumer is the prevailing party.

Some Don't See The Damage

However, the "What-Are-The-Damages" syndrome still plagues consumers who try to stand up for their rights under the FCRA.

Contrast Thomas' experience with that of Mary Harris, a Texas resident whose credit report had been fouled, off-and-on for 16 years, by the negative history of another Mary Harris, who lived in South Carolina.

---

[327] Safeco Ins. Co of America v. Burr, 127 S.Ct. 2201 (June 4, 2007)

Mary Harris first discovered her Equifax file was mixed in 1986 when her husband told her that their mortgage application for a South Carolina home had been held up because of her "bad credit." With the help of some in-laws, one of whom was a state judge and the other an employee of a credit bureau, Harris was able to dispute the errors and remove the inaccuracies.

In 1996, again applying for credit, Harris learned that more bad data from the other "Mary Harris" had returned to her credit report. This time when she called Equifax, Harris said an agent told her that Equifax merely reported the information creditors provided them and it was not Equifax's job to investigate errors. The agent told Harris that she had to contact the creditors, convince them to stop the errors, and direct Equifax to delete them.

Not knowing her rights to demand an investigation, Harris contacted Sears, Household Credit, Lane Bryant and Discover Card, all of whom eventually agreed that mistakes did not belong on Harris' report, and advised Equifax to delete them.

In 1999, Harris and her husband had already sold their farm in Louisiana and applied for a mortgage for a home in Texas. But the same negative accounts were back on her credit report, and their application was declined.

Under a tight deadline, Harris and her husband had to re-do the application so it was strictly in the husband's name. After staying in a camper on a fretful Sunday night in Houston, the Harrises learned their husband-only application had been approved.

In 2002, after applying for a home equity loan, Harris learned that the Sears, Household, Discover and Lane Bryant accounts had returned, along with American Express, MBNA, Providian and a collection account that was not hers. Inaccuracies also persisted in her name and address. This time the report was issued by CSC Credit Services, an Equifax affiliate that services Texas and other states in the South and Midwest. While CSC handles consumer disclosures and requests for reinvestigations, it relies on the Equifax database for credit reports.

Throughout 2002 and into 2003, credit report errors repeatedly prevented the Harrises from getting the best rates on home equity loans or refinancing packages at a time when those rates were heading to historic lows and millions of consumers were benefiting. Throughout the entire period, the situation was putting a great deal of stress on their relationship.

Somebody, Help Me

Harris finally complained about Equifax in June of 2002 to the Texas Attorney General, which tries to resolve complaints informally but does not have the authority to issue orders in individual cases. In October 2002, the office advised Harris that it had tried to contact Equifax on several occasions.

"Regretfully, we have not received any response to our inquiries. Informal complaint resolution is not effective when a business does not respond. Therefore, we must close the file at this time," wrote Bach Stephens, a complaint analyst in the Houston office of then Texas AG John Cornyn.

Stephens suggested that Harris might want to talk to an attorney. Harris finally did, and filed suit in federal court in Galveston.[328]

Initially, U.S. District Judge Sam Kent expressed disbelief that the inaccuracies could drag on for so long, Harris said. Judge Kent was considered friendly to plaintiffs, having heard many cases involving oil rig workers who were injured during explosions and other accidents in the Gulf of Mexico. Mary Harris thought she would finally get her day in court. She did – kind of.

---

[328] Harris was represented by Houston-area attorneys Steven L. Parker, and Jack and Jordin Nolan.

At her May 2003 trial in Galveston, about 40 minutes into her testimony, Judge Kent appeared to grow impatient. Harris said he interrupted her testimony, and curtly asked her to list her out-of-pocket expenses. Kent wrote them down and then ordered her lawyers, and the Equifax lawyers into his chambers. Symbolically, Harris was left sitting on the witness stand alone in the court room.

Back in his chambers, Judge Kent then advised her lawyers in no uncertain terms that he did not want to hear any more of her testimony, and advised them to settle the case right then and there. Harris felt she had no choice, and settled.[329] She got the impression that Judge Kent did not think the credit denials, the ongoing hassles and the emotional distress were all that damaging. She also got the impression that Judge Kent would not even consider whether Equifax was liable for punitive damages, recalling that she understood him to say something to the effect that he "didn't have authority to punish Equifax."[330]

Her long-awaited "day-in-court" aborted, Harris stood outside the Galveston courthouse, visibly shaken, and in tears.

"Help me!" she said, sobbing softly. "We are raised to believe that our legal system will protect the innocent. If the federal court cannot enforce the FCRA laws, then who can?" she asked.

Looking backs months later, Harris, commented on the power that CRAs have over consumers.

"Equifax controls our lives more than our own government. Equifax controls whether we have employment, housing, transportation, clothing, food, and most important, a good reputation with total and complete disregard to accuracy and accountability."

---

[329] The terms of the settlement were confidential

[330] <u>Mary M. Harris v. Equifax Information Services, L.L.C.</u>: U.S. Dist. Ct. – S. Dist. of Texas (Galveston) – No. 02-CV-753. Harris' attorneys waived a jury trial and opted for a "bench" trial.

She expressed concern that actions like Judge Kent's had the effect of giving Equifax the green light to conduct business under its own rules, and reduced its incentive to comply with the FCRA.

Privacy, Credit Reporting & 'FIPs'

Actually, there is an extensive body of research confirming that, for most people, it is very damaging to suffer the kinds of privacy invasions stemming from credit reporting, including inaccuracies and mixed files, impermissible access and disclosures, identity theft, failure to correct errors and reinsertion of previously deleted data.

It's important to understand that credit reporting is a "privacy" issue because privacy in the modern age is defined and evaluated according to principles of Fair Information Practices (FIPs). These principles, which serve as the foundation for most privacy laws in the United States and abroad, encompass access and correction, data accuracy and integrity, purpose specification and use limitation, data security, transparency and enforcement.[331]

---

[331] In 1980, the Organization of Economic Cooperation and Development (OECD), based in Paris, adopted the following eight principles of fair information practices, still referred to by some experts as the "Gold Standard" of privacy. These principles were endorsed by the Governments of the United States, Japan and most Western European countries in an OECD international accord. These principles effectively have been recognized by the United Nations in its work on privacy: (1) Collection Limitation; (2) Data Quality; (3) Purpose Specification; (4) Use Limitation; (5) Security Safeguards; (6) Openness (7) Participation and (8) Accountability.

Also see *Personal Privacy In The Information Age: The Report of the Privacy Protection Study Commission*, (July 1977; GPO Stock No. 052-003-00395) Herein referred to as the PPSC Report. The three general FIP principles endorsed by the PPSC were: (1) minimize intrusiveness; (2) open up record-keeping operations in ways that will minimize the extent to which recorded information about an individual is itself a source of unfairness in any decision about him made on the basis

The U.S. Privacy Protection Study Commission, in its 1976 report, noted the link between third-party recordkeepers, privacy, and the rights of individuals.

> The intrusiveness, unfairness and unrestricted disclosure characteristic of so much organizational record keeping today is largely the result of weaknesses in the relationship between the individual and those who need to know intimate details of his life . . . As long as America believes, as more than a matter of rhetoric, in the worth of the individual citizen, it must constantly reaffirm and reinforce its protections for privacy, and ultimately the autonomy, of the individual.[332]

In fact, Equifax explicitly recognized the importance of Fair Information Practices principles in its groundbreaking, 1990 public opinion survey, entitled, "Equifax Report on Consumers In The Information Age."[333]

---

of it (maximize fairness); and (3) create legitimate enforceable expectations of confidentiality.

Also see "The 1973 Report of the [HEW] Secretary's Advisory Committee On Automated Personal Data Systems." The five FIP principles set forth by the HEW task force were: (1) there must be no personal data recordkeeping systems whose very existence is secret; (2) there must be a way for an individual to find out what information about him is in a record and how it is used; (3) there must be a way for an individual to prevent information about him obtained for one purpose from being used or made available for other purposes without his consent; (4) there must be a way for an individual to correct or amend a record of identifiable information about him; and (5) any organization creating, maintaining, using, or disseminating records of identifiable personal data must assure the reliability of the data for their intended use and must take reasonable precautions to prevent misuse of the data.

[332] "Personal Privacy In An Information Society," Op. Cit.,

[333] "Equifax Report on Consumers In The Information Age, " (© Equifax 1990) "A national opinion survey conducted for Equifax, Inc. by Louis Harris & Associates and Dr. Alan F. Westin, professor of public law and government, Columbia University." Westin served as a consultant to Equifax for several yea

However, despite extensive literature on the subject, there is not general familiarity with it – outside of a small community of privacy experts and consumer advocates.

Starter List of Harms

Here's the short list of the ways in which consumers are damaged by inaccurate credit reports, non-responsiveness and faulty reinvestigations by CRAs and furnishers.

- Inaccurate data can lead to the unjust denial of credit or insurance.
- In the age of risk-based pricing, inaccuracies can result in the granting of credit or insurance on less favorable terms.
- Attempting to correct inaccuracies can be time-consuming, causing a loss of time, energy and opportunity.
- Often the most profound damage that consumers suffer is the emotional distress that accompanies the discovery of inaccuracies in one's credit report; and/or the frustrating process of trying to correct errors that were not of one's own making; and/or the unjust denial of credit; and/or of being told that false information has been "verified," and/or that information that was previously deleted as inaccurate was reinserted without notice.

With identity theft, all of the above damages apply, compounded by the fact that a criminal is joyriding on your good credit, ruining your name.

since the 1990 report. He was a special consultant to the PPSC and a member of the 1973 HEW Advisory Task Force.

History Offers Abundant Evidence

One of the first recognized harms resulting from inaccurate data is the unjust denial of credit, insurance or employment.

A 1994 House Banking Committee report on FCRA legislation said that an immediate damage from "inaccurate credit reports" was that they "can impede the ability of too many consumers to obtain credit or other benefits." Referring to the 1989 Williams study and the 1991 Consumers Union study, the Committee further specified one reason why inaccuracies were damaging: "Both studies defined serious errors to mean those that could, or did, cause the denial of credit, employment or insurance."

Similarly, the 1998 U.S. PIRG report stated:

In many instances, credit report errors cause consumers considerable harm. The results of mistakes can range from the rejection of a credit card application to the denial of a job. Also, errors often cause consumers to spend weeks – sometimes years – calling creditors, writing credit bureaus, and worrying anxiously in an effort to remove the inaccurate information from their record. One California victim of credit fraud who contacted PIRG was denied financing on her new car, even after she had contacted all three credit bureaus numerous times about the mistaken delinquencies on her credit report. Another California man had to hire an attorney to send a letter to the credit bureaus, "stating that I am who I am," before he could finally get a stranger's bad credit accounts removed from his credit report. While credit report errors almost always lead to a little consumer hassle, they also can create a ticking time bomb waiting to wreck an unsuspecting consumer's good name at any moment.

As TransUnion's Web site points out, a negative credit history will lower the credit score. A lower credit score means that a consumer will not be able to obtain credit or insurance, or will only be able to obtain them on less favorable terms.

The damage of inaccurate credit reports will become clearer to more and more consumers because in the era of risk-based pricing, the credit score will define the terms of credit. Again, the lower the credit score, the worse the interest rate or insurance premium.

Time Lost

The process of cleaning up an inaccurate credit report can be time-consuming. In its 1994 report, the House Banking Committee wrote, "Compounding this high error rate problem is the difficulty that consumers face when they attempt to correct inaccurate or incomplete information contained in their credit files."

The Committee cited the 1991 U.S. PIRG study, based on the review of 155 consumer report complaints on file with the FTC, which found that the average duration of complaints against CRAs was 22.5 weeks, or nearly 6 months. The 1991 PIRG report was entitled "Don't Call; Don't Write; We Don't Care."

Not Responsive

The dispute correction process is prolonged when the CRAs are not responsive. This is what one unnamed consumer told US PIRG for its 1990 report:

> After 5 1/2 months of phone calls and letters, the CRA has absolutely refused to rectify the incor-

rect information on my report. . . . I have submitted comments from institutions and from my own records that should clearly show that their report is incorrect. . . . This has caused me untold humiliation and embarrassment with banks and credit agencies from which I have tried to obtain credit.[334]

Nancy Ross, a *Washington Post* writer, had a similar experience:

For the past two years, I have been the victim in a case of mistaken identity that has ruined my credit rating. Despite my efforts to rectify the situation, I'm beginning to fear that my epitaph may read: 'Here lies a deadbeat.'[335]

On October 3, 1989, *Privacy Times* ran a lengthy story based on consumer complaints to the FTC regarding credit bureaus. One consumer's letter referred to the frustrating and time-consuming nature of fixing the problem. "[It] looks like another round of letters is in order," the consumer wrote.

The article noted that in several complaints, consumers referred to their attempts to correct errors as "humiliating and frustrating" experiences. One outraged consumer said 30 days after he had submitted corrections to TRW he received a reply stating that his "disputes are frivolous or irrelevant. Therefore, they will not be reinvestigated."

After a year, the consumer was convinced that TRW was violating the FCRA, but said he was "powerless to obtain their compliance," explaining, "The FTC advised me to seek private council (sic) and pursue a civil action, while, at the same time, the FTC advised me that they would 'short-

---

[334] "Nightmare On Credit Street, Or, How The Credit Bureau Ruined My Life," U.S. PIRG, June 12, 1990
[335] Ross, Nancy, *Washington Post*, May 31, 1990

ly' file an action against TRW for 'similar' and other violations of the FCRA.'"

"The Center for Law in The Public Interest advised me this was 'not the kind of case they do.' The law firm of Allred, Maroko, Goldberg & Ribicoff declined the case because the firm has 'no expertise in the field.' A meeting with an attorney provided by the L.A. County Bar Association yielded the opinion that 'it would be time-consuming and too costly to litigate.'"

The 1993 U.S. PIRG report, based upon consumer complaints to the FTC, found that 16% of "corrected" errors subsequently reappeared and that the average consumer had already contacted the credit bureau 3.6 times by phone call or letter without satisfaction before contacting the FTC.

The 1998 U.S. PIRG Report found that CRA non-responsiveness relating to basic communications and simple access to their consumer reports continued to cause frustration to a significant percentage of consumers. Moreover, inaccuracies continued to cause damage:

> If a consumer's credit report is inaccurate, she may appear to be a bad credit risk because of a variety of factors: because she appears to have been delinquent on accounts that she was never late on, because she looks like she has too many credit accounts open at one time, because she has court judgments against her that are actually against a stranger, or many other unfortunate scenarios. Credit report errors can cause the denial of not only credit, but also employment, insurance, housing or even the right to cash a check, use a debit card or open a bank account.. . . The most valuable thing we have is our good name.

Parallel With Identity Theft

As mentioned before, identity theft is a subcategory of Mixed Files, as the imposter-generated data are mixed into the consumer report of the innocent victim. Thus, the damages arising from identity theft, as they pertain to the interaction between consumers and CRAs, are similar to the damages arising from Mixed Files. In July 12, 2000 testimony before the Senate Judiciary Subcommittee on Technology, Terrorism and Government Information, Jodie Bernstein, then head of the FTC's Bureau of Consumer Protection, testified:

> The leading complaints by identity theft victims against the consumer reporting agencies are that they provide inadequate assistance over the phone, or that they will not reinvestigate or correct an inaccurate entry in the consumer's credit report. In one fairly typical case, a consumer reported that two years after initially notifying the consumer reporting agencies of the identity theft, following up with them numerous times by phone, and sending several copies of documents that they requested, the suspect's address and other inaccurate information continues to appear on her credit report. In another case, although the consumer has sent documents requested by the consumer reporting agency three separate times, the consumer reporting agency involved still claims that it has not received the information.[336]

In her March 7, 2000 testimony before the Subcommittee, Bernstein elaborated further:

> A consumer's credit history is frequently scarred, and he or she typically must spend numerous hours, sometimes over the course of months or even years, contesting bills and straightening out credit reporting errors. In the interim, the consumer victim may be denied loans, mortgages, a driver's license,

---

[336] www.ftc.gov/os/2000/07/idtheft.htm

and employment; a bad credit report may even prevent him or her from something as simple as opening up a new bank account at a time when other accounts are tainted and a new account is essential. Moreover, even after the initial fraudulent bills are resolved, new fraudulent charges may continue to appear, requiring ongoing vigilance and effort by the victimized consumer. . . .

Identity theft victims continue to face numerous obstacles to resolving the credit problems that frequently result from identity theft. For example, many consumers must contact and re-contact creditors, credit bureaus, and debt collectors, often with frustrating results.[337]

The General Accounting Office wrote in one of if its first reports on identity theft in 1998:

Identity theft can cause substantial harm to the lives of individual citizens -- potentially severe emotional or other non-monetary harm, as well as economic harm. Even though financial institutions may not hold victims liable for fraudulent debts, victims nonetheless often feel 'personally violated' and have reported spending significant amounts of time trying to resolve the problems caused by identity theft -- problems such as bounced checks, loan denials, credit card application rejections, and debt collection harassment," it wrote.[338]

---

[337] Prepared Statement of Jodie Bernstein, Director of Consumer Protection, FTC; http://www.ftc.gov/os/2000/03/identitytheft.htm

[338] (Identity Theft: Available Data Indicate Growth in Prevalence & Cost, GAO-02-424T, (www.gao.gov/new.items/d0242t.pdf)

FTC 2003 Survey

In its September 2003 survey, the FTC found that the longer it took to discover the identity theft, the greater the damages. While 63% had no out-of-pocket losses, victims reported a wide range of problems, including wrongful bank and credit card charges, harassment by collectors, loan or insurance rejection, cut off of utilities, civil lawsuits, and criminal investigations.

The FTC also found that credit bureaus were instrumental in gauging damage to victims. Among those victims who contacted a credit bureau, 58% said they were either "very" or "somewhat" satisfied, while 29% said they were somewhat dissatisfied and 9% said they were very dissatisfied. Of those consumer who contacted all three major credit bureaus, 49% said they were satisfied with all three, 20% said they were satisfied with some of them, and 31% said they were dissatisfied with all three.

Mental & Emotional Distress

Whether it be inaccuracies resulting from a mixed file, or identity theft, many of the studies above have alluded to what might be the worst damage to consumers: mental and emotional distress. It is evident in the testimony of victims that we cited in previous chapters.

Here is what two victims of mixed files described in U.S. PIRG's 1990 report, "Nightmare On Credit Street, Or, How The Credit Bureau Ruined My Life"

> **Michael Riley, *Time Magazine*.** "Suddenly, the credit-travel enticement had turned into a Kafkaesque nightmare of mistaken identities, computer screw-ups and human errors, all spilling out of the vast and powerful credit-reporting system. Not only was my credit a disaster, I was officially dead." (*Time Magazine*, April 9, 1990.)

> **Unnamed Consumer**. "Early part of last year I was denied because of wrongful report. . . This past December. . . I was denied again . . . I was furious as this was to have been corrected the first time. . . There are exactly seven accounts that do not belong on here and I want them removed for good. On January 23rd of this year I received my credit rating and again they have many accounts incorrect."

This author, along with other experts, not surprisingly has observed that invasion of privacy causes emotional distress. It is distressful to learn first hand that your good name and credit history have been tarnished, through no fault of your own, by the derogatory credit data of a complete stranger. It is distressful to find that, despite repeated efforts on your part, a credit bureau continuously fails to delete inaccurate or unverifiable data from your report, or a creditor continues to report false data. It is distressful to find that information, previously deleted because it was inaccurate, was inexplicably reinserted into your consumer report. It is distressful to be wrongly associated with highly derogatory credit data, and to have to clear your name. It also takes time and energy to try to correct the problem, often involving numerous phone calls and letters. It's distressful not knowing everyone who may have associated you with highly derogatory credit data. It can be difficult to maintain constructive personal relationships under stress.[339] It can be difficult to perform adequately at one's job.

ITRC Study

In September 2003, the Identity Theft Resource Center (ITRC) published research that enumerated the many harms that victims suffer, and concluded that the emotional

---

[339] In fact, the insurance industry says that stress, stemming from financial problems, can cause auto accidents, and therefore justifying its use of credit reports in setting insurance rates.

distress might be the worst of all. In the largest survey of its kind, the ITRC surveyed 173 actual victims of identity theft, and then had two experts review their responses.[340]

One was Paul Colins, a credit industry analyst. "The range of emotions is wide and rather painful to read. Three-fourths of victims were left with a feeling of financial insecurity, 88% experienced anger, and 75% expressed a feeling of helplessness," Colins commented.

"While these feelings do appear to subside a little over time, the survey clearly shows for many victims the feelings linger on. While most surveys have focused on the financial costs to victims, these psychological impacts are generally unreported. They may, however, have far worse consequences for victims."[341]

Dr. Charles Nelson, a licensed psychologist, and director of both the Crime and Trauma Recovery Program at the Family Treatment Institute, also reviewed victims' responses.

"Identity theft has been classified in many realms as a victimless crime," Nelson wrote. "This survey was designed to test the emotional impact of identity theft and to discover if sufferers of this crime exhibit similar responses as those of more commonly recognized victims including rape, repeated abuse, and violent assault victims. Many of the listed symptoms are classic examples of Post Traumatic Stress Disorder and secondary PTSD (from secondary wounding)."[342]

"While each crime has its own specific triggers and emotional responses, upon examination of these results, this study clearly proves that the impact of identity theft on its victims leaves similar scars and long-term impact as demonstrated by victims of violent crime.

---

[340] "Identity Theft: The Aftermath 2003," Identity Theft Resource Center (Sept. 2003); http://www.idtheftcenter.org/idaftermath.pdf
[341] *Id.*
[342] *Id.*

"This comes as no surprise to victims of identity theft. Although there is no direct physical injury in this crime, identity theft victims know all too well the psychological, emotional, and social destructive swath of pain that has been cut through their lives. Furthermore, it is clear that this crime has a ripple effect on the relationships in the victims' lives. This study found that numerous victims of this crime suffered a significant strain in the relationship with their significant other. Anecdotally, during ITRC focus groups, victims have shared that this crime was a major contributing factor in a divorce due to the intense strain on one or both of the partners," he continued.

Nelson noted that some ID Theft victims said they felt "dirty or defiled, guilty, ashamed or embarrassed, being an outcast, undeserving of assistance or having brought this crime upon myself – responses similar to the ones we saw after an extensive media information campaign on rape and sexual assault prevention."

"Consumers are being told that they are the responsible party, if a crime occurs. 'Top ten lists' of how to avoid victimization add to this perception," he wrote. "For the self-blaming response to stop, victims need to learn that they are not the responsible party for this crime. Victims are victims, each with his or her own fingerprint of painful responses to the crimes committed. There are commonalities within the victimization responses found in each category of crime victims. This study discovered that there are also far more response similarities that identity theft victims share with ALL victims than previously realized."[343]

It Shows In The Statistics

The high value that Americans place in protecting and preserving their good names is reflected in FTC complaint statistics. As the 1993 U.S. PIRG studies revealed,

---

[343] *Id.*

in the early 1990s, the leading cause of complaints to the FTC was inaccuracy in credit reports. Notice how complaints about mistakes, which do not always involve out-of-pocket loss, outpaced other categories which did entail loss of money.

1. Credit Bureaus (30,901);
2. Misc. Credit (22, 729);
3. Investment Fraud (12,809);
4. Equal Credit Oppt. (11,634);
5. Automobiles (6,901);
6. Truth-In-Lending (6,303);
7. Household Supplies (5,835);
8. Recreational Goods (5,747);
9. Mail Order (4,687)
10. Food/Beverage (2,738).

Starting in 2000, and continuing for four consecutive years, complaints about identity theft far exceeded all other categories. Again, notice how an issue that is more concerned with one's good name than it is with out-of-pocket loss, far exceeded categories where consumers lost money. Here are the 2001 numbers:

1. Identity Theft (42%);
2. Internet Auctions (10%)
3. Internet Services and Computer Complaints (7%)
4. Shop-at-Home and Catalog Offers (6%)
5. Advance Fee Loans and Credit Protection (5%)
6. Prizes/Sweepstakes/Gifts (4%)
7. Business Opportunities &Work at Home Plans (4%)
8. Foreign Money Offers (4%)
9. Magazines and Buyers Clubs (3%)
10. Telephone Pay-Per-Call/Information Services (2%)[344]

---

[344] http://www.ftc.gov/opa/2002/01/idtheft.htm

In 2002, 43% of the complaints concerned identity theft, and 13% related to Internet Auctions.[345] For 2003, 42% of the complaints were about identity theft. The FTC received more than half a million complaints in 2003, up from 404,000 in 2002.[346]

A Formula For Identifying and Measuring Damages

In a 2003 FCRA case,[347] plaintiff's counsel calculated that Plaintiff worried about, or was tormented for, 15 hours per week, or slightly less than 2.5 hours per day, about inaccuracies in her consumer report. While this was a good start, a more robust formula is needed to fairly gauge damages.

It seems logical that since we are relying so heavily on credit scores to summarize a consumer's creditworthiness, we also should have a scoring model for measuring the damages and costs to consumers caused by defects in the national credit reporting system. Perhaps such a scoring model would finally help the financial services industry appreciate the extremely damaging nature of credit report inaccuracy.

To that end, this author in 2003 unveiled the following proposed methodology, which first requires one to identify the applicable categories of damage in the given case, and then determine which of the factors listed below are appropriate multipliers.[348]

---

[345] http://www.ftc.gov/opa/2003/01/top10.htm

[346] http://www.ftc.gov/opa/2004/01/top10.htm

[347] Boris v. ChoicePoint: USDC-W.D. Kentucky (Louisville) – No. 3:01CV-342-H; March 14, 2003

[348] Prepared Statement of Evan Hendricks, "The Accuracy of Credit Report Information and the Fair Credit Reporting Act," Senate Banking Committee; July 10, 2003
http://banking.senate.gov/03_07hrg/071003/index.htm; and, Presentation of Evan Hendricks, "Information Flows: The Costs and Benefits to Consumers and Businesses of The Collection and Use of Consumer

Some Categories of Typical Damages/Costs of ID Theft & Inaccuracy

(1) Inaccurately described as not creditworthy to third parties
(2) Improperly denied credit because of inaccurate data
(3) Expended time and energy to correct errors not of one's making
(4) Wrongfully received debt collection calls
(5) Chilled from applying for credit
(6) Sleeplessness, physical symptoms
(7) Sense of helplessness, loss of control over personal data
(8) The *emotional distress stemming from, and associated, with all of the above*

I propose a formula that takes into account the following factors.

FACTORS

1)   The nature and substance of the category of damage
2)   Time & energy to solve the immediate problem
3)   The expectation that the problem was solved
4)   The number of recurrences
5)   The period of time over which the problem persists

In essence, the formula, like a credit scoring model, would need to "assign weights or points " to each factor and then multiply Factor (1) by Factor (2); then that result would be multiplied by Factor (3), and then by Factor (4), etc. The purpose is to measure the compounding nature of the damage.

As a preliminary example, take the "Category 1" – "inaccurate characterization." Let's say John Doe, a victim of identity theft, discovers in January 2001 that his credit report

Information." Federal Trade Commission National Workshop; June 18, 2003. http://www.ftc.gov/bcp/workshops/infoflows/030618agenda.html

was polluted with highly negative collection and charge-off accounts generated by a fraudster. This would be a momentous event, deserving a significant assignment of points under the formula. After all, the inaccurate credit report was not the result of anything done by John Doe and was totally unexpected, so the "shock value" (Category #8, emotional distress) was relatively high. Rather than routinely extending him credit, the system falsely branded him unworthy of credit. Further points are assigned because this inaccurate characterization coincided with the unjust denial of credit (Category #2). It's possible that this unjust denial resulted in being humiliated in front of a store clerk or others (Category #8), and with being unable to do anything about it (Category #7). Thus, the formula assigns a relatively large number of damage points for John Doe's first interaction under Factor #1, as compared to a consumer who only finds a few minor inaccuracies on his credit report that did not result in a denial of credit, humiliation and sense of helplessness.

If John Doe's credit report worsens because of the addition of an imposter-caused bankruptcy, Category 1 later earns additional points. The other multipliers come into play, as John Doe must expend time and energy to solve the problems (Factor 2), and develops an expectation that the problem was solved (Factor 3); instead, there are recurrences of being mischaracterized (Factor 4), and the problem persisted over a defined period of time (Factor 5).

Invasion of Privacy = Emotional Distress

Many thoughtful commentators have reached the conclusion that it is emotionally distressful, and therefore damaging, to have your privacy invaded. As Judge J. Michael Blane pointed out in his dissent in 4th Circuit's ruling in ***Doe v. Chao***, a Privacy Act case, "First, Congress created the statutory damages remedy as an incentive to suit because it recognized that damages from government invasions of privacy are hard to prove. Second, Congress recognized that the typical injury caused by the invasion of privacy is emotional distress."

The Members of Congress who were most active in the 2003 FCRA Amendments, known as the Fair and Accurate Credit Transactions Act (FACTA), consistently spoke of the harms flowing to consumers and to society from inaccurate credit reports and/or identity theft.

Shelby and Sarbanes

Senator Richard Shelby (R-AL), Chairman of the Senate Banking Committee opened the July 10, 2003 hearing by stating, "This morning, we take up one of the most important issues, if not the most important, associated with the FCRA: the accuracy of the information contained in consumer credit reports. Changes in our financial services industries have made accuracy more important than ever. Credit report information is increasingly used as the key determinant of the cost of credit or insurance... With the rewards for good credit so meaningful, and the penalties for bad credit so severe, it is absolutely critical that credit reports accurately portray consumers' true credit histories."[349]

Senator Paul Sarbanes, the panel's Ranking Democrat from Maryland, said, "Erroneous negative information on credit reports can often take a significant investment of time and money to remove. They can also be extremely costly to consumers by significantly raising borrower costs. Not only do such inaccuracies raise the cost of borrowing, but they may also actually cost the consumer a loan. Insurers, mortgage banks, and other financial institutions rely heavily on credit scores to make credit decisions. Inaccuracies in the underlying credit reports can therefore make it more difficult and significantly more expensive for

---

[349] Senate Banking hearing, July 10, 2003, op. cit.; http://banking.senate.gov/index.cfm?Fuseaction=Hearings.Testimony&TestimonyID=264&HearingID=49

Americans to purchase insurance, homes, cars, and other big-ticket items."[350]

Senator Debbie Stabenow (D-MI), stated, "In addition, when that information is not accurate, consumers need a quick and easy resolution process. In a fast-paced society like ours, unnecessarily long delays in correcting inaccurate credit reports have profound consequences. They can lead to denial of a mortgage to buy a home or the steering into a subprime loan. They can lead to the inability to get a credit card or an unwarranted increase in interest rates on an existing credit card. They can also create reduced work productivity and extreme stress as consumers must take off work and spend countless hours trying to correct mistakes that occurred through no fault of their own." [351]

On identity theft, Shelby said, "Soon thereafter, when the criminals' handiwork shows up on their credit reports, they face the considerable task of restoring their good name and credit. Plainly, this crime has many victims. Firms lose profits. Individuals lose time, money, and peace of mind when their good name and reputation are tarnished."

"In light of the serious nature of the consequences of identity theft, this issue would merit attention even if there were only a limited number of victims. Unfortunately, there are thousands of victims whose numbers are growing at an increasingly faster pace. Indeed, it has been asserted that identity theft is the fastest growing crime in America."

"This issue tracks across credit reporting in so many ways that it is essential that we consider it in the context of the reauthorization of the preemption provisions of the Fair Credit Reporting Act."[352]

---

[350] *Id.*
[351] *Id.*
[352] "The Growing Problem of Identity Theft and Its Relationship to the Fair Credit Reporting Act" June, 19 2003
http://banking.senate.gov/index.cfm?Fuseaction=Hearings.Testimony&TestimonyID=108&HearingID=43

Sarbanes agreed. "Americans have strong concerns about protecting their confidential information. Honest citizens who are victims of identity theft incur a high cost in money, time, anxiety and effort to correct and restore their spoiled credit histories and good names."[353]

Senator Michael Enzi (R-WY) said legislative solutions were "critical for somebody who is trying to put his or her life back together after the trauma of identity theft."[354]

It's Always Been Valued

In fact, none of this is new. As noted previously, Protecting one's good name is so fundamental to mankind that Shakespeare wrote about it some 400 years ago.

> Who steals my purse steals trash:
> 'Tis something, nothing;
> Twas mine 'tis his and has been slave to thousands.
> But he that filches from me my good name
> Robs me of that which not enriches him,
> And makes me poor indeed.[355]

---

[353] *Id.*
[354] *Id.*
[355] Othello, III,iii,157-61 (Iago)

Chapter 21

The 2003 FACTA Battle

"Politics isn't everything, but everything is politics."

> – James R. Klonoski
> Professor Emeritus, Political Science
> University of Oregon

For close followers of the Fair Credit Reporting Act, 2003 was both an unusual and exciting year.

It was unusual in the sense that the "opposing sides"—the financial services industry and the consumer privacy groups—both wanted legislation.

To the financial services industry, legislation was a top priority because key provisions of the FCRA which preempted State law were set to expire on December 31, 2003. These provisions dealt with issues affecting billions of dollars in commerce: pre-approved credit card offers, duties on creditors (furnishers) to report accurately and to reinvestigate, and the sharing of personal data among corporate affiliates. Industry expressed fears that if legislation was not passed and the preemption expired, state legislatures would begin passing conflicting laws that would raise compliance costs, and worse, interfere with profits.

To the consumer and privacy groups, legislation was long overdue because the 1996 FCRA Amendments were not getting the job done. All of the long-standing problems related to privacy and fair information practices persisted: inaccuracy, faulty reinvestigations, reinsertion, non-responsiveness, and lax security. More dramatically, identity theft had been crowned the nation's "fastest growing crime," and the biggest harm from identity theft, everyone knew, was to the privacy of credit reports. Citing Congress' slow and feeble response to identity theft, as well as the admirable work of states like California, the consumer privacy forces favored letting the FCRA's preemption expire and expanding the role of the states in protecting consumers.

Both sides wanted legislation, but not the same legislation. Industry wanted a simple, straightforward bill that would do nothing more than make FCRA preemption permanent.

Consumer privacy groups called for a detailed reform bill that would set a "floor" of new protections, but which would leave the states free to go further.

The game was on.

The Drama Builds

The scene was unusual in another sense: the burden was on industry to push legislation through Congress before preemption expired on December 31, 2003. Everyone knew it was much harder to pass legislation than to stop it.

Adding to the drama was the new committee lineup, due to the Republicans' regaining control of the Senate after the 2002 elections. Senator Richard Shelby (R-AL), for the first time became chairman of the Senate Banking Committee through which any FCRA legislation had to pass. His predecessor, Senator Paul Sarbanes of Maryland, in turn became the Ranking Democrat.

Together, Shelby and Sarbanes were two of the Senate's biggest privacy advocates, particularly on financial issues. In years past, Shelby had been responsible for landmark privacy legislation requiring that state motor vehicles departments stop selling drivers' data to the direct marketing industry without first obtaining consent. He also was the first Senator to sponsor opt-in legislation for customer data held by financial conglomerates.

Sarbanes also had an impressive track record. Like Shelby, he was an early sponsor of financial privacy legislation that went beyond the much-criticized Gramm-Leach-Bliley Act (GLB). And, he was responsible for the "Sarbanes Amendment" to GLB, which reserved the rights of states to pass stronger financial privacy laws.

At a September 19, 2002 Senate hearing, Sarbanes and Shelby warned representatives of the financial industry that American consumers overwhelmingly favored stronger privacy safeguards, and one day would prevail. Sarbanes likened the situation to the corporate neglect and wrongdoing that resulted in a series of accounting scandals, and the landmark Sarbanes-Oxley Law. He called on the industry to cooperate in creating a stronger financial privacy law. He also took issue with Fred Cate, a pro-industry, University of Indiana Law Professor, calling his argument against opt-in legislation "disingenuous."[356]

The financial services industry looked to Representative Michael Oxley (R-OH), then chairman of the House Financial Services Committee, to put a pro-industry preemption bill on the "fast track." But after the highly publicized corporate accounting scandals, Oxley demonstrated his ability to work with Sarbanes and other Democrats to fashion a publicly popular legislative solution.

Moreover, a Congressional aide to Oxley told an industry gathering that the price of extending FCRA preemption would be "very high," meaning that industry would have to agree to pro-consumer provisions.

"Industry described a failure to extend preemption as 'death,' and described making preemption permanent as

---

[356] "Financial Privacy and Consumer Protection," Hearing of the Senate Committee on Banking, Housing, and Urban Affairs, September 19, 2002

'everlasting life,'" said a Congressional source, looking back on the year. "Well, you don't get everlasting life for cheap."

These comments framed the debate, and foreshadowed the outcome. In hindsight, as it turned out, there was never much question that Congress was going to extend preemption. It was also obvious that the FCRA was in need of another major upgrade.

Still, at the time, any such outcome was very much in doubt. In January 2003, the stage was set for a very interesting legislative battle.

Industry Makes Its Move

Industry knew it had no time to waste. It called out its "top guns." On January 8, 2003, the corporate-sponsored[357] AEI-Brookings Joint Center For Regulatory Studies held a one-day discussion about the FCRA and preemption. Presiding over the affair were "the cream" of unabashed, pro-industry, anti-privacy academics: University of Indiana Law Professor Fred Cate;[358] Michael Staten, a Georgetown University Business School Professor,[359] and Robert Litan, of the Brookings Institution.[360]

A short time after, the team not surprisingly published a report[361] concluding that the FCRA struck the

---

[357] "Donors" to the AEI-Brookings Center include, Allstate. Arthur Andersen, AT&T, Cigna, Citigroup, Property and Casualty CEO Roundtable, State Farm and Visa USA

[358] For Cate's bio and writings, see http://www.law.indiana.edu/directory/fcate.asp

[359] Staten also is director of the Credit Research Center at the Georgetown's McDonough School of Business; his FCRA testimony is at http://financialservices.house.gov/media/pdf/050803ms.pdf

[360] Litan's bio is at http://www.brook.edu/scholars/rlitan.htm; in a previous work, Litan co-authored an attack on the European Union's Directive on Data Protection. See Swire and Litan, "None of Your Business," Brooking Institution, 1998

[361] "Financial Privacy, Consumer Prosperity, and the Public Good: Maintaining the Balance."
www.aei-brookings.org/wnew/index.php?menuid=2

right balance and that there was insufficient evidence of harm to consumers to upset that balance. Of course, this supported the industry view that Congress should merely extend preemption and not bother with additional consumer protections. The authors disregarded specific evidence of harm to consumers (starting with identity theft and inaccuracy). The paper was consistent with a pattern of industry-funded papers arguing that consumers' best interests are best served when industry gets its way.

Robert Gellman, a privacy consultant and former House staffer, called the AEI-Brookings Paper "shockingly incompetent."

"I found an incorrect citation. The paper describes key provisions of the FCRA, but it only represents the law as it passed originally in 1970, with no acknowledgment of later amendments. It keeps citing the views of privacy advocates, but doesn't name them or cite to their publications. Nobody is perfect, but the paper looks like a slapdash job that no one reviewed with any care," Gellman wrote. [362]

The Ad Campaign

In March, a newly formed industry coalition continued to turn up the heat on Congress by launching a Washington-based radio, newspaper, and subway poster advertisement campaign in support of legislation to reauthorize preemption under the FCRA. It may have been the first time that industry had undertaken such measures in regards to a federal privacy law. [363]

---

[362] Gellman, Robert, "No Fair Fight Over FCRA Provision," *DM News,* May 6, 2003
http://dmnews.com/cgi-bin/artprevbot.cgi?article_id=23811&dest=article
[363] However, in North Dakota in 2001, the industry spent over $150,000 in ads against a ballot initiative for an opt-in financial privacy law. The ads predicted economic doom for the state if the voters approved the initiative. The privacy law won 72 percent to 27 percent.

The radio ads, running on WTOP, the news radio station in Washington, warned that if Congress failed to "protect the national consumer credit system," consumers would find that the process of applying for credit will slow to a standstill. As the ad's narrator explained this, his voice slowed until it stopped, much like a defective recording. The ad never mentioned the FCRA by name. The industry also took out ads in *Roll Call*, a newspaper read widely in Congress.

The campaign was funded by "The Partnership to Protect Consumer Credit," whose members included Fannie Mae, the National Retail Federation, the Consumer Banker's Association, the American Financial Services Association, Capital One, Consumer Data Industry Association, Citigroup, Household International, JP Morgan Chase, Master-Card, MBNA, and Morgan Stanley-Discover Financial Services. The net worth of these member companies easily ran in the billions of dollars.[364]

"Unless Congress renews important Fair Credit Reporting Act provisions, the national credit system would be replaced by dozens of inconsistent state and local laws complicating the credit process for consumers and businesses, while hindering important identity theft and fraud protections," the group said on its Web site.[365]

Between the associations and all the banks, credit bureaus, insurers, and retailers, dozens upon dozens of well-heeled lobbyists were dispatched to Capitol Hill. Before the hearings had even started, many Members of Congress had heard first-hand that the entire financial services industry wanted prompt re-authorization of the FCRA's preemption of state law.

---

[364] www.protectconsumercredit.com
[365] *Id.*

The Consumer-Privacy Side

On the other side, those favoring stronger consumer protection and expansion of the state role included the U.S. Public Interest Research Group,[366] the Consumer Federation of America,[367] and Consumers Union,[368] which is publisher of the popular magazine *Consumer Reports*, the National Consumer Law Center;[369] and the National Association of Consumer Advocates.[370]

Aligned with these groups was the National Association of Attorneys General (NAAG),[371] representing state Attorneys General. Supporting roles were played by the Electronic Privacy Information Center, a well-respected organization based in Washington, D.C., [372] the Identity Theft Resource Center, the American Association for Retired People (AARP), and a handful of other groups and individuals with expertise in privacy, credit reporting, and/or identity theft.[373]

The House Goes First

It is customary for Congressional committees to hold public hearings before voting on legislation. Sometimes the

---

[366] Led by Consumer Programs Director Ed Mierzwinski

[367] Exec. Director Stephen Brobeck, Legislative Affairs Dir. Travis Plunkett, and Housing Director Brad Scriber

[368] Janell Mayo Duncan, Consumers Union legislative counsel; Shelley Curran, Policy Analyst, CU West Coast Regional Office; Gail Hillebrand, Senior Attorney, CU West Coast Regional Office; Ami Ghadia, Esther Peterson Fellow, CU Washington Office.

[369] Margot Saunders and Anthony Rodriguez

[370] Exec. Director Ira Rheingold and Newport News, Virg. attorney Leonard Bennett

[371] Led by Julie Brill, an Assistant AG of Vermont, and Susan Henrichsen, Asst. AG of California

[372] www.epic.org/privacy/fcra/

[373] Professor Joel Reidenberg, of Fordham Law School, Professor Peter Swire, Ohio State Univ. Law School and former senior privacy counselor of the Clinton Administration, and this author.

committee members already know how they will vote and the hearings are just a formality. But sometimes the testimony can actually have an impact.

A subcommittee[374] of the House Financial Services Committee opened hearings on May 8, 2003. The title of the hearing, "The Importance of the National Credit Reporting System to Consumers and the U.S. Economy," reflected the committee's pro-industry stance. The opening statement of Subcommittee Chairman Spencer Bachus reflected the pro-industry conclusions of the AEI-Brookings report:

"We will hear in detail today how our uniform credit system under the FCRA benefits consumers and the economy as a whole. Among the consumer benefits afforded by our national credit system are efficient and convenient access to credit and insurance, strong competition in the financial services marketplace, and lower costs of credit."[375]

The Republicans had the votes in the committee. The financial industry lobbyists had blanketed the Hill. Senator Tim Johnson (D-SD) and Rep. Patrick Tiberi (R-OH) had both introduced bills that would make preemption permanent and which were silent on consumer protection.[376] Everything seemed set for smooth sailing. Even Federal Reserve Board Chairman Alan Greenspan heartily endorsed keeping pre-emption of state law.[377]

---

[374] Subcommittee on Financial Institutions and Consumer Credit

[375] Opening Statement of Chairman Spencer Bachus, "The Importance of the National Credit Reporting System to Consumers and the U.S. Economy," May 8, 2003.

[376] No senator agreed to co-sponsor Johnson's bill. In praising the credit card industry at a June hearing, Tiberi said his father was an immigrant who used his credit card to buy everything and received cash back at the end of the year.

[377] Blackwell, Rob; "Greenspan Is 1st Regulator To Endorse FCRA Extension," The American Banker; February 13, 2003. Actually, Greenspan was quite vague, stating, "The system cannot function without ... the credit histories of individual borrowers," he said. "I should certainly hope that it is maintained." He did not address accuracy and reliability problems, even though his own researchers had found such problems. (See Footnote 27, Chapter 10 on history)

There was one problem. At the opening hearing, Assistant Treasury Secretary Wayne Abernathy stunned many Republicans when he testified that the Bush Administration had not yet finalized its position on the FCRA. Therefore, he said, he could not even say whether the Administration supported extension of the law's preemption provision, or whether new safeguards were needed to help consumers fight against identity theft.[378]

What happened? According to sources, "political higher ups" in the White House discovered through their polling data that the vast majority of Americans cared strongly about such issues as financial privacy, credit report accuracy, and identity theft. The polling data indicated it actually could be risky to endorse industry's wish for preemption without due consideration for consumers' interest. In other words, the Bush Administration was still at the drawing board. It was clearly a setback for the industry's fast-track timetable.

Despite the Administration's reticence, Committee Chairman Michael Oxley (R-OH) left no doubt that the committee's priority was reauthorizing preemption. While acknowledging that the committee had many issues to explore, he declared: "At the end of the day, this committee will act and will pass legislation reauthorizing the FCRA. That is job No. 1."

But Representative Bernie Sanders (I-VT), the Ranking Independent on the subcommittee, said that extensive inaccuracy in credit reports, coupled with growing identity theft, underscored the urgent need for stronger consumer protections. Sanders repeatedly said the place to start was "one free credit report per year." Vermont was one of the first states to have a law requiring one free credit report per year. Throughout the House's spring and summer hearings, Sanders continued to harangue committee members about the need for a federal right to a free credit report.

---

[378] "Bush Admin. Still Formulating Position; Oxley Vows Action," *Privacy Times*, Vol. 23 No. 10, May 13, 2003

Challenging Dogma

At the early hearings, pro-consumer witnesses quickly challenged industry claims that state laws were bad for commerce, or even that there were uniform national standards. Fordham Law Professor Joel Reidenberg, an author and expert on privacy law, testified that three states with the strongest credit-reporting laws—Vermont, Massachusetts, and California—ranked 50th, 49[th,] and 27th in bankruptcies. Moreover, those three States offered the lowest interest rates.[379]

Vermont Asst. Attorney General Julie Brill displayed three common ads from Vermont newspapers showing that "zero percent financing and instant credit for mortgages, car loans, and personal loans were widely available in the state."[380]

As every pro-consumer witness pointed out, it had been the states, and not Congress, that had enacted the best financial privacy, credit reporting, and identity theft protection laws. Preemption would shut off the key source of pro-consumer solutions to real and ever-changing problems, they argued.

None of this testimony deterred industry witnesses and some House Republicans from droning on about the "uniform national standards" and the "miracle of instant credit" made possible by the federal FCRA. By early June, the Bush Administration still had not announced its position.

On June 11, Representative Darlene Hooley (D-OR), long-time sponsor of identity theft legislation, upped the ante. Hooley, along with 11 other so-called "New Democrats," came out in support of reauthorizing preemption, provided four major conditions were met. In a letter to Committee Chairman Michael Oxley (R-OH), and Ranking

---

[379] Statement of Prof. Reidenberg, House hearing, May 8, 2003, op cit.

[380] Statement of Julie Brill, "Fair Credit Reporting Act: How it Functions for Consumers and the Economy," Subcommittee on Financial Institutions and Consumer Credit, June 4, 2003

Member Barney Frank (D-MA), Hooley and the New Dems said it was "imperative" that the legislation address problems that had arisen since the 1996 Amendments: (1) Identity theft and mitigation; (2) expeditious handling of consumer complaints and disputes; (3) greater accuracy in credit reports; and (4) consumers' access to their credit data.

The Hooley letter was significant because it signaled to Oxley that it was possible to reauthorize preemption with a bipartisan bill, but only if badly needed consumer protections were part of the package.

'Crippling Effects'

It was also a great prelude to the House subcommittee's June 24 hearing on identity theft, when the panel finally heard two victims describe the emotional distress and frustration they experienced spending hour upon hour trying to repair their reputations and clean up their credit reports.

"It seems rather incomprehensible that our previously impeccable credit reports, which clearly showed wise and careful use of credit along with a stable twenty year residence history, now showed over twenty five unauthorized credit inquiries and six out-of-state address changes, all of which had been entered on our credit reports between September and November of 1999," testified Maureen V. Mitchell, of Madison, Ohio.[381]

Commander Franklin D. Mellott described how the CRAs' voluntary system for fraud alerts failed to work. "I am even more concerned for those 19-year-old soldiers, sailors, and their families that are so easily victimized by this crime. Imagine their spouses, new to the ways of the military, trying to balance the day-to-day challenges of a young family with the crippling effects of identity theft and mistakes by the credit industry. Furthermore, I am concerned

---

[381] Statement of Maureen V. Mitchell, "Fighting Identity Theft – The Role of the FCRA," Subcom. On Fin. Inst., June 24, 2003

because I can see how it could be nearly impossible to fight these problems from overseas."[382]

The First Bill

At the end of June, Hooley and the New Dems joined forces with Oxley, Bachus, and other Republicans in sponsoring a bill (HR 2622) to make permanent the FCRA's preemption of state law, to provide consumers with one free credit report, to require fraud alerts, and to add other provisions to protect against identity theft and improve credit report accuracy. Senator Shelby called the bill a "good start." But consumer privacy groups said it fell short on several fronts, especially by not placing stronger duties on creditors, who are often culprits in causing inaccuracies.

Muris Calls For More

At a packed July 9 hearing on HR 2622, FTC Chairman Timothy Muris and Treasury Secretary John Snow said the Bush Administration and the FTC agreed that preemption should be reauthorized, and that new consumer protections were necessary. The pair endorsed the call for one free credit report per year.

Muris went further. He said that the reinvestigation standards that applied to CRAs should be extended to creditors. The change was significant because generally, disputing errors directly with creditors did not trigger liability. Although many may not have realized it, the current law required consumers to route all disputes through credit bureaus before they could enforce their rights.

Moreover, Muris said a new "risk-based pricing notice" was needed so consumers would know when their credit reports caused them to lose out on favorable interest rates or insurance premiums. Under current law, adverse

---

[382] Statement of Franklin D. Mellott, June 24, 2003. Mellott is the Military Victim Assistance Coordinator for the ID Theft Resource Center

action notices were only required when a consumer was denied credit and did not accept any counter-offers. This "counter-offer loophole" allowed creditors to avoid giving adverse actions. In such cases, consumers were not told their credit reports were causing them to lose out.

Enter Barney Frank

Until 2003, Rep. John LaFalce, from upstate New York, had been the ranking Democrat on the House Financial Services Committee. LaFalce was seen as a strong privacy advocate, having sponsored legislation to strengthen financial privacy after Gramm-Leach-Bliley. In fact, LaFalce's involvement in privacy went way back to 1978, when he played a role in the enactment of the Right to Financial Privacy Act, which regulated law enforcement agents' access to bank records.

Upon LaFalce's retirement,[383] Barney Frank assumed the position of the committee's Ranking Democrat. Frank was considered a pro-consumer, Massachusetts liberal, but most of his attention in the financial arena had been devoted to predatory lending, community reinvestment, and bankruptcy. At the outset of 2003, it was not clear how active he would be on FCRA and financial privacy. In the early FCRA hearings, the normally animated Frank was relatively subdued.

When Frank got his turn to speak at the packed July 9 hearing, he announced that he had taken advantage of the quiet July 4 holidays to read the mounds of FCRA written testimony of hearing witnesses. In a key moment of leadership, Frank said that HR 2622 did not adequately tackle the long-standing problems of credit report accuracy, or maintain the privacy of medical data. He noted that many of the reforms Congress made in 1996 had not even achieved their

---

[383]Despite LaFalce's retirement, some key staff members stayed on, and played an important role in ensuring that consumer voices were heard in the early hearings.

goal of improving CRA reinvestigations or reporting by creditors.

He also advised the financial industry and House Republicans that, given the fact that Shelby and Sarbanes had not committed to reauthorizing preemption, their chances of achieving that goal would be greatly enhanced if the committee would report out a more consumer-friendly bill that could win overwhelming approval on the House floor.

The Massachusetts Solution

Another unknown in 2003 was whether Oxley and Frank could work together. On some congressional committees, there can be an acrimonious relationship between the chairman and ranking member that hampers cooperation. Oxley and his staff were not sure what to expect from Frank.

But after the July 9 hearing, the two offices quickly began exploring a cooperative effort in advance of a hastily scheduled July 14 mark-up. Their collaboration resulted in several improvements in the bill, the most important of which might have been a much needed strengthening of the duty on creditors to report information accurately in the first place.

The 1996 FCRA Amendments were the first to place any duties on furnishers, but they were extremely weak. As the 2003 testimony indicated, and Frank noted, they had proven ineffective. Essentially, the 1996 provisions only prevented a creditor from reporting data it "knows or *consciously avoids knowing*" is inaccurate. Moreover, the FCRA generally did not permit consumers to sue creditors that violated this provision. It was only if the consumer sent a dispute to the CRA, <u>and</u> the CRA relayed the dispute to the creditor, <u>and</u> the creditor continued to report the information inaccurately, did the consumer then have the right to sue the creditor under the FCRA. Not surprisingly, it often seemed that some creditors did not take their FCRA compliance duties too seriously.

Frank noticed that the Massachusetts FCRA had a more common standard: a furnisher could not report data that it "knows or has reasonable cause to believe" was inaccurate. No company had ever complained about the Massachusetts standard in the many years it had been on the books. Working with Oxley, Frank and Representative Carolyn McCarthy (D-NY) succeeded in adding it to the House bill. Other pro-consumer changes were made relating to identity theft prevention, risk-based pricing notices, and medical data. Several studies about accuracy and credit scoring were mandated. The studies were to be conducted by the General Accounting Office, a research arm of Congress, or by the FTC and federal banking regulatory agencies.

At a July 24 mark-up, the committee rejected an amendment to extend preemption for 10 years, rather than make it permanent. By a 44-22 vote, the panel defeated a proposal by Bachus and Sanders to bar credit card issuers from raising their customers' interest rates based upon their payment history with a different creditor.

The Oxley-Frank compromise was approved 61-3, with Sanders and Representative Barbara Lee (D-CA) voting against it. They, like U.S. PIRG and several other consumer-privacy groups, felt the preemption of state law was not justified by the facts and that making it permanent was a clear case of overkill. On September 10, 2003, the bill passed on the House floor by a 392-30 vote.

Follow The Money

The growing list of consumer protections added to the House bill underscored the FCRA's importance to Americans. The result was somewhat impressive in light of the money and resources that the financial services industry poured into the legislative campaign.

Two of the leading groups were the Partnership to Protect Consumer Credit, which had sponsored the pro-preemption advertisement campaign, and Financial Services

Coordinating Council, which represents the biggest of the big banks. In September 2003, the *National Journal* reported that members of these two groups alone had contributed nearly $500,000 to members of the Senate Banking Committee, and had given a combined total of nearly $25 million to candidates, leadership PACs, and parties. The numbers were based upon research by the Center for Responsive Politics.[384]

The Senate Banking Committee

With Shelby and Sarbanes at the helm, the Senate Banking Committee was where the consumer privacy groups hoped to make even greater strides in advancing consumer protection, perhaps even limiting preemption rather than make it permanent. These hopes were boosted when Senators Charles Schumer (D-NY) and John Corzine (D-NJ) indicated they too would propose additional consumer protections for identity theft and accuracy.

But underneath this veneer was the reality that most of the members of the Senate Banking Committee were primarily friendly to banking interests. If push came to shove, the banking industry had the votes. This meant that the committee had some leeway to strengthen requirements on the credit reporting industry, but had to be cautious about reforms that might be perceived as too burdensome by the more powerful banking lobby.

Unlike his counterpart in the House, Shelby worked more deliberately. The Senate Banking Committee held its first "overview" hearing on June 19. He held a hearing on affiliate sharing later in June, and conducted hearings on identity theft, accuracy, and financial literacy in July.

The hearings built an impressive record, detailing the roots of such problems as credit report inaccuracy, CRA non-responsiveness, inadequate reinvestigations by creditors,

---

[384] The report can be found at http://www.capitaleye.org

identity theft, and the toll these problems take on consumers. They also revealed that the day-to-day operation of the credit reporting system was largely unregulated, or even unsupervised, by regulatory entities. In the early 1990s, the FTC had investigated the three CRAs and reached consent agreements with them that stayed in force for several years. Throughout the decade, the staff steadily turned out opinion letters in response to specific questions from industry. Another FTC enforcement action targeted the CRAs' failure to answer consumer phone calls.

But for the core issues of accuracy, disclosure standards, data integrity and furnisher reporting, the players in the credit reporting system were pretty much left to their own devices as long as they were not caught violating the FCRA. Further, although there were plenty of anecdotes and a series of studies over the years, the committee said more information was needed on the operation of all aspects of the credit reporting system.

Shelby: More Oversight Needed

Considering the complexity of the system and continuous impact on consumers, Shelby felt that tightening rules and increasing federal oversight of the daily operations was vital to improving credit reporting accuracy, fairness and privacy.

Shelby's draft legislation, unveiled in the form of a 98-page proposal and summary in early September 2003, reflected his emphasis on ongoing oversight. It was officially silent on the issue of extending preemption, but it was no secret Shelby would agree to it if he thought sufficiently strong national standards were enacted.

Under the proposal, for example, the FTC would have to compile complaints about credit report inaccuracy or incompleteness, and track resolution of consumer complaints referred to the "Big Three" credit bureaus. It would also study the effects of credit bureaus' use of "partial matching" criteria.

The Shelby-Sarbanes bill proposed that the FTC, along with the Treasury Department and Federal Reserve Board, issue rules as to when credit grantors would have to provide "counter-offer" notices to consumers whose negative credit histories made them ineligible for the best terms and rates. Similarly, the FTC and banking agencies would have to develop guidelines and promulgate rules regarding the accuracy and completeness of data furnished to credit bureaus, as well as rules to ensure that users of credit reports maintain the accuracy of consumer addresses. The Federal Reserve Board would conduct a study on the accuracy of credit report data and its impact on credit eligibility. The FTC would set rules to enhance opt-out notices for pre-screening. Federal banking agencies and the FTC would jointly conduct regular studies of financial institutions' data-sharing practices.

Beyond studies and regulations, the Shelby-Sarbanes draft strengthened identity theft victims' rights to block credit bureau dissemination of fraud-generated data, barred creditors from furnishing fraud data after being notified by CRAs, and required creditors to investigate identity theft data after receiving disputes directly from consumers. The measure also would require mortgage lenders to provide consumers with copies of credit reports and credit scores, rather than force consumers to go back to the bureaus.

The Shelby-Sarbanes bill, coupled with changes proposed in the House bill, signaled that the FCRA was headed for a major revamp.

Affiliate Sharing

For consumer privacy groups, there was one major disappointment. But it was not strictly about credit reporting. Instead, it was about "affiliate sharing." That is, the sharing of personal data among affiliates of huge financial conglomerates, without consumers' consent. It was an issue with a great deal of recent history. The 1996 FCRA Amendments preempted state law on affiliate sharing, but many people thought it only applied to credit reports—not the customer "transaction and experience" data that banks generate separately.

In 1999, Congress was preparing to finish years of work and eliminate depression-era rules preventing banks from operating securities and insurance businesses. However, a few scandals about banks selling credit card numbers to telemarketers drove home the point that tighter privacy rules were necessary. Shelby was one of the first to propose legislation to require banks to get customers' opt-in consent before selling their data to outsiders, or sharing it among affiliates.

As is sometimes the case, Congress responded to Shelby's "Gold Standard" with the lowest common denominator: the right to opt-out from selling to outside third parties, but no required notice or choice for affiliate sharing. The law, known as the Gramm-Leach-Bliley Act (GLB), resulted in financial institutions sending confusing notices to customers about their "privacy" policies and opt-out rights.

For consumer privacy groups, one of the best aspects of GLB was the Sarbanes Amendment, explicitly allowing states to go further than the federal law to protect privacy.

Senator Jackie Speier

One of the first officials to answer the call was California State Senator Jackie Speier. A Bay area legislator, Speier had regularly championed consumer and women's issues, and did not shy away from a good fight. Nearly 25 years earlier as a Congressional aide, she accompanied her boss, Congressman Leo Ryan, on an ill-fated trip to Guyana to visit the infamous cult leader Jim Jones. Ryan's Bay Area constituents were worried about family members who had joined the group, known as the People's Temple. Ryan's party was ambushed by Jones' followers. Ryan died in the gunfire. Speier took a couple of bullets, but survived.

Speier started with an opt-in bill. When California Governor Gray Davis said he could support the bill if it were changed to an opt-out for affiliate sharing, she modified it to win his support. But Davis eventually reneged on his word, and helped kill the bill in successive close votes. Coincidentally or not, Davis was receiving massive campaign contributions from the banks. The *San Francisco Chronicle* reported that the financial industry expenditures to defeat the Speier bill exceeded $20 million. Among the biggest spenders were Citigroup, which tallied $878,875 in expenses, the American Insurance Association, $310,662, and the giant credit card company, MBNA Corp., $500,871.[385]

The California Ballot Initiative

If Speier had hit a nerve, then Chris Larsen, CEO of E-Loan, the online lender, struck the central nervous system when he announced in July 2002 he was donating $1 million to gather signatures for a ballot initiative to create a statewide, opt-in financial privacy law. Larsen made his position clear: if the California Legislature was again unable to pass Speier's bill, the voters would create an even stricter law themselves.

Larsen's confidence in part stemmed from North Dakota, which in 2001 held the nation's first-ever statewide ballot initiative on an opt-in financial privacy law. The financial industry spent over $150,000 in advertising money attempting to convince the voters that the measure would re-

---

[385] *San Francisco Chronicle*, September 7, 2002; a *Chronicle* analysis of spending reports filed with the secretary of state's office shows that corporations opposed to the measure spent more than $8.8 million on political contributions during the last 18 months and another $12 million on lobbyists and related costs.

sult in economic doom for North Dakota. Thanks to a grant from the American Civil Liberties Union, hard-working state activists[386] were able to counter with $25,000 in radio ads. The privacy initiative won 72% to 27%.

Larsen's confidence also stemmed from the fact that opinion polls consistently showed support for the opt-in initiative, running between 80% and 90%. By July of 2003, with only halting progress on the Speier bill and with the deadline approaching, supporters of the California initiative were preparing to turn in the signatures.

Industry finally blinked. After a final round of negotiations, Speier and California Senate President John Burton hammered out the bill that was approved by a 78-1 vote. Davis, who was facing a recall drive that ultimately would oust him from office, finally supported the bill and signed it into law. It basically required a customer opt-in before banks could sell their data to outside third parties, and an opt-out for affiliate sharing. The ballot initiative was aborted.

As a last-ditch effort, major banks tried to persuade Speier to go along with an affiliate-sharing curb that only covered "marketing" data. But Speier stood firm. She recognized there was growing concern over the increasingly detailed consumer profiles that huge financial conglomerates were compiling through affiliate sharing. A marketing-only approach would not address the more profound issue of profiling.

As U.S. PIRG's Ed Mierzwinski often warned, affiliate sharing enabled large companies to create their own sort of "credit profile" beyond the reach of the FCRA.

Still, spokesmen for major banks said they could live with the bill. Jon Ross, a Citigroup lobbyist, told *The American Banker* on August 25, 2003, "We were part of this

---

[386] The initiative's proponents were led by Charlene Nelson, of the Constitution Party, and Rep. Jim Kasper, a Republican State Representative and small businessman. Kasper later traveled to California to explain the experience, and testified before the U.S. Senate as well in 2002.

and are pleased with the work done—it's a good fair result for everyone."

In an August 14, 2003 press release, the California Bankers Association (CBA), said, "We believe that, with the latest changes, this proposal qualifies as both reasonable and workable in many, but not all, aspects... We want to be clear that CBA would much prefer a national standard to a patchwork of state or local privacy laws."

But a new opportunity would arise to take an important part of the Speier bill "off the books."

Banks Win One In Court

Senator Jackie Speier's determined fight for privacy in Sacramento inspired several California counties and municipalities to pass ordinances granting residents opt-in rights for their financial data—both in relation to outside parties and affiliates. San Mateo and Contra Costa Counties, along with San Francisco and Daly City, all adopted local ordinances that went beyond what Speier proposed. Bank of America and other major banks filed suit, asking the courts to invalidate the local restrictions on affiliate sharing under the FCRA preemption of state law.

On July 29, 2003, U.S. District Judge Claudia Wilken ruled that the FCRA's preemption of affiliate sharing indeed barred states or localities from adopting opt-out rules for consumers. In a sweeping victory for industry, she held that the FCRA's preemption was unequivocal. The GLB's "Sarbanes Amendment" only preserved states' rights to adopt rules regarding third parties. The FCRA trumped GLB because it addressed affiliate sharing, while the GLB did not.

Although it upheld local ordinances requiring opt-in for third parties, Judge Wilken's ruling effectively meant that the affiliate-sharing provisions of the Speier bill were stillborn. The best way to restore them to life was for the FCRA Amendments either to clarify that the provisions were not preempted, or to adopt them as a national standard.

Meanwhile, Back At The U.S. Congress

To the biggest of the big banks and credit card companies, affiliate sharing was probably the priority issue in the FCRA debate. Major financial institutions view customer data as a "profit center." For a company like Citigroup, which has over 1,700 affiliates, the sharing of data helps one affiliate market to another affiliate's customers. The securities' division might want to promote to consumer banking customers. The credit card division might want to send hard-to-refuse offers to student loan recipients. In the mid-1990s, Nations Bank was caught and fined for marketing questionable securities to elderly depositors.

But marketing is only part of it. Affiliate sharing also helps major corporations make decisions about customers.

Several years ago, First Union, a bank, had developed a system enabling it to reduce the "hold-times" of preferred customers who called customer service representatives, and conversely, prolong the hold-times of less-preferred customers. The automatic number identification function would identify the customer from either the home or business phone that he was calling from, and then link to the customer's profile, enabling the system to apply something akin to "green," "yellow," or "red-light" status.

An Oct. 30, 2000 *Washington Post* article described how Capital One, the credit card company, had achieved success through superior use of customer data and computer modeling. For example, Capital One call centers received some 1 million calls per week from its 30 million customers:

> The Capital One computers make a calculated guess as to what the customer is calling about, and the company says the computers are right 70 percent of the time, up from 40 percent when the system was installed in 1998. Then they route the caller to the most appropriate available service representative among the company's 3,500, who are stationed at

five customer-service centers around the country, including Richmond and Fredericksburg. As the call is relayed, the customer's detailed credit history pops up on the rep's desktop computer... Once the customer's reason for calling has been addressed, the service rep morphs into a salesperson, clicking on a blue icon on the computer screen to see which products the computer has determined this customer might buy.

(In 1999) the company conducted 36,000 such tests; it estimates it will perform 45,000 (in 2000). All that information—coupled with data from billions of transactions by millions of cardholders over many years—has helped Capital One stratify consumers ever more finely. The company now offers thousands of credit card products that differ by price, fees, credit-line limits, and other features. Company executives hint that many other applications are possible by sifting through the mountain of consumer payment transactions they own, from which they can extract exact knowledge of what people buy, eat, and do, when they do it, where, and even why. For example, Fairbank and Morris told analysts last week, they can identify higher- and lower-risk candidates more precisely than the most widely used credit-scoring system, which was created by Fair, Isaac and Co. The FICO score is feared by every hopeful homebuyer looking for a mortgage.[387]

Clearly, such systems can be used to improve customer service or offer customers better products. But there can be a fine line between "offering" and "manipulating," and the danger of manipulation grows when a large organization holds detailed personal data on an individual and the individual does not realize it.

---

[387] *Washington Post*, October 30, 2000

At the Senate Banking Committee's June 26, 2003 hearing on affiliate sharing, Martin Wong, Citibank Global Consumer General Counsel confirmed that his company aggressively used affiliate data.

"Citigroup is able to use the credit information and transaction histories that we collect from affiliates to create internal credit scores and models that help determine a customer's eligibility for credit. This information supplements credit reports and FICO scores to paint the most accurate picture possible of a customer. For example, Citi-Mortgage underwriters have access to information from affiliates that includes a customer's deposit, loan, and brokerage account balances, as well as the customer's payment history and available lines of credit. This allows our credit analysts to verify the customer's credit worthiness quickly and efficiently, minimizing the burden on the customer associated with providing this documentation," Wong said.[388]

At the same hearing, Fordham Law Professor Joel Reidenberg warned that FCRA's current exemption for affiliate sharing had the potential to undermine the Act's privacy protections by creating a loophole for secondary use of customer data.

"Some companies justify this affiliate sharing provision by arguing that corporate families should be treated as one unit for consumer privacy purposes because corporate organizational structure does not have an effect on consumers. This claim is simply not credible. The existence of separate entities to avoid consolidated legal liability confuses operational responsibility for privacy, impacts consumers seeking to assure the fair treatment of their personal information, and undermines consumers seeking legal redress for violations. A confusing maze of companies helped Enron obscure its true behavior. The same holds true for affiliates' sharing of personal information," he said.[389]

---

[388] Statement of Martin Wong, Senate Banking Comm., June 26, 2003
[389] Statement of Joel Reidenberg, Senate Banking Comm., June 26, 2003

Flexing Their Muscle

There was great symbolism at the June 26 hearing on affiliate sharing. Shelby and Sarbanes were surrounded by the four committee members who had the reputations for being friendliest to big banks: Senators Robert Bennett (R-UT), Tim Johnson (D-SD), Elizabeth Dole (R-NC), and Thomas Carper (D-DE). These Senators could fairly be described as representing important constituents. Citibank had its credit card processing center in South Dakota. Bank of America and Wachovia were headquartered in North Carolina. MBNA and First USA were in Delaware. These Senators stayed at the affiliate sharing hearing longer than any other FCRA hearing. Their presence seemed designed to show that affiliate sharing was a major issue to major banks.

The Shelby-Sarbanes legislation included a provision requiring an opt-out for affiliate sharing, but only as it related to marketing data. Although an improvement over GLB, which did not include any opt-out rights for affiliate sharing, this was the same compromise that Speier had rejected as inadequate in California. In a mid-October mark-up in which the Committee gave final approval, Sarbanes said overall he thought the bill was a good one, but said he wished the committee could have accomplished more in the area of affiliate sharing.

Senators Dianne Feinstein and Barbara Boxer, both California Democrats, led an effort to restore the Speier affiliate-sharing provisions by making them the national standard under the FCRA. Their effort was defeated 70-24. The bill (S 1753) passed 90-2, with Feinstein and Boxer as the lone dissenters.

The industry got their "everlasting life" in the form of permanent preemption in the areas of affiliate sharing, pre-screening, duties on furnishers, and four other areas. Yet they had to "pay a high price" in new and substantial consumer protections designed to improve accuracy and fight identity theft. They also would have to live under a new set of federal regulations and await the outcome of several studies designed to shed light on their operations.

Consumer privacy groups hailed the new protections, but were disappointed that Congress did not at least "sunset" preemption so the issues would have to be revisited down the road. They were particularly disappointed about losing the Speier affiliate-sharing provisions, but knew the fight for them would resume another day.

In fact, privacy advocates won the next battle. On June 30, 2004 in Sacramento, U.S. District Judge Morrison C. England Jr. ruled that the FCRA did not preempt the affiliate sharing provisions of the California financial privacy law. In reaching the opposite conclusion of his judicial colleague, Judge England called Judge Wilken's reasoning "faulty." The FCRA only preempted state laws on affiliate sharing of credit reports; it did not "broadly preempt all State laws regulating information sharing by affiliates, whatever the purpose or context," he wrote.

But the victory was short-lived. The U.S. Court of Appeals for the Ninth Circuit reversed Judge England, finding the FCRA indeed preempted state laws on affiliate sharing.

President Bush Signs The Bill

On December 4, 2003, President George W. Bush held a small, hurriedly arranged signing ceremony in the White House for the Fair and Accurate Credit Transactions Act (FACT Act).

"The bill I'm about to sign will help make sure that hardworking, law-abiding citizens are treated fairly when they apply for credit," he said.[390]

"This bill also confronts the problem of identity theft. A growing number of Americans are victimized by criminals

---

[390] The President's full statement, with additional links to Treasury Dept. fact sheets, is at
http://www.whitehouse.gov/news/releases/2003/12/20031204-2.html.

who assume their identities and cause havoc in their financial affairs. With this legislation, the federal government is protecting our citizens by taking the offensive against identity theft," he said.[391]

"As we help people [get] access to credit, we're strengthening the protections that help consumers build and keep a good credit history. That good record is ruined when criminals steal identities and run up purchases under stolen names. Like other forms of stealing, identity theft leaves the victim feeling terribly violated. And undoing the damage caused by identity theft can take months," President Bush said.

"In an age when information about individuals can be found easily, sold easily, abused easily, government must act to protect individual privacy. And with this new law, we're taking action," he continued. "First, under this law, we're giving every consumer the right to get a copy of his or her credit report free of charge every year. That's important. The credit report is more than a record of past actions—it has great influence over a person's financial future. People should be able to check their credit report for accuracy, and to challenge any errors. The bill does just that."[392]

Appearing at the ceremony was Michael Berry, who discovered he was an identity theft victim in January 2002, and who "made countless calls to credit bureaus."

"He closed the credit card accounts as fast as he could, but applications for more credit in his name were being made every day. And many were getting approved. He had to call every credit card company to get each card canceled before it was issued. Nearly two years later, Michael is still fighting the effects of the fraud. The system was broken. Michael is living testimony to what I'm saying

---

[391] *Id.*
[392] *Id.*

when I said the system was broken. And Congress acted. I want to thank you all for stepping up and doing the right thing here," President Bush said.[393]

      Author's Note: For a preliminary version of the FCRA, as amended by the FACT Act, go to: www.ftc.gov/os/statutes/031224fcra.pdf

      For the text of the pre-2003 FCRA, go to: www.ftc.gov/os/statutes/fcra.htm

      The FTC's announcement of effective dates is: www.ftc.gov/opa/2004/02/fyi0410.htm and www.ftc.gov/os/2004/02/040203facta.pdf

---

[393] *Id.*

Chapter 22

Outer Limits: Missing Limits

Just because you're paranoid, doesn't mean someone isn't out to get you!

When it came to credit, Javiar Soler worked hard at being a "model consumer." In 1999, after attending Miami Dade College, he found himself saddled with nearly $5,500 in student loans. For the next few years, times were lean for the 27-year-old engineering student. The debt on his two Bank One credit cards climbed to nearly $9,000.

Determined to climb out of debt, Soler, in January 2004 set his own schedule for paying off his credit cards. He also signed up for Experian's Credit Expert program for monitoring his credit score and credit report. The big day came in August 2004 when he paid off the two Bank One cards. Around that time, Soler purchased about $90 worth of goods with his Capital One card, which he had used sparingly since he got it one year earlier. The Capital One card had a credit limit of $500. Soler's highest previous balance on the card was $151.

"I was so happy I did a happy little dance," Soler recalled.

By using the Credit Expert monitoring service to check his credit score at least twice a month, Soler watched his score gradually improve as he paid down his credit card debt over the first half of 2004. So with his two Bank One cards paid off, he enthusiastically went to check his credit score.

But Soler was flabbergasted to see that his credit score had dropped from 649 to 610 – meaning he went from "OK" credit to "sub-prime."

Then he noticed that while last month's $90 balance on his Capital One card was still on his Experian report, the $500 credit limit was not being reported. Instead, only the highest balance he'd ever carried, $151, was being reported as the "highest limit."

Soler was both mystified and annoyed. He understood that if Capital One correctly reported the $500 limit, his balance-to-limit ratio would be 18 percent, and would help his credit score. But with the $151 subbing as the credit limit, his "utilization ratio" had mushroomed to 60 percent and caused his credit score to plunge at a time when he expected it to go up.

"The missing Capital One credit limit was the only explanation," Soler said. "Nothing else had changed."

On his second attempt at calling Capital One, Soler said he spoke with "a very polite and helpful rep who informed me that Capital One's current policy is to NOT report credit limits, but that they are aware of the 'inconvenience' that it causes and are going to change their policy soon."

Cap One Changes

After years of criticism and a pair of potential class action lawsuits, Capital One announced in August 2007 that it would change course and finally report credit limits.

The change was a major step forward, but it did not eliminate all concern over the issue. As we will see, other major credit card issuers also did not report limits. Moreover, Capital One's change was "voluntary." If the lawsuits challenging the practice were dismissed, the company presumably would feel free to resort to its old ways.

Millions Impacted

Soler's experience was not a fluke. In 2004, three staff economists at the Federal Reserve Board studied a nationally representative, random sample of 301,000 individuals' credit files, and found that nearly half -- 46 percent -- of the consumers had files where at least one credit limit had been withheld by a creditor.[394]

The balance-to-credit limit factor, known as the "credit utilization ratio," has a major impact on a credit score. It is part of "Factor 2" of the FICO scoring model, which accounts for 30 percent of the score (see Chapters 1 and 2).

For example, if you had a $2,400 balance against your $2,500 limit, you'd have a very high (96 percent) utilization ratio, which would significantly lower your score for nearly being maxed out. On the other hand, your $250 balance against your $2,500 limit produces a low (10 percent) ratio -- and usually raises your score.

If there is no credit limit reported, then it becomes difficult, if not impossible, to properly calculate the ratio – usually to the detriment of the consumer's credit score.

Both Soler and the Federal Reserve Board researchers learned that when credit limits were not reported, most scoring systems "substitute the consumer's highest balance ever for the missing credit limit." This is because Equifax, Experian and Trans Union keep track of the highest balance in a separate field on the credit report.

Soler figured out that he could improve his score by "maxing out" his Capital One card and then paying it off immediately. To do this, he deposited a promotional "convenience" check that Cap One had sent him, and then promptly used the money to pay off his balance.

---

[394] Robert B. Avery, Paul S. Calem, and Glenn B. Canner, "Credit Report Accuracy and Access To Credit;" *Federal Reserve Bulletin* (Summer 2004)

Of course, most people have no idea that this is how the system works.

Richard Le Febvre, a pioneer in re-scoring and owner of the AAA American Credit Bureau Inc. in Flagstaff, Ariz., said one young couple – whom he would not identify by name – came to him to try to improve their credit score to qualify for a Fannie Mae mortgage with a three percent down payment.

"They were about 11 points short of what they needed to qualify," LeFebvre told the *American* Banker, an industry trade journal.[395] The couple had a $2,500 limit on their Capital One card, but it had not been reported to the three credit bureaus, Equifax, Experian, and TransUnion. Instead, only the couple's high balance of $113 appeared on their credit report.

"Just that one credit card made the FICO model think that the card was maxed out," Mr. LeFebvre said. "We got Capital One to report their credit limit and we moved them 31 or 32 points up by correcting that one issue."

The 2004 Federal Reserve study's finding that 46 percent of the consumers' files were missing at least one credit limit indicated the problem had worsened for consumers. A 2002 Federal Reserve Board review found that credit card limits were missing from 13 percent of accounts examined; in 1999, 33 percent of the revolving accounts lacked credit limits, the Fed found.

Cap One Not Alone

Internal industry research, from a source that asked not to be named, found that while some credit card issuers consistently reported credit limits, several major issuers often did not.

---

[395] Michele Heller, "FCRA Hearing To Shine Spotlight On Credit Process;" American Banker, June 12, 2003

The research indicated that Capital One was the worst offender. Based on a sampling of at least 150 credit reports from Equifax, Experian and Trans Union from 2002-2004, the review showed that the credit limit was missing from 100 percent of the 453 Capital One accounts that were identified.

Although some consumers were shocked to learn of this practice, it was no big surprise to industry insiders. After all, in 2003, company spokeswoman Diana Don told the *American Banker*, "Capital One has never reported credit limits, for proprietary reasons …We feel that it is part of our business strategy and provides competitive advantage."[396]

American Express did not report credit limits in a majority of cases between 2002-2003, the research found. Specifically, in those two years, it did not report limits to Equifax and Experian in about 80 percent of the cases, and did not report to Trans Union about 65 percent of the time. (Unlike standard revolving accounts, some types of American Express cards don't have credit limits.) In 2004, Amex credit limits were missing from 28 percent of the Trans Union accounts and 38 percent of the Experian accounts. But they were absent from 91 percent of the Equifax accounts, the research found.

Another offender was Citibank, although there were important differences among its subsidiaries. The credit card giant was found to report limits for its gas cards and for its CitiFinancial personal finance subsidiary.

"CITI does not report credit limits in its Citibank NA and Citibank South Dakota NA subsidiaries, but almost always does for its other subsidiaries," researchers wrote.

The statistics for Citibank underscores how difficult it is for consumers to "know the score." The numbers on the next page reflect the percentage of cases that Citibank did not report credit limits.

---

[396] Id.

Missing Citi Credit Limits[397]

	Trans Union	Experian	Equifax
2002	24%	39%	30%
2003	22%	44%	75%
2004	16%	42%	66%

Calling CITI

This author noticed on all three of his credit reports that credit limits were not being reported for his Citi AAdvantage MasterCard (American Airlines mileage card), even though the credit limit was $7,440.

When told of this, a very polite Citi customer service representative said she did not understand how this could be, since "all credit cards have credit limits and they're always reported to the (credit) bureaus."

She suggested that the omission might be a simple mistake by the credit bureaus. But I informed her that some credit card companies intentionally do not report credit limits. She admitted that she did not know her company's policy, but referred me to Citi's "Credit Bureau Dispute Unit," P.O. Box 6241, Sioux Falls, S.D., 57117. She said that I needed to include the credit report with a dispute letter that identified the account number in question. She said the dispute unit did not take phone calls.

(By the way, if you were to include your credit report as part of a dispute to Citi or another creditor, remember to black out all of your other tradelines and inquiries. Although creditors might like to have that information, they certainly are not entitled to it.)

---

[397] Based on review of 357 Citi tradelines by researchers who asked to remain anonymous

Household & Discover

Household Bank's pattern was somewhat similar to Citibank's, according to the researchers.

Missing Household Credit Limits[398]

	Trans Union	Experian	Equifax
2002	22%	42%	72%
2003	50%	31%	88%
2004	23%	21%	87%

Over the same three-year period, Discover tradelines were missing credit limits on Experian reports less than 20 percent of the time. For Trans Union reports, 36 percent of Discover tradelines lacked credit limits in 2002, while 15 percent lacked them in 2004, according to the researchers.

However, in Equifax reports, Discover tradelines were missing credit limits 100 percent of the time.

Equifax & Credit Limits

The higher incidence of missing credit limits in Equifax reports can be explained at least in part by the fact Equifax requires creditors to fill in an extra box in order to report a credit limit, researchers said. Specifically, creditors must fill in the "AZ" narrative field in order to instruct Equifax that the amount in the H/C (High Credit) column is a credit limit, they explained.

If it is true, as this preliminary data suggests, that Equifax credit reports more often lack credit limits, then the

---

[398] Based on a review of 270 Household tradelines by researchers who asked to remain anonymous

question arises as to whether credit scores for consumers' Equifax reports are generally lower than those from other bureaus.

Back To Basics: The Dispute

"Jamie" really wanted to buy a new Volkswagen. But his 680 credit score was not good enough to qualify him for the 0% interest rate that made the deal affordable to him. He sought help from Veracity Credit Consultants, a Denver firm specializing in credit report issues (see Chapter 11).

Jamie's case illustrated how even when there are no late payments on a credit report, the credit score can be significantly lowered by credit utilization factors.

Veracity discovered that Jamie had three basic problems. First, his report showed a Citi credit card account with a $4,000 balance. Jamie said he didn't even have a Citi credit card.

Second, because Capital One was not reporting Jamie's $3,000 credit limit, his credit report showed him maxed out at $400. Third, his First USA Mileage Plus card's $10,000 limit was missing from his credit report, making him look maxed out at the $1,000 balance.

Thus, Jamie was showing 100% usage of a reported $5,400 limit.

Veracity's J. Madison Ayer said its disputes resulted in the removal of the mysterious Citi account from Jamie's report, and the reporting of accurate credit limits for both the Capital One and First USA accounts. Jamie's credit score went from 680 to 740. He got the Volkswagen at 0%.

Ayer said that Veracity was regularly finding missing credit limits on its clients' credit reports. But it also said it was regularly having success in restoring accurate credit limits by disputing their absence with the CRAs and credit card companies.

"Once we dispute it, we're not getting much resistance from the credit card companies," Ayer said. "The credit limits are usually restored."

Ann Schleifley was not as lucky. After signing up for a credit monitoring service, the Seattle-area resident noticed that her FICO score seemed lower than it should have been. Why? Her monitoring service advised her she was using over 50% of her available credit.

Then Schleifley saw why. Neither Capital One nor Discover were reporting her credit limits. She tried disputing with all three parties by mail and by phone.

"It was the most ridiculous run-around I'd ever seen," Schleifley recalled. "Capital One would blame Equifax; Equifax would blame Capital One and Discover. It went on for months. It was very frustrating. I just wanted it fixed!"

Schleifley finally contacted the Washington State Attorney General's office. She said she was fortunate enough to find two experienced consumer attorneys who, in April 2004, filed a federal lawsuit in Seattle, charging that Capital One, Discover and Equifax failed their reinvestigation duties under the Fair Credit Reporting Act. The case was pending when this book went to print.[399]

What's A Consumer To Do?

Wouldn't it be nice if there were a ready and dependable list of credit card companies that always reported credit limits? Unfortunately, that might not be possible. It's a fast-changing situation, and it appeared to be changing for the worse by the beginning of 2005.

For example, the researchers who identified those companies that were not reporting limits wrote, "If you want your credit limit reported, it seems best to get a card from MBNA, Chase, Bank One, First USA, Providian or Sears." They quickly added, "Even they have some missing credit

---

[399] Schleifley was represented by Christopher Green of Seattle, and O. Randolph Bragg, of Horwitz & Associates, Chicago.

limits on Equifax, but they seem very good about reporting credit limits to the other two bureaus."

Other sources provided this author with anecdotes about missing credit limits from MBNA, Bank One, First USA and Sears credit report tradelines (though it was not clear if this was due to the Equifax factor cited above).

One fear, of course, is that competitive pressures will mount, prompting more and more credit card companies to follow the path of the highly successful Capital One. On the other hand, why would an educated consumer use a credit card that has a greater likelihood of lowering their credit score?

Why Don't They Report Credit Limits?

The common reason given for credit card companies not reporting credit limits is to make their customers look less attractive to competitors who might try to solicit them with pre-approved credit card offers. But no credit card company official has actually said that this was the reason. One of Capital One's only public comments was the one to the *American Banker* cited earlier, where Diana Don said, "Capital One has never reported credit limits, for proprietary reasons ...We feel that it is part of our business strategy and provides competitive advantage."[400]

But what does that mean, exactly?

Your Limits, Our Trade Secrets

On the Motley Fool discussion board, a participant who described herself as a Capital One employee, said her company was not trying to lower its customers' credit scores.

"The policy is not designed to screw customers, but to protect our credit policy from competitors. Yes, we have had many debates over whether or not this is necessary, and

---

[400] Id.

that is probably why the rep mentioned that the policy might change, but I promise we are not out to get you," said the participant, who went by the screen name "DBAVelvet74."[401]

In other words, reporting credit limits would enable Cap One's competitors to figure out its standards, or underwriting criteria, for granting credit.

Capital One essentially confirmed this in Dec. 2004 when it told the *Washington Post's* Kenneth Harney "it did not report any customers' limits because "we consider [limits] proprietary" information, and "because we do not think it would be appropriate to impact the individual's Fair Isaac score, positively or negatively, by reporting them."[402]

It was not clear how Capital One's practices could positively impact its customers' credit scores. But Capital One declined to discuss the issue with this author.

Follow The Money

The practice of not reporting credit limits must be viewed within the context of other industry trends. After a rash of bankruptcy filings hurt profits in the mid-to-late 1990's, credit card companies gravitated towards "universal default" as an industry standard. Under universal default, any late payment – to a phone or utility bill or another credit card – or just carrying too much debt, was justification for credit card companies to raise cardholders' interest rates.

Of course, this was possible because companies could conduct monthly "account reviews" of cardholders' credit reports and, more importantly, their credit scores. These policies were spelled out in the fine print of credit card agreements.

---

[401] "DBAVelvet74" did not respond to e-mail requests, so it was never confirmed that she/he actually worked for Capital One.
[402] Kenneth Harney, "Credit Card Limits Often Unreported," *Washington Post*, December 25, 2004

In its in-depth article on Universal Default, the *New York Times*, told the story of Steve Strachan, a flower importer in York, Penn. Strachan nearly always used his U.S. Bancorp WorldPerks Visa card for business travel to Europe in order to accumulate rewards in Northwest Airline's frequent-flier program. As a good customer, his credit limit was raised to $54,000 at a low interest rate. Despite heavy usage, he said he "never paid a penny of interest" because he paid it off each month.

But when the economy wilted in 2000, Strachan started using other credit cards. Although still paying on time, and maintaining a FICO score above 730, he was unable to pay off all of his balances every month.

It wasn't long before US Bank advised that it was raising the rate on his WorldPerks Visa card to 20.21 percent, nearly quadrupling the existing rate of 5.25 percent.

"I wasn't late, and I didn't go over the credit limit, and I didn't write bad checks," Mr. Strachan told the *Times*. A representative of US Bank told him he was using too much of his available credit, he said. (A US Bank spokesman declined to comment, the *Times* reported.)

John Gould, a former MasterCard International executive who conducts research for TowerGroup said it was "absurd" that 44 percent of credit card companies tell their customers that they might be penalized for one or two late payments with maximum rates that now exceed 28 percent.

The Nilson Report, a consumer payments newsletter, estimated that three out of four customers do something that violates the cardholder agreement and lose a favorable balance transfer rate, according to a 2003 article in the *Dallas Morning News*.[403]

Louis Freeh, MBNA general counsel, defended these practices in a statement to the *New York Times*: "If we see indications that a customer is taking on too much debt, has missed or is late on payments to other creditors, or is

---

[403] Anuradha Rahunathan, "Bait and Snitch?" *Dallas Morning News,* Aug. 8, 2003

otherwise mishandling their personal finances, it is not unreasonable to determine that this behavior is an increased risk. In the interest of all of our customers, we must protect the portfolio by adjusting a customer's rate to compensate for that increased risk."

Bottom Line: 'Rate Optimization'

Of the estimated 144 million cardholders in the U.S., 85 million Americans are considered "revolvers," meaning they don't pay their balances off every month. These are the most profitable customers. If they start at a low interest "teaser" rate, but are taken to a double-digit rate and they continue to pay, they are that much more profitable.

Some call it "rate optimization." It has helped card issuers reach record pre-tax profits, like $2.5 billion in 2003.

Card issuers regularly find justification for raising rates in the credit report. If it's not a missed payment with another creditor, it's rising balances with other issuers.

According to Consumer Action's Linda Sherry, who conducted the group's 2004 survey on credit cards, 44% of the card issuing banks surveyed used credit report data to identify so-called risky cardholders and raise their interest rates, even if they never made a late payment. The 2003 survey found 39% of banks had universal default policies.

The banks in the 2007 survey with universal default policies included Chase, Citi, Commerce Bank, Discover, EverBank, Franklin Templeton Bank, GE Money Bank, HSBC, Metropolitan National Bank and US Bank.[404] But Citi announced in March 2007 it dropped universal default.

Those that did not raise interest rates solely because of credit report data included American Express, Bank of

---

[404] Consumer Action's 2004 & 2007 Surveys are at: www.consumer-action.org/English/CANews/2004_May_CreditCard/#Topic_01; and www.consumer-action.org/news/articles/2007_credit_card_survey/

America, California Bank & Trust, State Farm and BB&T, according to the survey.

The survey found that Capital One also did not practice universal default, Sherry said. But it still appears to use credit reports. For example, a 2004 Cap One promo boldly offered "2.99% fixed APR FOR LIFE."

In the fine print on the back of the offer, the offer stated, "All your APRs may increase to a rate up to the default APR (24.9%) if you default under this Card Agreement ... because you fail to make a payment to us when due, you exceed your credit line or your payment is returned for any reason... Factors considered in determining your default rate may include *your general credit profile,* existence, seriousness and timing of the defaults under any Card Agreement that you have with us, and other indication of the account usage and performance."

Thus, under the stated policy, it's only after you miss a payment with them or exceed your limit that your credit report could be used to determine how much higher your interest rate goes. Capital One is free to change its policy.

Self-Fulfilling Prophecy

There is something troubling about card issuers not reporting credit limits, and then using credit reports as a justification for hiking their customers' interest rates.

After all, by not reporting credit limits, those issuers could very well be lowering their customers' credit scores. To then turn around and base an interest rate hike on a manipulated credit score seems like a subversion of the system – at least as it is portrayed by the financial services industry. And, if a primary goal of issuers is "rate optimization," there is a real danger that such practices will become more common.

Advocates warn that missing credit limits are patently unfair, and represent a ticking time bomb for unsuspecting consumers – and the system as a whole.

"We need legislation to guarantee completeness by all furnishers. We're not asking that furnishers be required to report, but if they do report they should be subject to accuracy and completeness standards," U.S. PIRG's Ed Mierzwinski told the *American Banker* in 2003.[405]

In its September 24, 2004 comments to the Federal Reserve Board, the National Association of Mortgage Brokers strongly endorsed a requirement for the complete reporting of "the high credit limit (not the highest credit used or some arbitrary number)."

"Furnishers of credit should be required to report complete information on each account, as many of the current practices today can be devastating to a consumer's credit score," the NAMB wrote.[406]

Providian

One company that chose the high road on this issue was Providian Financial, a top-ten credit card issuer based in San Francisco. In addition to fully reporting credit limits, Providian, in an unprecedented move in March 2004, began offering its cardholders free access to their Trans Union FICO score. Cardholders must register at the company Web site to start accessing their FICO scores. The program, dubbed "Providian Real Information," also permits cardholders to use a score simulator so they could see how much their score would change with certain behaviors, like paying down balances or late payments. They could also sign up to receive e-mail alerts if their credit score changed by more than 10 points.

---

[405] Heller, op. cit.

[406] Letter, NAMB President Bob Armbruster to Jennifer Johnson, Secretary, Federal Reserve Bd., Sept. 24, 2004. NAMB also endorsed full factual accurate information about the date an account was opened and date of last activity.

Providian officials said there had been tremendous customer response to the service.

Providian gained prominence by targeting the more risky sub-prime market. In years past, it had to settle several lawsuits over unwarranted late fees and other anti-consumer practices.

The FICO service is part of the company's pro-consumer makeover. "After listening to mainstream Americans across the country, we found some major gaps between how consumers say they want to be treated by their credit card company, and how they are actually being treated," said Warren Wilcox, Providian's vice chairman of planning and marketing.

It was also a shrewd use of resources. Like other credit card companies, Providian regularly purchased its cardholders' FICO scores from Trans Union when it conducts monthly "account reviews." Under the program, Providian could leverage that expense into a customer benefit.

The Ball's In Your Court

Capital One's decision to bow to criticism and finally begin reporting credit limits was a victory for American consumers. However, there's no way of knowing how long it will follow the policy. It's also unclear if all credit card issuers would agree to report credit limits.

Like so many other aspects of the system, the burden generally remains on consumers, first to become educated as to how the system works, and then to take the appropriate corrective actions.

Chapter 23

Conclusion

*Live in such a way that you would not be
ashamed to sell your parrot to the town gossip.*

– Will Rogers

A goal of this book was to describe the credit scoring and credit reporting system. Given the enormity of the system, the task of describing it took precedence over the task of analyzing it more thoroughly.[407] The purpose of this conclusion is to offer a few thoughts about the system.

Here To Stay

For the foreseeable future, it's safe to say that the credit reporting and credit scoring systems are here to stay. Although there has not been a final tally, it is clear that in 2003 the financial services industry invested millions of dollars in the FCRA-FACTA legislative debate to preserve the existing system, and to prevent states from interfering with it through enactment of new consumer protections.

And for good reason. On the front end, the credit scoring system increases profitability on a number of fronts:

---

[407] The author is hopeful that more analysis can be provided in future editions of the book.

better segregation of consumers and credit risk, lower cost through automation and faster decision-making. But one fundamental dilemma has not been adequately addressed, and it relates to the "general rule" set forth on Page 1 of this book: If lenders can charge more to those with lower credit scores, then will the system have a bias towards lowering scores? Perhaps we can begin to find answers to this by examining financial conglomerates that have significant and direct impact on a consumer's credit score, like a major mortgage lender that also operates its own credit bureau and re-scoring shop. Or we can look at Capital One, which reportedly had the effect of lowering some of its customers' credit scores by not reporting credit limits, making customers look more "maxed out" on their cards than they actually are. Many believe that the advantage to Capital One is that this practice makes its customers look less attractive to other credit card companies who might want to "cherry pick" them through pre-approved credit card offers.

On the back end, the credit reporting system provides great leverage to lenders. If consumers don't pay their bills on time, they will be reported to the credit bureaus. The entry of recent derogatory data has a very detrimental impact on credit scores. An educated consumer will avoid this scenario, as the damage to creditworthiness is potentially more costly than the debt in question. It certainly is not improper for creditors to inform customers that late payments should be avoided for precisely this reason. As we have seen, however, some lenders and debt collectors cross the line, and improperly attempt to use credit reporting as a tactic to force consumers to pay debts that they do not really owe. Many consumers have been abused because of *the manner* in which some lenders and collectors view credit reporting as an arm of debt collection.

Consumer Vigilance

The current system, and the law governing it, generally puts the burden on the individual if he or she wants to ensure that all is right. Accordingly, the first plank of protection under our national policy is *knowing* what is in one's credit report. This requires consumers to be vigilant in exercising their right of access to their credit reports. A wide range of commentators, including the Federal Reserve Board, regularly advise consumers to get their credit reports. Congress has sought to encourage this by entitling all Americans to one free credit report per year.

Taking advantage of modern technology, access can address important problems, like accuracy and identity theft. Before Congress, Treasury Assistant Secretary Wayne Abernathy spoke of the advantages of having "150 million Americans auditing" their own credit reports. If consumers were "plugged into" their own reports, enjoying the same kind of ongoing, online access to their reports that creditors currently have, then they quickly could spot errors, or better yet, detect signs of identity theft. Imagine that you live in Ohio, and that your monitoring service alerts you via e-mail that a car dealership in Arizona has pulled your credit report. You would know that immediate action was in order. Research shows that the longer it takes a victim to learn that his or her identity was stolen, the worse the damage.

How Much?

Equifax, Experian and Trans Union all offer some form of online subscription and fraud alert monitoring services. The services appear profitable, possibly grossing $1 billion annually. But at $89 to $119 per year, the prices of these services are exorbitant. Moreover, in an age of escalating identity theft, shouldn't at least some of these services be required of the Big Three consumer reporting agencies (CRAs) simply to assure "maximum possible accuracy" under the Fair Credit Reporting Act?

To no avail, this author strongly recommended to Congress that it cap the price of the Big Three's monitoring services, just as the 1996 Amendments capped the price of credit reports. Hopefully, this recommendation someday will be seen as being ahead of its time.

The debate will continue to rage over the apparent gap between industry practices and the FCRA's requirements that (1) disputes are investigated, or that (2) previously deleted information not be reinserted, or (3) that CRAs forward to the creditor all relevant information provided by the consumer. Several recent pro-consumer court decisions, including the Fourth Circuit's landmark opinion in <u>Johnson v. MBNA</u> (see Chapter 9), indicate that the law might actually be closing in on questionable industry practices. After more than 30 years, one would certainly hope so.

But what will industry do? Will it continue to cling to unpopular and discredited practices? Will the industry only change these practices if it is hit with tobacco-styled litigation and tobacco-like verdicts? That appears to be what the industry is inviting.

Other Personal Data

The problems and solutions learned from credit reporting should guide our policies on other personal records. For instance, along the lines of the CRA monitoring services, consumers should enjoy ongoing and affordable access to information about them held by medical providers, government agencies, employers, creditors, utilities, and database and marketing companies. But neither policy nor organizational practice is anywhere close to making such a fundamental right as access to one's own records universal.

In "post-911 America," we must also remain alert to ill-advised efforts to dump non-credit data onto credit reports. Take the case of Sandra Cortez, a grandmother who was ready to buy a car until a Colorado car salesman advised her that, according to TransUnion, she was on the Treasury Dept.'s watchlist for international drug dealers and terrorists. It turned out that TransUnion had begun selling names of suspects from Treasury's Office of Foreign Assets Control (OFAC), placing potential "matches" directly on the credit reports of applicants like Ms. Cortez. The problem was that the name from the OFAC list was a *Sandra Cortes Quintero*, of Cali, Columbia, with a birth date some 27 years later. Yet TransUnion took no steps to block Quintero's criminal data from appearing on Ms. Cortez's TU report.

Worse, when she tried to dispute it, TU operators said there was nothing they could do because the OFAC information was not incorporated into TU's credit reporting database. Instead, a vendor obtained it from the Treasury Dept., sold it to TransUnion, which then slapped it directly onto Ms. Cortez's TU report. In response to her lawsuit, TransUnion argued that its use of OFAC data wasn't covered by the FCRA because it wasn't in her TU file. Judge John Fullam, Sr. disagreed, and a jury awarded Ms. Cortez $50,000 in compensatory damages and $750,000 in punitive damages. The jury forewoman took the extraordinary step of writing on the verdict form, "The Trans Union business process needs to be completely revamped with much more focus on customer service and the consumer."[408]

Not Self-Enforcing

Considering the FCRA's age and what's at stake for consumers, enforcement of the FCRA, with a few exceptions has been abysmal. The Federal Trade Commission was most

---

[408] Judge Fullam reduced the punitive award to $100,000, ruling in plaintiff's case that the punitive damages should not be more than double the actual damages. Sandra Cortez vs. Trans Union, LLC.,: USDC – No. 2:05 CV-05684-JF; judge's opinion Sept. 13, 2007; jury verdict April 26, 2007 (The author testified as Cortez's expert.)

active in the early 1990s, when its enforcement actions resulted in landmark consent decrees, and set the table for the 1996 legislative amendments strengthening the law. To be fair, the FTC must oversee a wide array of consumer issues at a time when the privacy agenda, which includes the FCRA, is more than enough to keep it overworked. All developed countries, except the United States, have a national "Office of Privacy Commissioner" to handle the load. The FTC has opposed creation of such an office.

Enforcement is most glaringly absent when it comes to inaccurate reporting by creditors. On this issue, Congress did not give individuals the ability to enforce accuracy, that is, the right to sue. Instead, the 1996 Amendments generally permit creditors to report inaccurate data without liability. [409] Enforcement was left to the Office of the Comptroller of the Currency (OCC), and other U.S. banking agencies. But the OCC has never enforced this section of the law. We shouldn't be surprised. The OCC is a bank regulator, not a consumer protection agency.

Thus, if Americans want better compliance with the FCRA, they themselves will also need to become more vigilant about enforcement. In a recent law review article, St. Johns University Law Professor Jeff Sovern said this goal would be greatly enhanced if we moved toward a legal standard of "strict liability," particularly in the area of identity theft. The FCRA's current standard of "reasonable procedures" is too convoluted, Sovern wrote. What is needed, he said, was to make CRAs strictly liable for attributing the transactions of identity thieves to innocent consumers, and to make creditors liable for reporting the transactions of imposters as transactions of others. Sovern argued that this would create a simpler system of "loss allocation rules" that would "spread the consumer losses caused by identity theft more equitably."

---

[409] Exceptions include when reporting is done with "malice" or is egregious in some other way.

Sovern's straightforward proposal deserves serious attention.[410] But in the short run, it will have a difficult time getting any in Congress, given the strength of the financial services lobby.

Still, the FCRA, as much as any other federal statute, gives consumers important enforcement tools, which in very recent years, have begun to demonstrate their effectiveness.

Looking Ahead

Should we be so accepting of the system? Is there a danger that a credit score, with so much riding on it, will become an "internal passport" for American consumers? What about people who handle their money responsibly, but prefer to avoid the consumer credit system, and all the fees and surveillance that go along with it? Has the easy availability of our personal data in turn made too much credit too easily available, to the detriment of too many consumers?

These questions ultimately go to the fundamental importance of credit reports and personal information in 21st Century America. Throughout the latter half of the 20th Century to the present, governmental and corporate entities, along with our system of law, largely viewed personal information as a *commodity*. Sure, it might be your name, or information about you, but if a company collected or otherwise obtained it, that company owned it. In short, when held by a large organization, you did not even "own" your own name, or your personal data.[411] The FCRA, the Privacy Act and other statutes were created to give individuals *procedural* rights in relation to their personal information that was controlled by large organizations.

---

[410] Sovern, Jeff, "The Jewel of Their Souls: Preventing Identity Theft Through Loss Allocation Rules," *University of Pittsburgh Law Review* (Winter 2003)

[411] U.S. v. Miller 425 U.S 435 (1976)

Is this traditional approach adequate in an age where our personal information is the "lifeblood" of our consumer-based economy? Is there too much at stake to leave so much discretion to large entities, and only provide procedural rights to individuals? If so, then what are the alternatives?

Some observers have suggested that many of these problems could be cured by giving individuals a *property right or interest* in their personal data. On a theoretical level, such a right or interest would give individuals much greater standing to exert control over their information. But in situations where individuals found themselves in a weak bargaining position, they very likely would succumb to "coerced consent." In other words, to get the job, or the mortgage, or insurance, you must "consent" to revealing details you normally would not consent to revealing. This all too common scenario is contrary to the Fair Information Principle of "collection limitation." More broadly, should society and its system of laws allow a fundamental human right such as privacy be bartered away so easily?

Personal Data – A Natural Resource

Most would agree that the intimate details about our private lives are more than just a commodity. This book should help make clear that in the context of the United States' information-age economy, our personal information is a new type of *natural or public resource*. Defining it as such would seem to have dramatic implications for public policy. At earlier times in history, the conclusion that electricity, or water, or the airwaves were public resources resulted in the development of new infrastructures for administration and enforcement. Those infrastructures in no way ended the debate over how the resources were distributed and used, as new controversies arose through the years.

In theory, while it might be true that collectively, our personal information is a natural resource, it can never be overlooked that each piece of it is linked directly to a given individual. Accordingly, there can be no disputing that the collection, use and disclosure of our personal information are ultimately human rights issues.

These issues, in turn, cannot be separated from the consumerism dominating our society. If consumers use credit to buy things they cannot afford, then there is a stronger chance that they are heading for credit problems.[412]

Some have learned the hard way that the "miracle of instant credit" is a curse. Of course, Fair Isaac says this is precisely the type of problem that its scoring model successfully predicts.

So be careful what you buy, or what you buy into. There is a system out there waiting for you. By understanding how it works, you improve your control over how it portrays you. If the system treats you unfairly, or even abuses you, the law gives you rights. How you exercise them is up to you.

---

[412] For sound, common-sense advice, see Michelle Singletary's popular book, "Spend Well, Live Rich: How to Get What You Want with the Money You Have" (Ballantine Books), originally published as "7 Money Mantras for a Richer Life."

About The Author

Since 1981, Evan Hendricks has been Editor/Publisher and founder of Privacy Times, a newsletter based in the Washington, D.C. area. Through the newsletter alone, he has published nearly 3,000 pages covering a wide range of privacy and information law subjects, including the Fair Credit Reporting Act.

Mr. Hendricks regularly testifies before Congress, with four appearances in 2003.[413] He is a regular presenter at Federal Trade Commission workshops.[414] He has been qualified by the courts as an expert witness in FCRA and identity theft cases. Mr. Hendricks has served as a consultant on privacy issues to federal and state governmental organizations, and businesses. He has been a featured American presenter at events in Paris, France, Venice, Italy, Cardiff Wales, London, England and Ottawa, Ontario. He is regularly quoted in the mainstream media and trade press.

Mr. Hendricks has a Bachelor of Arts from Columbia College, Columbia University. He attended there after transferring from University of Oregon.[415]

---

[413] http://banking.senate.gov/03_07hrg/071003/index.htm
http://financialservices.house.gov/hearings.asp?formmode=detail&hearing=229
http://financialservices.house.gov/hearings.asp?formmode=detail&hearing=202
http://judiciary.senate.gov/testimony.cfm?id=983&wit_id=2790
[414] http://www.ftc.gov/bcp/workshops/infoflows/030618agenda.html
[415] Go Ducks!